GOD AND MAN

AT YALE

50th Anniversary Edition

GOD AND MAN AT YALE

The Superstitions of "Academic Freedom"

WILLIAM F. BUCKLEY JR.

Gateway Editions
REGNERY PUBLISHING, INC.
WASHINGTON, D.C.

First printing of the fiftieth anniversary paperback edition: 2002

Austin W. Bramwell's "The Revolt Against the Establishment: *God and Man at Yale* at Fifty" originally appeared in the Fall 2001 issue of *The Intercollegiate Review*, published by the Intercollegiate Studies Institute (ISI). Grateful acknowledgment is made to ISI for permission to reprint.

ISBN: 0-89526-692-X

Published in the United States by
Gateway Editions
A Division of Regnery Publishing, Inc.
One Massachusetts Avenue, NW
Washington, DC 20001

Visit us at www.regnery.com

Distributed to the trade by
National Book Network
4720-A Boston Way
Lanham, MD 20706

Printed on acid-free paper

Manufactured in the United States of America

10 9 8 7 6

Books are available in quantity for promotional or premium use. Write to Director of Special Sales, Regnery Publishing, Inc., One Massachusetts Avenue, NW, Washington, DC 20001, for information on discounts and terms or call (202) 216-0600.

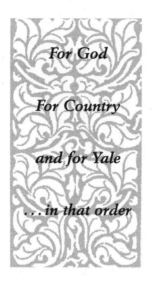

For God

For Country

and for Yale

. . . in that order

Contents

❧

The Revolt Against the Establishment: *God and Man at Yale* at Fifty

by Austin W. Bramwell

༄

The year 2001 marked the golden anniversary of the publication of one of the seminal books in modern American conservatism, William F. Buckley Jr.'s *God and Man at Yale*. Without it, one could fairly say, the conservative movement would not exist today. Soon after winning national attention with this controversial polemic, Buckley deployed his youth, charm, and intellect to unite a motley crew of cantankerous intellectuals into a viable conservative movement. Less than a generation after Lionel Trilling famously opined that "in the United States at this time liberalism is not only the dominant but even the sole intellectual tradition," Buckley had in large part caused the liberal consensus to unravel.

For all its fame, however, *God and Man at Yale* is as noteworthy as a failure as it is as a success. Buckley's call for Yale alumni to withhold financial support until Yale ceased to undermine her students' faith in Christianity and the free market went almost entirely unheeded; today Yale is more secular and left-wing than ever. Nonetheless, it would be a mistake to view the book as a mere historical artifact, for Buckley's tocsin rings as loudly today as it did then, and the controversy over the book's argument is well worth revisiting.

So decisive has been the rout of Christianity at Yale that any-one under the age of fifty now can hardly imagine how Buckley's book could have caused as much controversy as it did, much less why Buckley should have become at the time the object of such intense vituperation. McGeorge Bundy called Buckley a "violent, twisted, and ignorant young man," and questioned both the "hon-esty of his method" and the "measure of his intelligence." Frank Ashburn, founder of the Brooks School, called him "Torquemada, reincarnated in his early twenties," and insinuated that he should be wearing not academic robes but those of the Ku Klux Klan. Henry Sloane Coffin, the former president of Union Theological Seminary who chaired a blue-ribbon committee to respond to Buckley's charges, wrote snidely that Buckley, a Roman Catholic, "should have attended Fordham or some similar [Catholic] institution."

If these attacks seem personal, that is because they were. All of the major players in the effort to discredit Buckley hailed from old-line Yale families. Many of them, including Coffin, Bundy, and Ashburn, belonged (like Buckley himself) to Skull and Bones. Charles Seymour, the president of Yale while Buckley was an undergraduate, was himself a Bonesman, while A. Whitney Gris-wold, the Yale president when the book was published, came from a Bones family. Buckley's attackers thus saw themselves as custodians of a great tradition; their religion was liberal Protes-tant, their outlook modern, and their sensibility elitist. To them, Roman Catholicism, like Evangelical Protestantism, was the reli-gion of the lower classes—publicly tolerated but privately derided. Buckley in consequence was not so much a Torquemada as a latter-day Alaric who, upon being invited into the very citadel of northeastern WASP prestige, had the gaucherie to question its continued legitimacy.

Part of the difficulty in understanding the controversy over *God and Man at Yale* is that the class distinctions that made Buckley such an unwelcome guest have become blurred since the 1960s. Students today associate religious conservatism with Establishment stuffiness, whereas in truth the leaders of the American Establishment at mid-century contemned both religious enthusiasm and religious orthodoxy. To be sure, the social prestige of men such as Bundy and Coffin could only exist within a Christian society whose mainline churches dominated the universities, and in turn, the government and the culture. Ironically, had the old Yale scions only followed Buckley's prescriptions, they might not have seen their regime crumble around them in the 1960s. Perhaps an even greater irony is that Buckley's urbanity and charm have made him perhaps the last living icon of the traditional high-WASP temperament.

In 1951, however, he was but a barbarian who had somehow found his way into the inner temple. His arguments in *God and Man at Yale* were straightforward: first, Yale was undermining students' faith in Christianity; second, Yale was promoting economic collectivism; and third, alumni should exert their influence to reverse the course of pedagogy at Yale. His critics refused, however, to take these points at face value, but rather insisted that the book was not what it seemed. Fulminated Ashburn, "[*God and Man at Yale*] stands as one of the most forthright, implacable, typical, and unscrupulously sincere examples of a return to authoritarianism that has appeared. Under the guise of liberty it attacks freedom; under the guise of knowledge it denies the privilege of free investigation and dissent; under the guise of defending capitalism and religion it uses the technique of Dr. Goebbels; under the guise of academic freedom it hides the somber robes of theocracy."

How did a book about pedagogy at Yale inspire a philippic against totalitarianism? Ashburn was not alone in leveling such charges at Buckley; every one of his critics construed the book as an attack not only on Yale, but also, despite Buckley's professed belief in democracy and freedom, as a veiled attack on the very nature of a free society. Certainly they could not have inferred this insidious purpose from the substance of Buckley's arguments. In reaching the book's first two conclusions, Buckley was scrupulous almost to a fault in examining Yale department by department, professor by professor, in order to assess the effect each was having on students' spiritual lives and political convictions. Indeed, much of the debate over the book focused not so much on questions of fact but on questions of interpretation. Buckley found that the drift of Keynesian economics was collectivist; his critics insisted that Lord Keynes merely defended the free market from itself. Buckley presupposed that Christianity entailed adherence to the orthodox tenets of the faith; his critics thought that mere interest in Christian spirituality sufficed to demonstrate the strength of religion on campus. Although in each case Buckley upheld the more rigorous view, the differences were surely not so great as to put him in the camp of Dr. Goebbels.

God and Man at Yale's third charge—that alumni should exercise control over the teaching at Yale—was more controversial still. Buckley deconstructed the idea of academic freedom from two angles. First, pure academic freedom was a mirage, he claimed, for Yale would (quite rightly) never allow an anthropologist to teach theories of Aryan racial superiority. Thus, the question was not whether academic freedom should be restricted, but to what extent. Second, romantic notions to the contrary notwithstanding, truth does not always win out in the free marketplace of ideas. Both Italy and Germany, Buckley observed, had the option to elect democratic leaders or authoritarians, but both chose the latter rather than the former. If we indeed know that democracy is superior to totalitarianism, then we have a duty to defend and advance this truth rather than to maintain a falsely "open" question. In sum, Buckley argued, Yale should restrict academic freedom such that Christianity and political freedom always upheld.

In response, Buckley's critics only blustered. Bundy, after falsely accusing Buckley's father of sending a copy of *God and Man at Yale* to every Yale alumnus, wrote that "Mr. Buckley does not seem to know what academic freedom is" and that "he leaps from one view to another, as suits his convenience." Never, however, did Bundy bother to define *his* understanding of academic freedom, nor did he respond to either of Buckley's principal arguments for restricting academic freedom. The same went for Ashburn: "[Buckley's] thesis, stripped to its essentials, is that the way to academic freedom is dogmatism and that the way to save capitalism is by way of indoctrination." Ashburn's only follow-up, however, was purely ad hominem: "[Buckley's] point of view [is] shared, of course, by Marshal Stalin as a staunch supporter of what millions of people sincerely call democracy."

Ashburn and Bundy could not respond to Buckley's arguments for the simple reason that their own position was deeply mired in contradiction. While they agreed with Buckley that Yale was or should be a Christian university, they also believed that, as Coffin put it, "[i]n the ideal university all sides of any issue are presented as forcefully as possible." If Yale were equally open to all ideas, it could not also promote Christianity above all other comprehensive worldviews; if Yale were devoted to promoting Christianity above all other comprehensive worldviews, it could not also be equally open to all others. Buckley's critics could defend Christianity or they could defend openness, but not both. Contrary to Bundy's assertion, it was he and not Buckley who leapt from one view to the other, as suited his convenience.

Hindsight reveals that, as Buckley no doubt suspected, Yale's elite preferred openness to Christianity. In the late 1960s, Yale president Kingman Brewster (who himself came from a family of Bonesmen) took liberal modernism to its logical conclusion and, finding no grounds on which to oppose violent student radicals, propitiated them, going so far as to opine at the time of the Bobby Seale trial that a black man could never get a fair trial in the United States. McGeorge Bundy, in turn, rushed to Brewster's defense. Alas for Yale, since the Great Disruption on American campuses, the university has suffered a marked decline in prestige. Having lost its unrivaled social cachet, Yale has struggled to keep up with Harvard in becoming an elite research university and has failed to reestablish an identity for itself (other than, perhaps, as a haven for an obstreperous homosexual community).

In a sense, then, Buckley's critics were right to infer from *God and Man at Yale*'s attacks on openness in the academy an attack on the open society in general. The conflict over the role of the university paralleled a conflict over the nature of American society just as much in the early 1950s as it did in the late 1960s. Buckley had a radically different understanding of the nature of totalitarianism from that of his critics. In his most notorious passage, he wrote that "the duel between Christianity and atheism is the most important in the world . . . [and] the struggle between individualism and collectivism is the same struggle reproduced on another level." Elsewhere, he quoted approvingly Yale president Charles Seymour, who as late as 1937 could respond to the events in Germany by proclaiming that Yale had a duty to fight "selfish materialism" through the "maintenance and upbuilding of the Christian religion as a vital part of university life." In other words, according to Buckley, totalitarianism arises from a philosophical denial of God which leads to a denial of any higher authority for human institutions. The state thus has absolute authority over all other institutions—family, church, market—all of which can be manipulated for the social or scientific ends of the state.

Though these comments had little to do with the central argument of the book, they set in high relief the most fundamental differences between Buckley and his critics. Ashburn and Bundy thought that the problem of totalitarianism arises not from the dominance of a secular orthodoxy, but rather from the dominance of any orthodoxy whatsoever. Their argument is familiar to the point of banality: anyone who makes an exclusive claim to the truth will then attempt to impose this truth upon everyone else. All dissent will be eliminated, to the point where a single orthodoxy is imposed, as in a one-party totalitarian government. Buckley's understanding of a free society would require that a certain public orthodoxy—which celebrates the West's Christian and liberal heritage—be upheld. Not only are an "open society" and the "free society" not identical; in Buckley's view, it was the "open society" which paved the way to modern totalitarianism.

Which understanding was correct? Theory and history vindicate Buckley. Ashburn's liberalism shares with "selfish materialism" an antipathy to markets, or at least to any claim that the state has only a limited right to interfere in the market. As in communist or fascist ideology, all institutions are understood as mere human inventions, and individuals do not have any rights apart from those granted by men. Thus, no institution or person has any authority independent of or prior to the state. Bundy, Ashburn, et al. may have objected to full-blown collectivism, but they could only do so on prudential grounds. Buckley's "individualist" notion that the state's authority has moral limits was alien to them.

Consequently, it was not the secular liberals with their gentlemanly theories of engagement and détente who at length brought about the defeat of communism in our time, but leaders such as Thatcher, Reagan, and Karol Wojtyla (Pope John Paul II), all of whom shared the conviction that the Soviet Union was the "evil empire" of the century just past. Without the fundamentally moral attack on communism that Bundy et al. found so apparently distasteful, its defeat would have been impossible. Interestingly, just as it took an outsider such as Buckley to reveal what was going on at Yale, so it took an outsider such as Reagan to bear witness to the true nature of communism. Only by ignoring the wisdom of this country's secular liberal elites and taking their case directly to the people could Buckley's and Reagan's conservative movement have succeeded. Buckley may have first learned about the moral flaccidity of the American elite from his Yale mentor, the "Appalachians to the Rockies" American, Willmoore Kendall; but he also experienced that lack of moral resolve firsthand in the controversy over *God and Man at Yale*.

The only question remaining is why the WASP elites ever adopted a philosophy—that of the open society—that not only harmed their country but also undermined their very position as leaders of a Christian society. Part of the reason may have been nothing more than social snobbery. The more enthusiastic the religion of the masses became, the more modernist and liberal became that of the upper crust. This explanation, however, is not decisive, for it sometimes happens, as in the Victorian era, that the upper classes, which can always afford to flirt with libertinism, nonetheless adopt the rigorist morality of the lower or middling classes.

The best explanation may be simply that the last scions of the old-line WASP families were mediocre men. They found the philosophy of the "open society" congenial because it did not demand much of them. They preferred governance to politics, policy to ideology, and prudence to moral aspiration. Buckley offended them because he called them to a higher duty than they were prepared to assume. Little did they realize, however, that the moral capital from which they drew their authority—built by the generations of men who had founded, defended, and advanced this nation—was nearly depleted. Buckley the "barbarian" was, despite their protestations, their last, best hope to defend the heritage that they took for granted.

After half a century, *God and Man at Yale* remains a testament to the power of one man to stand up for the truth. Few realize today what courage it must have taken for Buckley to write such a book, knowing how much it would offend the very men who had tapped into the Yale elite. Buckley's philosophy of "Christian individualism," which combined a distrust of the omnicompetent state with a defense of the truths of the Judeo-Christian tradition, remains as much the core of American conservatism—and, indeed, of the American tradition—in our own time as it did in 1951. Let us hope that fifty years from now Buckley's exemplary defense of the American patrimony will continue to inspire.

Austin W. Bramwell, currently a student at Harvard Law School, graduated from Yale in 2000. He was an Honors Fellow of the Intercollegiate Studies Institute, whose flagship journal, The Intercollegiate Review, *originally published a version of Mr. Bramwell's anniversary assessment of* God and Man at Yale.

Introduction to the Twenty-Fifth Anniversary Edition

by William F. Buckley Jr.

꧁

I was still familiar with the arguments of *God and Man at Yale* when Henry Regnery, its original publisher, asked whether I would furnish a fresh introduction to a reissue of it. But I had not seen the book since I finally closed its covers, six months after its publication in the fall of 1951. It had caused a most fearful row and required me over a period of several months to spend considerable time rereading what I had written, sometimes to check what I remembered having said against a reviewer's rendition of it; sometimes to reassure myself on one or another point. The prospect of rereading it a quarter century later, in order to write this introduction, was uninviting.

Granted, my reluctance was mostly for stylistic reasons. I was twenty-four when I wrote the book, freshly married, living in a suburb of New Haven and teaching a course in beginning Spanish at Yale University. I had help, notably from Frank Chodorov, the gentle, elderly anarchist, friend and disciple of Albert Jay Nock, pamphleteer, editor, founder of the Intercollegiate Society of Individualists, a fine essayist whose thought turned on a single spit: all the reasons why one should be distrustful of state activity, round and round, and round again. And help, also, from Willmoore Kendall, at that time a tenured associate professor of political science at Yale, on leave of absence in Washington, where he worked for an army think tank ("Every time I ask Yale for a leave of absence," he once remarked, "I find it insultingly cooperative").

Kendall had greatly influenced me as an undergraduate. He was a conservative all right, but invariably he gave the impression that he was being a conservative because he was surrounded by liberals; that he'd have been a revolutionist if that had been required in order to be socially disruptive. Those were the days when the Hiss-Chambers case broke, when Senator McCarthy was first heard from, when the leaders of the Communist Party were prosecuted at Foley Square and sentenced to jail for violating the Smith Act. That conviction greatly incensed Kendall's colleagues, and a meeting of the faculty was called for the special purpose of discussing this outrage on civil liberties and framing appropriate articles of indignation. Kendall listened for two hours and then raised his hand to recite an exchange he had had that morning with the colored janitor who cleaned the fellows' suites at Pierson College.

"Is it true, professor"—Kendall, with his Oklahoma drawl, idiosyncratically Oxfordized while he studied as a Rhodes scholar in England, imitated the janitor—"Is it true, professor, dat dere's people in New York City who want to... destroy the guvamint of the United States?"

"Yes, Oliver, that is true," Willmoore had replied.

"Well, why don't we lock 'em up?"

That insight, Kendall informed his colleagues, reflected more political wisdom than he had heard from the entire faculty of Yale's political science department since the meeting began. Thus did Kendall make his way through Yale, endearing himself on all occasions.

Kendall was a genius of sorts, and his posthumous reputation continues to grow; but not very long after this book was published he proposed to Yale that the matter of their mutual incompatibility be settled by Yale's buying up his contract, which Yale elatedly agreed to do, paying over forty thousand dollars to relieve itself of his alien presence. Willmoore Kendall went over the manuscript of *God and Man at Yale* and, as a matter of fact, was responsible for the provocative arrangement of a pair of sentences that got me into more trouble than any others in the book. Since any collusion or suspected collusion in this book was deemed a form of high treason at Yale, I have always believed that the inhospitable treatment of Kendall (after all, there were other eccentrics at Yale who survived) may in part have traced to his suspected association with it and to his very public friendship with me (he became a founding senior editor of *National Review* while still at Yale).

You see, the rumors that the book was being written had got around. They caused considerable consternation at Woodbridge Hall, which is Yale's White House. Yale had a brand-new president, A. Whitney Griswold, and he had not yet acquired the savoir faire of high office (when the controversy raged, Dwight Macdonald would comment that Yale's authorities "reacted with all the grace and agility of an elephant cornered by a mouse"—but more on that later). I remember, while doing the research, making an appointment with a professor of economics who privately deplored the hot collectivist turn taken by the economics faculty after the war. At Yale—at least this was so when I was there—the relation between faculty and students (properly speaking I was no longer a student, having graduated in the spring) is wonderfully genial, though (again, this is how it *was*) there was no confusing who was the professor, who the student. I told him I was there to collect information about the left turn taken in the instruction of economics, and he reacted as a Soviet bureaucrat might have when questioned by a young KGB investigator on the putative heterodoxy of Josef Stalin. He told me, maintaining civility by his fingernails, that he would simply *not* discuss the subject with me in any way.

It was not so, however, in the research dealing with the treatment of religion at Yale, perhaps because I ambushed my Protestant friends. I asked the then president of Dwight Hall, the Protestant student organization, if he would bring together the chaplain and the half dozen persons, staff and undergraduate, centrally concerned with religion to hear one afternoon my chapter on religion at Yale. Everyone came. I read them the chapter that appears in this book—save only the paragraph concerning Yale's chaplain, the Reverend Sidney Lovett. (I did not want to express even the tenderest criticism of him in his presence.) Three or four suggestions of a minor kind were made by members of the audience, and these corrections I entered. I wish I had recorded the episode in the book, because a great deal was made of the alleged singularity of my criticisms and of the distinctiveness of my position as a Roman Catholic. All that would have been difficult for the critics to say if they had known that the chapter had been read out verbatim to the half dozen Protestant officials most intimately informed about the religious life of Yale, all of whom had acknowledged the validity of my findings, while dissociating themselves from my prescriptions.

I sent the completed manuscript to Henry Regnery in Chicago in April, and he instantly accepted it for publication. I had waited until then formally to apprise the president, Mr. Griswold, of the forthcoming event. We had crossed paths, never swords, several times while I was undergraduate chairman of the *Yale Daily News*. The conversation on the telephone was reserved, but not heated. He thanked me for the civility of a formal notification, told me he knew that I was at work on such a book, that he respected my right to make my views known. I was grateful that he did not ask to see a copy of the manuscript, as I knew there would be eternal wrangling on this point or the other.

But a week or so later I had a telephone call from an elderly tycoon with a huge opinion of himself. William Rogers Coe is mentioned in the book. He advised me that he knew about the manuscript and had splendid tidings for me: namely, I could safely withdraw the book because he, Mr. Coe, had got the private assurance of President Griswold that great reforms at Yale were under way and that conservative principles were in the ascendancy: so why bother to publish a book that would merely stir things up? I gasped at the blend of naïveté and effrontery. But although I had observed the phenomenon I was not yet as conversant as I would quickly become with the ease with which rich and vain men are manipulated by skillful educators. As a matter of fact, men who are not particularly rich or vain are pretty easy to manipulate also.

I did attempt to make one point in a correspondence with Mr. Coe that especially bears repeating. It is this, that a very recent graduate is not only supremely qualified, but uniquely qualified, to write about the ideological impact of an education he has experienced. I was asked recently whether I would "update" this book, to which the answer was very easy: this book cannot be updated, at least not by me. I could only undertake this if I were suddenly thirty years younger, slipped past the Admissions Committee of Yale University in a red wig, enrolled in the courses that serve as ideological pressure points; if I listened to the conversation of students and faculty, participated in the debates, read the college paper every day, read the textbooks, heard the classroom inflections, compared notes with other students in other courses. For years and years after this book came out I would receive letters from Yale alumni asking for an authoritative account of "how the situation at Yale is now." After about three or four years I wrote that I was incompetent to give such an account. I am as incompetent to judge Yale education today as most of the critics who reviewed this book were incompetent to correct me when I judged it twenty-five years ago. Only the man who makes the voyage can speak truly about it. I knew that most of my own classmates would disagree with me on any number of matters, most especially on my prescriptions. But at another level I'd have been surprised to find disagreement. Dwight Macdonald was among the few who spotted the point, though I don't think in his piece for the *Reporter* on the controversy he gave it quite the emphasis it deserved. But he did say, "... Nor does Buckley claim any sizable following among the undergraduates. They have discussed his book intensively—and critically. Richard Coulson ('52) notes in the Yale Alumni Magazine that 'it is a greater topic of serious and casual conversation than any philosophical or educational question that has been debated in quite a few years.... In contrast to many of their elders the majority has not been blinded with surprise or carried away with rage at either Buckley or the Corporation by his claim that individualism, religion and capitalism are not being propounded strongly both in and out of the classroom. The undergraduate feels that this particular observation is correct."

Well then, if this is so, why republish *God and Man at Yale* in 1977, if it tells the story of Yale in 1950? The question is fair. I suppose a sufficient reason for republishing it is that the publisher has experienced a demand for it. Not, obviously, from people who desire to know the current ideological complexion at Yale—they will have to probe for an answer to that question elsewhere—but by whoever it is who is curious to know how one student, a Christian conservative, experienced and reacted to a postwar education at Yale University, and wants to read the document that caused such a huge fuss; and those who are curious—

the purpose of this introduction, I suppose—about what, a quarter century later, the author might have to say (if anything) about his original contentions, and the reaction to them. I do have some thoughts about the arguments of this book (which I have reread with great embarrassment at the immaturity of my expression—I wish Messrs. Chodorov and Kendall had used more blue pencil) and about the sociology of the educational controversy. It is extremely interesting how people react to the telling of the truth. We all know that, but should not tire of learning even more about it. But the problems raised by *God and Man at Yale* are most definitely with us yet. Some of the predictions made in it have already been realized. Some of the questions are still open. Some of the arguments appear antiquarian; others fresh, even urgent.

First, something on the matter of definitions. Several critics, notably McGeorge Bundy (whose scathing article-length review in the *Atlantic Monthly* was adopted unofficially by Yale as its showcase defense) objected to the looseness of the terms on which I relied. Throughout the book I used a term briefly fashionable after the war, commonplace at the turn of the century, which however now has ebbed out of most polemical intercourse. It is "individualism." I have mentioned Chodorov's Intercollegiate Society of Individualists. Well, about ten years ago even that society changed its name (to Intercollegiate Studies Institute). The term *individualism* was once used as the antonym of "collectivism." Today the preference is for more individuated terms. We hear now about the *private sector*. About *free market* solutions, or approaches. "Individualism" has moved toward its philosophic home—it always had a metaphysical usage. One would expect to hear the word nowadays from disciples of Ayn Rand, or Murray Rothbard; Neo-Spenserians. In any case, if I were rewriting the book I would in most cases reject it in preference for a broader (e.g., "conservative") or narrower term (e.g., "monetarist"). Even so, though it is unfashionable, "individualism" is not, I think, misleading as it here appears.

Now it was very widely alleged, in the course of criticizing the book's terminology, that the position of the authors of the economics texts cited here was misrepresented. For instance, Frank Ashburn, reviewing *Gamay* (the publisher's useful abbreviation in office correspondence) in the *Saturday Review*, wrote: "One economist took the trouble to extract quotations out of context from the same volumes Mr. Buckley used so freely, with the result that the texts seemed the last testaments of the robber barons." That statement puzzles me as much today as when I first read it. After all, on page 44 I had written, "All of these textbook authors take some pains to assure the student that they have in mind the 'strengthening' of the free enterprise system. Not one of them, I am certain, would call himself a socialist or even a confirmed collectivist. Witness, for example, [Theodore] Morgan's eulogy [in *Income and Employment*]." I went on to quote Morgan:

> ... it is our general assumption that government should not do anything which individuals or voluntary associations can more efficiently do for themselves [p. 184].... Capitalist, or dominantly free-enterprise economies, have succeeded very well in the Western World in raising tremendously the volume of production [p. 176].... Obviously, the American public does not want a nationalized economy or a totalitarian unity. We want to give up no segment of our area of freedom unless there is clear justification [p. 177].... There are both economic and non-economic reasons for preserving a dominantly wide area of free enterprise [p. 193].

It is hard to understand how any critic, laboring the point that I had suppressed professions of allegiance to the free enterprise system by the authors under scrutiny, could do so persuasively in the face of the plain language quoted above. The technique of associating oneself for institutional convenience with a general position but disparaging it wherever it is engaged in wars or skirmishes along its frontiers is as old as the wisecrack about the man and woman who got on so splendidly during their married life, having arrived at a covenant that she would settle minor disagreements, he major: "We have never had a major disagreement," the husband ruminates. In this textbook Mr. Morgan, having professed his devotion to the private sector, went on to call for "diminishing the inequality of income and wealth," later revealed as a tax of 75 to 99 percent on incomes over one hundred thousand dollars; the elimination of the exemption for capital gains; confiscatory taxes on inheritance "aimed at the goal of ending transmissions of hereditary fortunes"; the nationalization of monopolies, the universalization of social security coverage; family allowances from the government; and government guarantee of full employment. The preferences of this economist would even in 1977 be viewed as left of center. In 1950 they were very far to the left of anything the Democratic Party was calling for. To suggest, as Mr. Ashburn and others did, that there was distortion in representing such as Morgan as "collectivist" is, simply, astonishing; but at another level it is consistent with the public perceptions. Frank Ashburn was a trustee of Yale when he wrote. Yale University was thought of (and still is, though to a lesser extent) as a "citadel of conservatism" (*Time* magazine's phrase). Therefore what emerges to the myth-preserver as principally relevant is less the left-salients in a book like Morgan's than the obeisances to orthodoxy. Very well. But who's misleading whom?

Now other reviewers graduated their criticism from misrepresentation to misunderstanding. These would stress that economics is a scientific discipline; that Keynes (for instance) could no more be called a left-wing economist than Buckminster Fuller could be called a collectivist architect.

Philip Kurland, writing in the *Northwestern Law Review*, was emphatic on the point. He quotes with some relish a statement by the author of another book reviewed in *Gamay*, Professor Lorie Tarshis. "A word must be said, before we begin our analysis, about the political implications of the Keynesian theory. This is necessary because there is so much misinformation on the subject. The truth is simple. The Keynesian theory no more supports the New Deal stand or the Republican stand than do the newest data on atomic fission. This does not mean that the Keynesian theory cannot be used by supporters of either political party; for it can be, and if it is properly used, it should be. The theory of employment we are going to study is simply an attempt to account for variations in the level of employment in a capitalist economy. It is possible, as we shall see later, to frame either the Republican or the Democratic economic dogma in terms of the theory."

This point, variously stated, was not infrequently made by reviewers. But, in fact, by the end of the 1940s the analysis of John Maynard Keynes was the enthusiastic ideological engine of the New Economics. There is documented evidence that Keynes himself was unhappy about the lengths to which "Keynesians" were going, presumably under his scientific auspices. Kurland, via Tarshis, was telling us in 1951 that Keynes was all technician. As a matter of fact even that is in dispute. It is not disputed that Keynes formulated an analytical vocabulary for addressing certain kinds of economic problems, and the universalization of this vocabulary is as much a fait accompli as the universalization of Freud. But there is continuing dispute over what it is to be "a Keynesian." A long series was published in the sixties in *Encounter* magazine under the title "Are We All Keynesians Now?" One contributor to that series—to demonstrate the confusion—maintained that one could not properly qualify as a "Keynesian" unless one believed that the apparatus of the government should be used to maintain low interest rates. Others argued that Keynes had higher—indeed much higher—priorities. Richard Nixon, early in his second term, made the statement, "We are all Keynesians now." Even in 1973 that statement shocked the orthodox. For a Republican to have said such a thing in 1950 is inconceivable— as inconceivable, to quote Professor John Kenneth Galbraith, as to have said, "We are all Marxists." Whatever a Keynesian was, at least he was the archenemy of the balanced budget, the trademark of conservative economic thought.

It is especially significant that anti-Keynesian analyses of some gravity had been published at the time the class of 1950 graduated from Yale University. These were both technical and political. But the work of Robbins, Mises, Hutt, Anderson, Röpke—to mention a few—was not called to the attention of students of economics. The operative assumption was that the business cycle was the result of an organic deficiency in the market system and that interventionism was the only cure. We know now that the factor of the money supply looms larger in causing contraction and expansion than anyone surmised at the time. The texts reviewed in *Gamay* were, I am saying, heavily ideological, and "Keynesian" was the correct idiomatic word to use to describe economists who inclined to interventionist solutions for economic problems and, while at it, social problems as well.

I do not mean to give the impression that critics were united in their disdain of my analysis of economic education at Yale. Max Eastman, who had himself written books on socialist theory, was amusingly impatient, in his obstinate atheism, with the chapter on religion ("For my part, I fail to see why God can not take care of Himself at Yale, or even for that matter at Harvard. To me it is ridiculous to see little, two-legged fanatics running around the earth fighting and arguing in behalf of a Deity whom they profess to consider omnipotent"). But he was forthrightly enthusiastic about the economic section: "His second chapter, Individualism at Yale, is by contrast entirely mature. And it is devastating." There were others, schooled in economics, who applauded the chapter, e.g., Felix Morley, Henry Hazlitt, John Davenport, Garret Garrett, and C. P. Ives.

Max Eastman's dichotomization brings up the heated reaction to a book that professes concurrently a concern over the ascendancy of religious skepticism and political statism. I spoke earlier about a set of sentences that many critics found especially galling. When I saw the suggested formulation, written out on the margin of my manuscript in Willmoore Kendall's bold green script, I suspected they would cause difficulty. But there was a nice rhetorical resonance and an intrinsic, almost nonchalant suggestion of an exciting symbiosis, so I let pass: "*I believe that the duel between Christianity and atheism is the most important in the world. I further believe that the struggle between individualism and collectivism is the same struggle reproduced on another level.*" The words "the same struggle reproduced on another level" were not originally my own. In the prolonged defense of the book I did not renounce them, in part out of loyalty to my mentor, in part, no doubt, because it would have proved embarassing to disavow a formulation published over one's signature, never mind its provenance. But in part also because I was tickled by the audacity of the sally and not unamused by the sputtering outrage of its critics.

They were, no doubt, particularly spurred on to lambaste the suggested nexus by their knowledge of its popularity in certain Christian-conservative circles, my favorite of them being the American Council of Christian Laymen in Madison, Wisconsin, which quoted the two sentences in its publication and then sighed,

"No Solomon or Confucius or other wise man of the ages ever spoke or wrote truer words than the sentence just quoted." It was the very first time I had been compared to Solomon *or* Confucius.

The widespread objection was not only on the point that to suggest an affinity between the eschatological prospects of heaven and hell and the correct role of the state in achieving full employment was something on the order of blasphemy. It was fueled by the ideological conviction of many Christian modernists that the road to Christianity on earth lies through the federal government. Although these criticisms flowed in copiously from Protestant quarters, they were on the whole most bitter in the fashionable Catholic journals; and indeed my being a Catholic itself became something of an issue.

McGeorge Bundy, in his main-event review in the *Atlantic*, wrote directly on the point:

> Most remarkable of all, Mr. Buckley, who urges a return to what he considers to be Yale's true religious tradition, at no point says one word of the fact that he himself is an ardent Roman Catholic. In view of the pronounced and well-recognized difference between Protestant and Catholic views on education in America, and in view of Yale's Protestant history, it seems strange for any Roman Catholic to undertake to speak for the Yale religious tradition. . . . It is stranger still for Mr. Buckley to venture his prescription with no word or hint to show his special allegiance.

On this point Dwight Macdonald commented: "Buckley is indeed a Catholic, and an ardent one. But, oddly enough, this fact is irrelevant, since his book defines Christianity in Protestant terms, and his economics are Calvinist rather than Catholic. One of the wryest twists in the whole comedy is that the Catholic press has almost unanimously damned Buckley's economic views."

Macdonald exaggerated, but not entirely. "He quite unwittingly succeeds in contravening Catholic moral doctrine as applied to economics and politics on almost every topic he takes up," the Jesuits' *America* had editorialized, concluding, "Mr. Buckley's own social philosophy is almost as obnoxious to a well-instructed Catholic as the assaults on religion he rightly condemns." (Who is flirting with the nexus now?) *Commonweal*, the Catholic layman's journal of opinion, was right in there. "The nature of Mr. Buckley's heresies were pointed out again in the Catholic press, but apparently the young man remains unmoved. He continues to peddle his anti-papal economics without any noticeable changes often under the auspices of Catholics. . . ." Father Higgins, the labor priest, objected heatedly to my "attempt to identify the heresy of economic individualism with Catholic or Christian doctrine."

I am obliged to concede, at this distance, that, the attacks from the Catholics quite apart, it is probably true that there was a pretty distinct anti-Catholic animus in some of the criticism of this book. The Reverend Henry Sloan Coffin, former head of the Union Theological Seminary, former chairman of the Educational Policy Committee of Yale, former trustee of the Corporation, chairman of a committee commissioned by the Yale Corporation to investigate my charges about Yale education without ever acknowledging them (see below), was so incautious as to write to an alumnus who had questioned Coffin about my book, "Mr. Buckley's book is really a misrepresentation and [is] distorted by his Roman Catholic point of view. Yale is a Puritan and Protestant institution by its heritage and he should have attended Fordham or some similar institution."

Now there are three strands to the Catholic point. The first has to do with the allegedly distinctive Catholic definition of Christianity; the second with the allegedly distinctive Catholic understanding of the role of the university; and the third, most simply stated, was ad hominem, i.e., an attempt to suggest that by "concealing" my Catholicism I told the discerning reader a great deal about my deficient character and, derivatively, about the invalidity of my criticisms and arguments.

Taking the third point first, a semantic advantage was instantly achieved by those who spoke of my having "concealed" my Catholicism. By not advertising it—so ran the planted axiom—I was concealing it. Inasmuch as, on writing the book, I saw nothing in the least distinctively Catholic about the points I made, I had thought it irrelevant to advert to my Catholicism. Even as I was criticized for "concealing" my Catholicism, I could have been criticized had I identified myself as a Catholic on the grounds that I had "dragged" in my Catholicism as if it were relevant.

But see, for instance, Professor Fred Rodell (of the Yale Law School) writing in the *Progressive*, probably (though there are close runners-up—Arthur Schlesinger in the *New York Post*, Vern Countryman in the *Yale Law Journal*, Herman Liebert in the *St. Louis Post-Dispatch*, Theodore Greene in the *Yale Daily News*, Frank Ashburn in the *Saturday Review*) the most acidulous review of the lot: "...most Catholics would resent both the un-Christian arrogance of his presentation and, particularly, his deliberate concealment—throughout the entire foreword, text, and appendices of a highly personalized book—of his very relevant church affiliation." Ah, the sweet uses of rhetoric. "No mention" of Catholicism elides to "concealment" of Catholicism elides to "deliberate concealment" (a tautology, by the way). That my affiliation was "very relevant" spared Mr. Rodell the pains of having to explain its relevance. By the same token would it have been relevant for a reviewer of a book by Fred Rodell on the *Supreme Court and Freedom of Religion* to accuse the author of "deliberate concealment" of the "very relevant" fact that his name used to be Fred Rodelheim, and that his interpretation of the Freedom Clause was tainted in virtue of his lifetime's concealment of his having been born Jewish? That would have gone down—quite properly—as anti-Semitism.

If one pauses to think about it, it is difficult to be at once an "ardent" Catholic, as everyone kept saying I was, and to "conceal" one's Catholicism (unless one worships furiously and furtively). The only place in the book in which I might unobtrusively have said that I am a Catholic is on page 28 where I mention an Inter-Faith Conference held in the spring of 1949 sponsored by Dwight Hall (Protestant), St. Thomas More (Catholic), and the Hillel Foundation (Jewish). I was the Catholic co-chairman of that conference, which is hardly the way to go about concealing one's affiliation. But even to have mentioned in this book that I had been co-chairman would have been irrelevant, perhaps even vainglorious. Should I have mentioned that I was the son of a wealthy father, in order to explain a prejudice in favor of capitalism?

With respect to the second point, I accepted as the operative definition of "Christianity" (see page 7) that of the World Council of Churches, supplemented by a definition of Dr. Reinhold Niebuhr—an organization, and an individual, never accused of being closet Catholics.

As to the remaining point, namely the purpose of education, it is hard to know what the Reverend Henry Sloan Coffin had in mind when he suggested that Yale's "Puritan and Protestant heritage" was responsible for a "distortion" that grew inevitably out of my Roman Catholicism, or McGeorge Bundy, when he referred to the well-recognized difference between Protestant and Catholic views on education in America. I am aware of no difference, celebrated or obscure, with reference to the purpose of a *secular college*, about which I was writing. Yale was indeed founded as a Protestant institution, but the bearing of that datum on this book underscores rather than subverts its thesis. The man who was president of Yale while I was there said in his inaugural address, "I call on all members of the faculty, as members of a thinking body, freely to recognize the tremendous validity and power of the teachings of Christ in our life-and-death struggle against the force of selfish materialism." That wasn't Pope Pius IX talking. And, later, President Charles Seymour said, "Yale was dedicated to the training of spiritual leaders. We betray our trust if we fail to explore the various ways in which the youth who come to us may learn to appreciate spiritual values, whether by the example of our own lives or through the cogency of our philosophical arguments. The simple and direct way is through the maintenance and upbuilding of the Christian religion as a vital part of university life." Maybe Charles Seymour should have been made president of Fordham.

I have mentioned that the reaction to the publication of *Gamay* was quite startling. Louis Filler wrote in the *New England Quarterly*, "This book is a phenomenon of our time. It could hardly have been written ten years ago, at least for general circulation." He meant by that that no one ten years earlier (a) was particularly alarmed by, or interested in, ideological trends in higher education; and that therefore (b) nobody would have bothered to read a book that examined those themes, let alone one that focused on a single college.

So that the book's success as an attention-getter first surprised, then amazed. It was infuriating to the hostile critics that a man as eminent as John Chamberlain should have consented to write the introduction to it, and indeed Fred Rodell held him personally responsible for the notoriety of the book. ("It was doubtless the fact of a John Chamberlain introduction that lent the book, from the start, the aura of importance and respectability. . . .") But it was too late to ignore it. *Life* magazine did an editorial (cautious interest in the book's theme), *Time* and *Newsweek* ran news stories; the *Saturday Review*, a double review; and after a while there were reviews and news stories about the reviews and news stories. The critic Selden Rodman, although he disagreed with the book and its conclusions, had said of it in the *Saturday Review*, "[Mr. Buckley] writes with clarity, a sobriety, and an intellectual honesty that would be noteworthy if it came from a college president." (Compare Herman Liebert, from the staff of the Yale Library, writing for the *St. Louis Post-Dispatch*: "... the book is a series of fanatically emotional attacks on a few professors who dare to approach religion and politics objectively." Note that collectivist economics and agnostic philosophy suddenly became the "objective" approaches. That they were so considered at Yale was of course the gravamen of the book which this critic, in his fustian, was witless to recognize.) Oh, yes, Fred Rodell: "I deem it irresponsible in a scholar like Selden Rodman to dignify the book as 'important' and 'thought-provoking.'" Max Eastman had written, in the *American Mercury*, "He names names, and quotes quotes, and conducts himself, in general, with a disrespect for his teachers that is charming and stimulating in a high degree.... This perhaps is the best feature of his book, certainly the most American in the old style—its arrant intellectual courage." (From the encephalophonic Mr. Rodell, his voice hoarse: "... I deem it irresponsible, in a scholar like Max Eastman, to shower the book with adulatory adjectives....")

And so on, for months and months. Official Yale took no official position but was very busy at every level. The *Yale Daily News* ran analyses of the book by six professors, only one of whom (William Wimsatt) found anything remotely commendable about the book. The series was introduced by an editorial of which a specimen sentence was "When the Buckley book has succeeded in turning the stomachs of its readers and lining up Yale men categorically on the side of that great 'hoax' academic freedom, Bill Buckley will, as Professor Greene suggests, have performed a great service to Yale."

In the *Yale Alumni Magazine* the book was treated with caution, but I was offhandedly coupled with a notorious and wealthy old crank called George Gundelfinger, a gentleman who had gone off his rocker a generation earlier and periodically drowned the campus with nervous exhalations of his arcane philosophy, which heralded as the key to the full life a kind of platonic masturbation ("sublimate pumping" he called it). Copies of McGeorge Bundy's review were sent out to questioning alumni. Meanwhile, in the trustees' room, a plan had been devised to commission an inquiry by a committee of eight alumni into "the intellectual and spiritual welfare of the university, the students, and its faculty." The chairman, as mentioned, was Henry Sloan Coffin. And among its members was Irving Olds, then chairman of the board of United States Steel Corporation, thus effecting representation for God and man. The committee was surreptitiously set up during the summer, in anticipation of *Gamay*'s appearance in the fall, but its clear function of unsaying what this book said was acknowledged even in the news stories.

Yale didn't have an easy time of it. Too many people knew instinctively that the central charges of the book were correct, whatever the inflections distinctive to Yale. Felix Morley, formerly president of Haverford College, had written in *Barron's*, "[Buckley's] arguments must be taken seriously. As he suggests, and as this reviewer from personal knowledge of scores of American colleges can confirm, the indictment is equally applicable to many of our privately endowed institutions of higher learning. Mr. Buckley, says John Chamberlain in the latter's foreword, is incontestably right about the educational drift of modern times." It is confirmation of Morley's generalization that, twenty-five years later, references to religion and politics that were then eyebrow-raising seem utterly bland: almost conservative, in a way. What is unthinkable in the current scene isn't that an economics teacher should come out for 100 percent excess profits tax, or that a teacher of sociology should mock religion. What is unthinkable today is an inaugural address by a president of a major university containing such passages as I have quoted from Charles Seymour.

So that Yale had that problem—that most people suspected that heterodoxy was rampant—and an additional problem which it needed to handle most deftly (and, on the whole, did). I made the suggestion in this book that the alumni of Yale play a greater role in directing the course of Yale education. That they proceed to govern the University, through their representatives, even as the people govern the country through theirs. This suggestion had a most startling effect. Yale's challenge has always been to flatter its alumni while making certain they should continue impotent.

The purpose of a Yale education, never mind the strictures of this book, can hardly be to turn out a race of idiots. But one would have thought that was what Yale precisely engages in. Walking out of the Huntington Hotel in Pasadena during the hottest days of the controversy, I espied the Reverend Henry Sloan Coffin walking in. I introduced myself. He greeted me stiffly, and then said, as he resumed his way into the hotel, "Why do you want to turn Yale education over to a bunch of boobs?" Since Mr. Coffin had been chairman of the Educational Policy Committee of the Corporation, it struck me that if indeed the alumni were boobs he bore a considerable procreative responsibility. Certainly his contempt for Yale's demonstrated failure was far greater than my alarm at its potential failure.

He was not alone.

Bruce Barton, the anti–New Dealer at whose partial expense President Roosevelt had composed the rollicking taunt, "Martin, Barton, and Fish," saw the need for reform. But by *alumni*? "As for Mr. Buckley's cure—letting the alumni dictate the teaching, what could be more terrifying? Are these noisy, perennial sophomores, who dress up in silly costumes and get drunk at reunions, who spend their thousands of dollars buying halfbacks and quarterbacks, and following the Big Blue Team—are they to be the nation's mental mentors?" I really had had no idea the contempt in which "alumni" qua alumni were so generally held.

My notion, as elaborated in the book, was that alumni would concern themselves with the purpose of a university; that, if mind and conscience led them to the conclusion, they would not only be free, but compelled, to decide that certain values should be encouraged, others discouraged. That, necessarily, this would give them, through their representatives, the right to judicious hiring and firing, precisely with the end in mind of furthering broad philosophical objectives and cultivating certain ideals—through the exposure of the undergraduate body to (President Seymour's phrase) cogent philosophical arguments.

There are many grounds for disapproving the proposal of alumni control. But the description, by some critics, of the state of affairs I sought led me to question my own sanity and then, finding it in good order, to question that of my critics. Consider the near-terminal pain of Frank Ashburn as he closed his long piece for the *Saturday Review*: "The book is one which has the glow and appeal of a fiery cross on a hillside at night. There will undoubtedly be robed figures who gather to it, but the hoods will not be academic. They will cover the face."

Gee whiz. Now it is important to remember that Frank Ashburn is a very nice man. He is, moreover, quite intelligent. He founded a successful boy's preparatory school, Brooks School, and, years later, in his capacity as headmaster, he invited me to address the student body, proffering the customary fee. And I did, arriving without my hood; and, to the extent it is possible to do so under less than clinical conditions, I probed about a bit, and Frank Ashburn was to all appearances entirely normal. But that's the kind of thing *Gamay* did to people, especially people close to Yale. I did mention that Frank Ashburn was a trustee?

I must not let the point go, because one *has* to ask oneself *why* it is that supervision of the general direction of undergraduate instruction is so instinctively repugnant to nonjuveniles. I do not know whether Robert Hatch, who wrote for the *New Republic*, is a Yale graduate, but in terms of horror registered he might as well have been. He took pains, in his review, to try to explain what, in fact, I was *really* up to with my bizarre proposals. "It is astonishing," he wrote, "on the assumption that Buckley is well-meaning, that he has not realized that the methods he proposes for his alma mater are precisely those employed in Italy, Germany, and Russia. An elite shall establish the truth by ukase and no basic disagreement shall be tolerated."

It really wasn't all that astonishing that I did not spot the similarities in the methods I proposed and those of the Fascists, Nazis, and Communists, because there are no similarities. My book made it plain that alumni direction could be tolerated only over the college of which they were uniquely the constituents; that alumni of institutions that sought different ends should be equally free to pursue them. Moreover, the ideals I sought to serve were those that no authoritarian society would regard as other than seditious—namely, the ideals of a minimalist state, and deference to a transcendent order.

But the notion that the proposals were subversive was jubilantly contagious. Four months after the publication of *Gamay*, Chad Walsh was writing in the *Saturday Review*: "What Mr. Buckley really proposes is that the alumni of Yale should turn themselves into a politburo, and control the campus exactly as the Kremlin controls the intellectual life of Russia." "Exactly," in the sense used here, can only be understood to mean "analogously." Obviously there are no "exact" parallels between a state directing

all education and enforcing a political orthodoxy and the constituency of discrete educational institutions, within a free and
pluralist society, directing the education of its own educational
enterprise. Indeed, so obviously is it inexact to draw the parallel,
the heretical thought suggests itself that conventional limitations
on alumni are closer to the authoritarian model. A free association, within a free society, shaping an educational institution
toward its own purpose, is practicing a freedom which totalitarian
societies would never permit it to do. An obvious example would
be a German university under Hitler which prescribed that its faculty, in the relevant disciplines, should preach racial toleration and
racial equality; or, in the Bolshevik model, a constituency backing
a university that, athwart the political orthodoxy, insisted on
preaching the ideals of freedom and pluralism.

I find it painful, at this remove, to make points so obvious.
But if *Gamay* is to be republished, it must surely be in part for
the purpose of allowing us to examine specimens, however
wilted, of the political literature of yesteryear; and to wonder
what was the madness that seized so many people of such considerable reputation; and to wonder further that such profound
misinterpretations were not more widely disavowed. Were these
people lefties?—shrewdly protecting their positions by theoretical incantations? Yes, one supposes, in some cases. But surely not
in others: Frank Ashburn was an Establishment figure, in lockstep
with the Zeitgeist, who probably shed a wistful tear or two in private over some of the departed virtues. They are the enigma. The
left was of course especially scornful. When, fifteen years later, a
number of our colleges and universities were given over to the
thousand blooms of the youth revolution, which demanded that
colleges be "relevant"—i.e., that they become arms depots for the
anti-Vietnam war—many of the same people who sharpened
their teeth on *Gamay* were preternaturally silent.

They feasted on ideological reticulation. Michael Harrington was in those days a socialist and a Christian. He would in due course repeal the laws of progress by reaffirming the one faith and renouncing the second. He wrote his review for Dorothy Day's *Catholic Worker*: "The frightening thing is that Mr. Buckley is not yet realistic enough for fascism. Mr. Buckley's aims can only be secured by fascist methods—coercion in favor of capitalists—a realistic conclusion which Mr. Buckley's five years in New Haven did not educate him to make." Neither five years' education in New Haven nor twenty-five years' education outside New Haven. The case for capitalism is infinitely stronger in 1977 than in 1950, having profited in the interim from the empirical failures of socialism, as from the scholarly accreditation of the presumptions of the free market. Besides which, the word "fascism" loses its pungency when it is used to mean, pure and simple, the exercise of authority. Mr. Harrington, even then, was flirting with heresy, which would become his succubus.

Authority is licitly and illicitly acquired by the democratic canon; and, once acquired, is then licitly and illicitly exercised. The "authority" to apprehend, try, and punish a lawbreaker is licitly acquired in the democratic circumstances of a society which, after popular consultation, makes its own laws, prescribes its own judicial procedures, and stipulates its own punishments—all subject to the rule of law. The line between licit and illicit authority in a secular society is, however, elusive, though it is generally acknowledged in the Judeo-Christian world that there is such a line, most resonantly affirmed by Christ's distinction between Caesar and God. It is an unusual experience for a libertarian to be catechized by a socialist on the theme of the dangers of coercion. Harrington's oxymoronic formulation—"coercion in favor of capitalists"—reminds us of the fashionable jargon in the commodity markets of the left (alas, not greatly changed). His sentence is on the order of "coercive freedom," or "the slavery of the bill of rights." Unless a "fascist method" can be distinguished from a plain old "method" by which the will of the entrepreneurial unit prevails over the will of the individual resolved subversively to gainsay that will, then paradoxically you are left without the freedom of the collectivity. The interdiction of that modest freedom on the grand piano Mr. Harrington is used to playing on in his fullthroated crusade for state socialism is not only inconsistent, it is positively unseemly.

It is worth pursuing the matter yet one step further, I think, in order to notice the review by T. M. Greene. Professor Greene was a considerable character on the Yale campus. I think he was the most quintessentially liberal man I ever came upon, outside the pages of Randall Jarrell's *Pictures From an Institution*. As master of the largest residential college at Yale (Silliman), he one day issued an order, in the interest of decorum, requiring students who ate dinner in the dining room to wear coats and ties. He was dismayed by the trickle of criticism, and very soon indignantly repealed his own order, apologizing for his lapse into *dirigisme*. He taught, as an explicit Christian, a course in the philosophy of religion which was widely attended; but I remarked (see page 7) that in the opinion of his students he was engaged, really, in reteaching ethics, not religion. (There's nothing against teaching ethics, but of course it isn't exactly the same thing.)

His reaction to *Gamay*, as published in the *Yale Daily News*, fairly took one's breath away. He fondled the word "fascist" as though he had come up with a Dead Sea Scroll vouchsafing the key word to the understanding of *God and Man at Yale*. In a few sentences he used the term thrice. "Mr. Buckley has done Yale a great service" (how I would tire of this pedestrian rhetorical device), "and he may well do the cause of liberal education in America an even greater service, by stating the fascist alternative to liberalism. This facist thesis... This... pure fascism... What more could Hitler, Mussolini, or Stalin ask for...?" (They asked for, and got, a great deal more.)

What survives, from such stuff as this, is ne plus ultra relativism, idiot nihilism. "What is required," Professor Greene spoke, "is more, not less tolerance—not the tolerance of indifference, but the tolerance of honest respect for divergent convictions and the determination of all that such divergent opinions be heard without administrative censorship. I try my best in the classroom to expound and defend my faith, when it is relevant, as honestly and persuasively as I can. But I can do so only because many of my colleagues are expounding and defending their contrasting faiths, or skepticisms, as openly and honestly as I am mine."

A professor of *philosophy!* Question: What is the (1) ethical, (2) philosophical, or (3) epistemological argument for *requiring* continued tolerance of ideas whose discrediting it is the purpose of education to effect? What ethical code (in the Bible? in Plato? Kant? Hume?) requires "honest respect" for any divergent conviction? Even John Stuart Mill did not ask more than that a question be not considered as closed so long as any one man adhered to it; he did not require that that man, flourishing the map of a flat world, be seated in a chair of science at Yale. And this is to say nothing about the flamboyant contrast between Professor Greene's call to toleration in all circumstances and the toleration *he* showed to the book he was reviewing. An honest respect by him for my divergent conviction would have been an arresting application at once of his theoretical and charitable convictions.

The sleeper, in that issue of the *Yale Daily News*, was William Wimsatt. The late Professor Wimsatt, the renowned critic and teacher, was... a Catholic! Not an uppity Catholic. He was, simply, known by the cognoscenti to be one, and his friends found that charming. But under the circumstances, the pressure on Professor Wimsatt to Tom must have been very nearly unbearable, and his conciliatory motions must be weighed charitably under the circumstances. He denounced *Gamay* as "impudent," inasmuch as its author "used the entree and confidential advantage of a student and alumnus to publicize so widely both embarrassing personalities and problems of policy which are internal to the relation between administrative officers and alumni." A so-so point which, it happens, I dealt with in the book itself, in my discussion of the emasculating hold the Yale administration exercises over its alumni; but, in a sense, also a point gainsaid by the universal interest provoked by the book, which interest focused not on its gossip value involving any one or more professors (only three of the hundred reviews I have reread bother even to mention by name any individual professor named in the book).

Protected by such rhetorical cover, Professor Wimsatt went on to say some very interesting things. He began, for instance, by suavely blowing the whole Coffin–Bundy–Dwight Hall–Yale position about religion at Yale. "The prevailing secularism of the university is palpable," wrote Professor Wimsatt matter-of-factly. That's what *I* said. But lest that should shock, he added, What-else-is-new? "What else did Mr. Buckley expect when he elected to come here?" He went on to say, in effect, that a "modern" university cannot orient itself other than to fashion. "What would he expect of any modern American university large enough to be the representative of the culture in which he has lived all his life?"

Mr. Wimsatt is here carefully avoiding the point. Obviously a modern, acquiescent, college will tend not to buck the Zeitgeist. This begs the question whether under certain circumstances it might do so; and certainly begs the question whether idealistically active alumni are entitled to apply pressure on it to do so.

But, despite himself, Professor Wimsatt was getting hotter and hotter. "It is more fundamental to ask...what is actually right, and how far any individual may in good conscience tolerate or assist the teaching of what he firmly believes wrong. If I knew that a professor were teaching the Baconian heresy about Shakespeare, I should think it a pity. If I knew that a professor were preaching genocide, I should think it a duty, if I were able, to prevent him—even though his views were being adequately refuted in the next classroom." That buzz saw ran right through the analysis of Professor Greene, adjacent on the page, leaving it bobbing and weaving in death agony. But nobody noticed. "As Mr. Buckley so earnestly pleads, it is indeed very far from being a fact that the truth, in such matters of value, is bound 'to emerge victorious.' It would be easy to name several doctrines, not only genocide but the less violent forms of racism, for instance, or an ethics of premarital sexual experiment—which the present administration of no university in this country would tolerate." (From the 25th Reunion Yearbook of the Yale Class of 1950, published in 1975, Questionnaire #13: "Are you in favor of or opposed to: . . . People living together out of wedlock? Oppose, 42%. Favor, 43%.") Although Professor Wimsatt was hardly quotable as an endorser of *Gamay*, the passages here reproduced take you exactly as far as I go in every theoretical point. Everything else he said was in the nature of social shock absorption.

It is worth it, before making a final comment on the grander points involved, to climb out of the polemical fever swamps and look with a little detachment on the purely economic question. When I wrote this book, there were reviewers who defended the factual generalities, indeed went so far as to say the points I made were obvious. Yale's teachings were distinct from Yale's preachings—"this rudimentary fact of life," Dwight Macdonald commented, "Buckley is rude enough to dwell on for 240 pages." On the other hand, very few reviewers (certainly not Macdonald) were prepared to associate themselves with my prescriptions—though some of them acknowledged nervously that any way you look at it there was a paradox in the circumstance of alumni agitatedly supporting the cultivation of values different from their own. I think it safe to say that no fully integrated member of the intellectual community associated himself with my position on academic freedom. In March of this year Irving Kristol, a professor, editor, author, philosopher of unassailable academic and intellectual standing, included in a casual essay in his regular series for the *Wall Street Journal* (which space he shares with such other scholars as Robert Nisbet and Arthur Schlesinger Jr.) the comment: "Business men or corporations do not have any obligation to give money to institutions whose views or attitudes they disapprove of. It's absurd to insist otherwise—yet this absurdity is consistently set forth in the name of 'academic freedom.'" The prose is an improvement on my own in *God and Man at Yale*, but the point is identical. Yet no one rose to say of Professor Kristol that he should be wearing a hood and that he was introducing fascism to American education.

Indeed the educational establishment, although it rose to smite my book hip and thigh, has since then tended to find it more useful to take the advice of that generic class of prudent lawyers who counsel their clients to say "No comment." Even now I rub my eyes in amazement at the silence given to events—historical, sociological, and even judicial—that tend to confirm and reconfirm the factual claims of my book, and to give support to its theoretical arguments. There was, for instance, the A. P. Smith case of 1953 (*A. P. Smith Manufacturing Company* v. *Barlow*). I should like to be able to refer to it as the "celebrated A. P. Smith case." But it is not celebrated at all. It is unknown.

What happened was that a New Jersey manufacturer of valves and hydrants made a gift of fifteen hundred dollars to Princeton University, and a group of minority stockholders sued, saying in effect, What does Princeton University have to do with the fortunes of the A. P. Smith Company? The case was tried and most vigorously defended, with star witnesses moving in and out of the witness stand. Not because of the fifteen hundred dollars, obviously, but because the precedent was deemed very important.

Well, Princeton and the management of the A. P. Smith Company won. Two courts, the superior court of New Jersey and the Supreme Court of that state on appeal, affirmed the corporate validity of the gift. Why then is the case not more greatly celebrated?

Because the price of victory was academic freedom as commonly understood. The A. P. Smith Company, in its defense brief, took the position that by giving money to Princeton it was advancing its corporate purposes strictly defined. The defense brief said: "The Smith Company turned to philanthropy not for the sake of philanthropy but for the sake of selling more valves and hydrants." *How's that again?*

But there was no recorded objection from representatives of Princeton University. Expert witnesses were called. One of them was: Irving Olds. Our old friend! Chairman of the board of United States Steel! Mr. Olds testified soberly on the stand that "our American institutions of higher learning can and do perform a service of tremendous importance to the corporations of this and other states, through acquainting their students with the facts about different economic theories and ideologies. With the good educational facilities provided by these institutions, the courses of instruction will and do lead the student body to recognize the virtues and achievements of our well-proven economic system; and, on the other hand, to discover the faults and weaknesses of an arbitrary, government-directed and controlled system of production and distribution."

That testimony by Mr. Olds was given approximately on the first anniversary of the release of the report of the Yale committee to investigate the charges levelled in this book, and Mr. Olds had then put his signature on a document that said: "A university does not take sides in the questions that are discussed in its halls. The business of a university is to educate, not to indoctrinate its students. In the ideal university all sides of any issue are presented as impartially and as forcefully as possible. This is Yale's policy." Now the only course in comparative economic systems being taught at Yale at that time is described in this book. The professor who taught it proclaimed himself an ardent socialist in the British tradition, and defended the socialist alternative to the free market system, which one would suppose is not the system that, in the understanding of A. P. Smith, the lower court, the higher court, and Irving Olds, promotes the "selling of more valves and hydrants."

The worst was yet to be. The lower court, in authorizing the gift, ruled: "It is the youth of today which also furnishes tomorrow's leaders in economics and in government, thereby erecting a strong breastwork against any onslaught from hostile forces which would change our way of life either in respect of private enterprise or democratic self-government. The proofs before me are abundant that Princeton emphasizes by precept and indoctrination [*precept and indoctrination!*] the principles which are very vital to the preservation of our democratic system of business and government. . . . I cannot conceive of any greater benefit to corporations in this country than to build, and continue to build, respect for and adherence to a system of free enterprise and democratic government, the serious impairment of either of which may well spell the destruction of all corporate enterprise." I cannot think of a more excruciatingly embarrassing victory in Princeton's history.

Dumb judge? I invite you to find a denunciation of him by an official of Princeton University. The decision was appealed and went on to the Supreme Court of New Jersey, where *another* dumb judge affirmed the lower court's decision, and made it all worse. Because *he* reminded the "objective stockholders" that they had "not disputed any of the foregoing testimony" asserting the service Princeton is performing in behalf of free market economy; and the court reminded them, paternalistically, that "more and more they [private corporations] have come to recognize that their salvation rests upon a sound economic and social environment which in turn rests in no insignificant part upon free and vigorous nongovernmental institutions of learning." Princeton didn't take its fifteen hundred dollars and go hang itself, but one can imagine the gloom in the panelled office where they all met to open that judicial valentine.

The educators were saying, in response to this book, that college is a cultural sanctuary from the commerce of life. That such concessions as periodically were made by university officials were purely rhetorical—President Seymour, enjoining the faculty to cultivate the doctrines of Christ at inaugural ceremonies; Princeton deans, nodding their heads acquiescently when the court upholds a financial award on the grounds that Princeton is "by precept and indoctrination" committed to spreading the gospel of free enterprise. Actually, they were saying, no interference is possible. All ideas must start out equal. (All ideas *are* equal!) To make demands on a college is totalitarian, fascist, communist, condemned by all men of understanding, reaching back to Thomas Jefferson. How widely he was used during the controversy! "Subject opinion to coercion," Philip Kurland quoted him; "whom will you make your inquisitors? Fallible men; men governed by bad passions, by private as well as public reasons. And why subject it to coercion? To produce uniformity. But is uniformity of opinion desirable? No more than of face and stature... difference of opinion is advantageous." And, of course, who would disagree that men are fallible? But does that mean we can rely, at the margin, other than on men? On whom was Jefferson relying for remedies when in 1821 he wrote to General Breckinridge to complain of "seminaries [where] our sons [are] imbibing opinions and principles in discord with those of their own country." Did Jefferson wish to do something about it? Or was he describing only a situation which could not be corrected, because men are fallible, dominated by passion? No. Jefferson continued, "This canker is eating on the vitals of our existence, and if not arrested at once, will be beyond remedy." If not arrested by whom? Surely not the state. We would all agree on this? Not quite all. The state would prove to have its uses. President Seymour warned urgently and repeatedly against accepting federal aid to education on the grounds that it would bring federal interference. President Seymour retired in 1950. In the succeeding generation major private universities became totally dependent on federal funds. Remove the federal subsidy to Yale (35%), or to Harvard (25%), or to MIT (65%), and what would happen to them? The notion of mere trustees influencing the choice of textbooks was—and is—thought scandalous: by the same people who, calling such interference fascism, backed, or were indifferent to, legislation which twenty-five years later would permit the attorney general of the United States (ironically, a former college president, in a Republican administration, executing laws passed by a Democratic Congress) to pry out of a thoroughly private association—the American Institute of Real Estate Appraisers—the promise to destroy a textbook called *The Appraisal of Real Estate*, in which appraisers are advised that the ethnic composition of a neighborhood in fact influences the value of real estate. Under the proposed consent decree, the Institute agrees to strike from the present (sixth) edition of its textbook all the improper language. Specific textbook revisions have been prepared. These changes "will be included in the seventh edition of the text" not later than September 5, 1978. Sixty days after the decree is entered, the Institute "will commence a review of all booklets, manuals, monographs, guides, lexicons, and...other instructional material published under its auspices" to assure that they too conform with the text revisions. And they called fascistic a summons to free citizens freely associated, exercising no judicial or legislative power, to communicate their ideals at a private college through the appropriate selection of texts and teachers.

"Unless the great concepts which have been traditional to the western world are rooted in a reasoned view of the universe and man's place in it, and unless this reasoned view contains in its orbit a place for the spirit, man is left in our day with archaic weapons unsuited for the problems of the present." I don't know who wrote that sentence, which appeared in an editorial in the *Boston Pilot*, but I know I wish I had written it because with great economy of expression it says, really, everything my book sought to say. It leaves unsaid only this. Is there a role for the nonacademician in formulating that "reasoned view"? Or if not that, in catalyzing that "reasoned view"? Or if not that, in providing genial ground in which to cultivate that "reasoned view"? It is on this point that I declare myself, a generation after the event, on the side of the university with a mission.

In recent months I have been asked by representatives of Yale University to make a public declaration urging contributions to the University's capital fund. I dealt with the first such communication most tactfully, uttering an evasion, stuttering off like a member of the Drones Club. It did not work. A second request came in. I had, this time, to say No, but I begged off giving the reasons why. A third request came in, and there was then nothing to do—I was backed up against the wall: my correspondent had never learned Machiavelli's axiom that you should not cut off the enemy's line of retreat.

I have always held in high esteem the genial tradition, and I hope it is something other than sentimentality that inclines me to believe that one of the reasons I was so happy at Yale was that geniality is—forget, and forgive, the intemperances necessarily recorded here—as natural to Yale as laughter is to Dublin, song to Milan, or angst to the *New York Review of Books*. Mostly I prefer nowadays to contend with the slogan, rather than with the man who hoists it. But sometimes there are no alternatives (in particular as the anthropomorphization of public life proceeds—you do not talk about the Democratic Party, you talk about Kennedy, Johnson, Carter). So, in my third communication, I answered directly.

"In the ideal university all sides of any issue are presented as impartially and as forcefully as possible." This was Official Yale's answer to *Gamay*. In a world governed by compromise, in which opportunism can be virtuous—such a world as our own—I am obliged to confess: I would probably settle for such an arrangement. A truly balanced curriculum, in which as much time, by professors as talented as their counterparts, in courses as critical as the others, was given to demonstrating the cogency of the arguments for God and man. This book establishes that nothing like that balance obtained twenty-five years ago. But the allocation of ideological and philosophical commitments aside, I cannot come to terms with a university that accepts the philosophical proposition that it is there for the purpose of presenting "all sides" of "any issue" as impartially and as forcefully as possible. That will not do, for the reasons Professor Wimsatt gave.

And so I was driven to write, in what I swore until I was seduced to write this essay would be my last exchange on the Yale question. And what I said was: "What's the problem? Why doesn't Yale donate itself to the State of Connecticut?"

The mechanical problem, as it happens, is virtually nonexistent. There is a thing called the Yale Corporation. It literally "owns"

Yale. If the trustees of Yale were to vote tomorrow to give "Yale" to the State of Connecticut, there would be lots of amazement and thunderstorms of indignation—and no recourse. Obviously the State of Connecticut would accept the gift. We are talking about several hundred million dollars of real property, and a half billion or so in endowments.

What then would happen?

To tell the truth, I don't know that anything much would happen. Obviously there would be changes at the corporate level. Instead of fourteen trustees, eight of them elected by their predecessors, the balance by the alumni, there would, presumably, be fourteen (or more, or less) trustees named by the governor of Connecticut (who is already *ex officio* a trustee), and confirmed by the state legislature. Would these be a scurvy lot? That is hard to say. If you look at the board of trustees of the University of California you would not find a significant difference in the profile of its membership and that of Yale today. The University of California, particularly in recent days, has its share of flower children; but, lo, so does Yale.

What else would be different? Standards of admission?

Why? The University of California at Berkeley is as hard to get into as Yale. A state university can be "elitist" and get away with it provided there are other universities within the system that will accept the less gifted students.

The curriculum would be less varied?

I don't think that would necessarily follow. There is a luxurious offering at Yale of courses in the recondite byways of human knowledge, wonderful to behold. But—that is also true of the University of California.

Excellence of faculty? But the University of California has the highest concentration of Nobel Prize winners in the country. It is simply no longer true that the most gifted scholars insist on join-

ing the faculties of privately run universities. As for the maintenance of a Yale tradition within the faculty, the incidence of
Yale-educated members continues to decline, consistent with the
de-traditionalization of Yale.

What about the quality of undergraduate instruction?

There are a lot of complaints about the mega-university, large
lecture courses, graduate-student instruction. But these complaints are also increasingly lodged against Yale and Harvard as
well as Berkeley, and as the economic noose tightens, economiz-
ing at the expense of the student is likelier at private colleges,
whose resources are limited, than at the public universities,
whose resources are less limited.

The quality of undergraduate life? Why should it be affected?
Yale has insisted it can show no geneological preferences—neither
would the State of Connecticut; neither, of course, does Berkeley.
Would state ownership interfere with undergraduate social life?
How? There is only a single fraternity surviving in Yale; there are
dozens in many state colleges. Yale's senior societies are unique,
but they are privately owned; and, in any case, their survival (so
heatedly opposed, for instance, by the recent chaplain of Yale,
among others) would hardly be the pivotal justification for with-
holding the gift of Yale to the State of Connecticut.

And consider the advantages! Yale's painful annual deficit is a
mere added calorie in the paunch of Connecticut's deficit. Those
who desire to contribute to Yale to promote specific activities
within Yale could continue to do so, even as there are private
endowments at Berkeley.

And—the most interesting point of all, I think—what, in the
absence of specific objections, are the philosophical objections? The
sense of the swingers in the social science faculty even twenty-five
years ago was to prefer the public sector over the private sector. I
cannot think what arguments most of the distinguished teachers

mentioned in this book would use to oppose in principle turning Yale over to the public sector.

Now, having said all that, let me say that *I* know why Yale shouldn't be turned over to the state. Because there are great historical presumptions that from time to time the interests of the state and those of civilization will bifurcate, and unless there is independence, the cause of civilization is neglected. Individual professors can raise their fists and cry out against the howling of the storm; but professors so inclined are resident alike at Berkeley as at New Haven. The critical difference is the corporate sense of mission. At Berkeley that sense of mission is as diffuse and inchoate—and unspecified and unspecifiable—as the resolute pluralism of California society. At the private college, the sense of mission is distinguishing. It is, however, strangled by what goes under the presumptuous designation of academic freedom. It is a terrible loss, the loss of the sense of mission. It makes the private university, sad to say, incoherent; and that is what I was trying to say when, two months out of Yale, I sat down to write this book.

August 1977

Foreword

by John Chamberlain

❧

I first ran into the name of William F. Buckley Jr. when I spent a week on the Yale campus in 1949 as part of a preparation for doing a *Life* magazine editorial on education. Both undergraduates and professors seemed fascinated by Mr. Buckley. Some of them called him a "black reactionary"; others said he was a true liberal in the old, traditional sense of the word. His editorials in the *Yale Daily News* (of which he was chairman) were debated, reviled, and praised. Clearly he was someone. But, the temper of the times being what they were, practically everyone I talked with thought young Mr. Buckley was fighting a losing fight. He was on the side of the "past."

Maybe so, but there is no compulsion on the decent human being to be "with history" when history is driving headlong toward an abyss. The compulsion to be "with history" denies the moral freedom of man. Mr. Buckley's chief sin, as this book will make plain to the discerning, is to hold certain ancient truths to be self-evident: that the free economy is better for both the individual and the group than the "planned" or the controlled economy; that man has a definite nature, which includes intimations of a moral and religious character; that to live solely for "others" is not only an impracticability but an insult to the average human being's need and capacity for self-reliance. It is also self-evident to Mr. Buckley that, in a democracy, the customer (who pays the bills) must have the right to exercise his free choice when he is out shopping in the marketplace. The autonomy of the customer should hold whether he is buying toothpaste, tennis rackets—or education for his children.

But, so a mighty chorus tells us, there is Academic Freedom to be considered. The professor must have the right to pursue the truth as he sees fit. Mr. Buckley does not deny that right; indeed, he thinks any coercion of a *researcher* is a pretty silly and self-defeating business. But should the right to pursue the truth be construed as a right to inculcate values that deny the value judgments of the customer who is paying the bills of education? Must the customer, in the name of Academic Freedom, be compelled to take a product which he may consider defective?

Professor Henry Steele Commager of Columbia University, who thinks that the university faculties, not the alumni or the parents of the students, should have final control over the aims of education, has virtually stated that the customer has no rights in the educational marketplace. Pursued to its logical conclusion, the Commager theory would end by setting up an *elite* of professorial Untouchables. The *elite* would perpetuate itself as it chose. Departments would select their staffs without reference to alumni or parental or undergraduate opinion. This is caste rule as applied to education; it might be unkind to call it "Fascism," but it is certainly not democracy.

Mr. Buckley's analysis and argument are circumscribed by the boundaries of the Yale University campus. That is his field of reference for his "case" study. He finds that Yale has sometimes professed to have no teaching "orthodoxy." "Objectivity" is its shibboleth. He finds also that Yale has an unadmitted orthodoxy; it *does* attempt to inculcate values. And what are these values?

Mr. Buckley finds that they are agnostic as to religion, "interventionist" and Keynesian as to economics, and collectivist as applied to the relation of the individual to society and government.

Whether Mr. Buckley overstates his specific argument is not for me to say: I have only spent a few days at Yale since my graduation in 1925, whereas Mr. Buckley has just come from spending five years at the place. But Mr. Buckley is incontestably right about the educational drift of modern times. And I must say that the case Mr. Buckley makes against Yale's economics department is devastating on its face. It is certainly a case that can and should be made against modern economics teaching as a whole. The quotations he chooses from the textbooks used in the Yale undergraduate economics courses would seem to speak for themselves. They are quotations that support price-fixing, virtually unlimited taxation, government monopoly, all the things that have been brewed out of Keynes, the Fabians, and Karl Marx himself. The quotations might be justified if they were part of a teaching technique aimed to expose the student to "both sides" of the question. But where are the countervailing quotations from Röpke, von Mises, Hayek, Frank Knight, the Walter Lippmann of *The Good Society* and other believers in the economics of free customer choice? Mr. Buckley says they can't be produced in any significant volume from the texts used at Yale. The Yale economics faculty is roughly 8 to 2 for economic collectivism on the evidence of this book.

Mr. Buckley would not be against this if it could be demonstrated that the customer, the one who is paying the bills for education, demands it. But does the Yale alumni body want Keynesian interventionism to dominate the economic value judgment taught to Yale students? Does it want to see the values of Christian individualism skimped or denied? Does the Yale Corporation, which represents the education-buying customer, want any such thing? Do the parents of the students want it? Do the undergraduates themselves want it prior to their indoctrination by Keynesian professors?

That is the question, as Mr. Buckley sees it. He has taken no Gallup Poll of the alumni, but he rather guesses that Yale is giving the sources of its endowment something they wouldn't vote for if they were consulted in advance. His book is a ringing call to the alumni to exercise their right to customers' choice. If they should vote for collectivism Mr. Buckley would admit defeat. But he is rather inclined to think that they wouldn't vote for any such thing. He believes the traditional values of the Christian and individualist West are still the predominant American choice. It could be. But the choice will never prevail if people, including the alumni body of Yale, refuse to stand up on their hind legs and fight.

Author's Preface

&

During the years 1946 to 1950, I was an undergraduate at Yale University. I arrived in New Haven fresh from a two-year stint in the Army, and I brought with me a firm belief in Christianity and a profound respect for American institutions and traditions. I had always been taught, and experience had fortified the teachings, that an active faith in God and a rigid adherence to Christian principles are the most powerful influences toward the good life. I also believed, with only a scanty knowledge of economics, that free enterprise and limited government had served this country well and would probably continue to do so in the future.

These two attitudes were basic to my general outlook. One concerned the role of man in the universe; the other, in all its implications, the role of man in his society. I knew, of course, of the existence of many persons who had no faith in God and even less in the individual's capacity to work out his own destiny without recourse to the state. I therefore looked eagerly to Yale University for allies against secularism and collectivism.

I am one of a small group of students who fought, during undergraduate days, in the columns of the newspaper, in the Political Union, in debates and seminars, against those who seek to subvert religion and individualism. The fight we waged continues even though little headway was made. The struggle was never more bitter than when the issue concerned educational policy.

As opportunity afforded, some of us advanced the viewpoint that the faculty of Yale is morally and constitutionally responsible to the trustees of Yale, who are in turn responsible to the alumni, and thus duty bound to transmit to their students the wisdom, insight, and value judgments which in the trustees' opinion will enable the American citizen to make the optimum adjustment to the community and to the world. I contended that the trustees of Yale, along with the vast majority of the alumni, are committed to the desirability of fostering both a belief in God and a recognition of the merits of our economic system. I therefore concluded that it was the clear responsibility of the trustees, as our educational overseers, to guide the teaching at Yale toward those ends.

The reaction to this point of view has been violent. A number of persons affiliated with the University, all the way from President-emeritus Charles Seymour to a host of students, have upheld what they call "academic freedom," by which they mean the freedom of the faculty member to teach what he sees fit as he sees fit—provided, of course, he is "honest" and "professionally competent." Here the argument rested when I left Yale.

A number of persons sympathetic to this point of view have urged me to deal at greater length with the problem. I was not disposed to do this, in part because I lack the scholarly equipment to deal with it adequately, in part because I was unwilling to spend the necessary time. I finally decided to make an attempt, largely because I fell victim to arguments I have so often utilized myself: that the so-called conservative, uncomfortably disdainful of controversy, seldom has the energy to fight his battles, while the radical, so often a member of the minority, exerts disproportionate influence because of his dedication to his cause.

I *am* dedicated to my cause. At the same time, I cannot claim to have approached this project with the diligence and patience of a professional scholar. As far as pure scholarship is concerned, it is best said of me that I have the profoundest respect for it, and no pretension to it. As witness to this, I propose, in the nontheoretical portion of this book, to confine myself to Yale. Ideally, my observations would be based on an exhaustive study of the curricula and attitudes of a number of colleges and universities. Instead, I have confined myself to the university that I know firsthand.

I do this confidently, let me add, because Yale, I judge deservedly, has earned a reputation as a citadel of "triumphant conservatism," as *Time* magazine recently put it. By comparison with many others, I believe it is. This would suggest that what is amiss at Yale is more drastically amiss in other of our great institutions of learning. Yet on this point I will not insist. It is not here my concern. I propose, simply, to expose what I regard as an extraordinarily irresponsible educational attitude that, under the protective label "academic freedom," has produced one of the most extraordinary incongruities of our time: the institution that derives its moral and financial support from Christian individualists and then addresses itself to the task of persuading the sons of these supporters to be atheistic socialists.

I ought to add that what little experience I have had with the purposefulness and tenacity of the mid-twentieth-century conservative gives me few grounds for hope that this paradox will be remedied. So it is that for consolation I have turned frequently to a few sentences of Arthur Koestler:

> Art is a contemplative business. It is also a ruthless business. One
> should either write ruthlessly what one believes to be the truth,

or shut up. Now I happen to believe that Europe is doomed. . . .
This is so to speak my contemplative truth. . . . But I also happen
to believe in the ethical imperative of fighting evil, even if the
fight is hopeless. . . . And on this plane my contemplative truth
becomes defeatist propaganda and hence an immoral influence.

I have some notion of the bitter opposition that this book
will inspire. But I am through worrying about it. My concern
over present-day educational practice stems from my conviction
that, after each side has had its say, we are right and they are
wrong; and my greatest anguish is not in contemplation of the
antagonism that this essay will evoke from many quarters, but
rather from the knowledge that they are winning and we are
losing.

I shall insert here what may seem obvious: I consider this battle of educational theory important and worth time and thought
even in the context of a world-situation that seems to render
totally irrelevant any fight except the power struggle against
Communism. I myself believe that the duel between Christianity
and atheism is the most important in the world. I further believe
that the struggle between individualism and collectivism is the
same struggle reproduced on another level. I believe that if and
when the menace of Communism is gone, other vital battles, at
present subordinated, will emerge to the foreground. And the
winner must have help from the classroom.

I should also like to state that I am not here concerned with
writing an *apologia* either for Christianity or for individualism.
That is to say, this essay will not attempt either to prove the divinity of Christ or to defend the advantages of conducting our lives
with reference to divine sanctions. Nor shall I attempt to demonstrate the contemporary applicability of the principal theses of
Adam Smith.

Rather, I will proceed on the assumption that Christianity and freedom are "good,"* without ever worrying that by so doing, I am being presumptuous.

The first duty, of course, is to arrive at a judgment as to whether or not there exists at Yale an atmosphere of detached impartiality with respect to the great value-alternatives of the day, that is, Christianity versus agnosticism and atheism, and individualism versus collectivism. My belief is that such impartiality does not exist. I shall document this opinion. What is more, for practical reasons I have restricted my survey to the undergraduate school, even though some of the graduate departments, the Yale Law School in particular, would provide far more flamboyant copy.

The question then arises: If there is a bias does it coincide with the bias of the educational trustees of Yale? In other words, if there is not impartiality, does the net impact of Yale education encourage those values probably held by the alumni? My opinion is that on the contrary, the emphases at Yale are directly opposed to those of her alumni.

I shall then ask if impartiality—assuming it to be possible—is desirable in classroom treatment of conflicting ideologies. I shall go on to question what so many persons consider axiomatic, namely the proposition that "all sides should be presented impartially," that the student should be encouraged to select the side that pleases him most. I hope to point out that this attitude, acknowledged in theory by the University, has never been practiced, and in fact, can never and ought never to be practiced.

---

* In point of fact, the argument I shall advance does not even require that free enterprise and Christianity be "good," but merely that the educational overseers of a private university should consider them to be "good."

In one respect, I have spared no pains. Although some of the matter that appears in this book is elusive, I have made every effort to be accurate. In fact, several friends, intimately associated with Yale over the past few years, believe I have bent over backwards almost grotesquely in my effort to avoid distortion. Be that as it may, I have worked with the clear realization that exaggeration would bring only unwarranted damage to an institution of which I am almost irrationally fond, and personal humiliation to myself.

Nor should this book be interpreted as a comprehensive indictment of Yale life. Volume after volume, each many times the bulk of this one, could justly be written commending the virtues of countless aspects of Yale's education. But it is not the diligence or patience of her scholars, or the kindness and understanding of her administrators, or the joys and sustaining pleasures of the friendships she makes possible that are the subject matter of this book. These deserve tribute, and I give mine without reservation. Notwithstanding, something greater, I think, is at stake: the net impact of Yale education. It is to this problem that I address myself.

I have made extensive use of Appendices for documentation, for theoretical but pertinent digressions, and for references of various kinds. It is naturally the hope of every writer that the Appendices should be consulted fastidiously. Notwithstanding, many, including myself, must admit that an understanding of the thesis does not require familiarity with appendix material.

Finally, I must ask indulgence for the frequent references in the text to myself and my personal experiences at Yale. If there were a way out, I should willingly have taken it. But a great deal of the material that I have summoned, and of the insights that I have received, has been a result of personal experiences. To avoid mention of these would be not only coy, but restrictive. For these reasons I ask patience; and further, I approach my thesis with profound humility and with the desperate hope that even those who disagree emphatically will acknowledge that I could have no motive other than a devotion to Yale, a recognition of Yale's importance, and a deep concern for the future of our country.

August 1951

GOD AND MAN

AT YALE

Chapter One

RELIGION
AT YALE

I call on all members of the faculty, as members of a thinking body, freely to recognize the tremendous validity and power of the teachings of Christ in our life-and-death struggle against the forces of selfish materialism. If we lose that struggle, judging from present events abroad, scholarship as well as religion will disappear.

—President Charles Seymour,
Inaugural Address, October 16, 1937

In evaluating the role of Christianity and religion at Yale, I have not in mind the ideal that the University should be composed of a company of scholars exclusively or even primarily concerned with spreading the Word of the Lord. I do not feel that Yale should treat her students as potential candidates for divinity school. It has been said that there are those who "want to make a damned seminary" out of Yale. There may be some who do, but I do not count myself among these.

But we can, without going that far, raise the question whether Yale fortifies or shatters the average student's respect for Christianity. There are, of course, some students who will emerge stronger Christians from any institution, and others who will reject religion wherever they are sent. But if the atmosphere of a college

is overwhelmingly secular, if the influential members of the faculty
tend to discourage religious inclinations, or to persuade the student
that Christianity is nothing more than "ghost-fear," or "twentieth-
century witchcraft," university policy quite properly becomes a
matter of concern to those parents and alumni who deem active
Christian faith a powerful force for good and for personal happiness.

I think of Yale, then, as a nondenominational educational
institution not exclusively interested in the propagation of Christianity. The question must then arise whether or not the weight
of academic activity at Yale tends to reinforce or to subvert Christianity, or to do neither the one nor the other. It is clear that
insight into this problem cannot be had from counting the number of faculty members who believe as opposed to those that do
not believe. Some instructors deal with subject matter that has
little, if any, academic bearing upon religion. Some have more
influence than others. Some teach classes that as a matter of
course attract a large number of students, while others seldom
address more than a half dozen or so.

The handiest arguments of those who vaunt the pro-religious
atmosphere at Yale is that the University has a large religion
department, a great number of strong and influential men whose
beliefs are strongly pro-Christian on its faculty, and a powerful
and pervasive "religious tradition."

To a greater or lesser extent, these statements are true. And
yet, it remains that Yale, corporately speaking, is neither pro-
Christian, nor even, I believe, neutral toward religion.

To begin with, it is impossible to gauge the Christian purpose
of a college by counting the number of courses offered in religion.
It is, of course, of interest that such courses are offered, because
this serves as an official indication, at least, that the University recognizes religion as an important field of learning, worthy of the
student's academic endeavor. But it is important to remember that

a student may major in Christianity and not be pro-Christian, just as he can major in Far Eastern Studies and be anti-oriental.

Also relevant is the number of students who are influenced by the religious department of a university or avail themselves of the college's religious facilities. Professor Clarence P. Shedd, of Yale, speaking on the radio program "Yale Interprets the News" on August 15, 1948, insisted upon the dramatic upswing in postwar religious interest, but added: "I talked with a chaplain in a large state university only last week who asserted that all the religious influences in his university were not significantly influencing more than ten percent of the undergraduates. My own figure for the large university situation nationally has been fifteen percent."

The degree to which a college is pro-Christian depends then, not so much on the number of religion courses it offers or even the number of students electing such courses, but on the orientation and direction given to the students by the instructors in these courses, and, most especially, in other courses that deal or should deal with religious values.

THE DEPARTMENT OF RELIGION

Even as with chapel, the bare figures of the presence of courses in religion are no reliable guide as to the value of the work offered.[1]

At Yale, the religion course which consistently attracts the greatest number of students is entitled the Historical and Literary Aspects of the Old Testament. Mr. Lovett, the widely admired university chaplain,* teaches this course; but he does not proselytize the Christian faith or, indeed, *teach* religion at all. Even the title of the

---

* "No aspect of my administration [President Seymour has written] has brought deeper satisfaction than the devoted and fruitful service

course does not call for understanding of, or even sympathy with, Christianity. Mr. Lovett, to be sure, has both; but he apparently feels that it would be presumptuous to speak on behalf of Christianity in a course so dispassionately designated. Strictly speaking he is right, though the cause of Christianity suffers to a certain degree from a treatment which focuses upon the Bible as a "monument over the grave of Christianity." It must be acknowledged that Mr. Lovett's personal interest in religion can be, and frequently has been, quietly contagious. Through the years, many students, impressed by his faith and goodness, have sought out religion on their own. And some of these have ended up at divinity schools.

My point is that a Bible course no more bespeaks an influence on behalf of Christianity than a course on *Das Kapital* would necessarily indicate an influence on behalf of Marxism. Attendance at Dr. Lovett's classes is deceptive in itself, because far from signifying an interest in "religion" it indicates, on the part of many undergraduates, nothing more than a fruitful search for a "gut." It is notorious that far less is expected of a student in this course than in most others in the University, as, it seems, is the case in many other colleges:

---

of Mr. Lovett in the maintenance of religious values on our campus. Not merely as pastor of the church and as Woolsey Professor of Biblical Literature, but in his personal contacts and with his genius for stimulating cooperative effort, he has unobtrusively and effectively brought religious interest into the center of college life" (*Report of the President of Yale University to the Alumni*, 1949–1950, p. 32). Mr. Seymour here pays tribute to Mr. Lovett in two distinct senses. The first acknowledges his devoted service and personal interest, and I cannot see two points of view about this; the other applauds his religious influence and the results it has had on the Yale campus. This is, as I hope to point out, another thing entirely.

All that glitters in the catalogues is not mentally respectable gold, and courses in religion, as any experienced observer knows, are often "snaps" or "crips."...Put purely on the basis of grades, seldom is it as difficult to get an A in religion as it is in philosophy or biology or economics. Yet God is a God of judgment as well as of mercy.[2]

We move to the next largest course in the Religion Department, the Philosophy of Religion taught by Professor T. M. Greene. While Mr. Greene is a Christian by a great many definitions (he replies ambiguously when asked if he believes in the divinity of Christ), his course is largely a completely nondogmatic examination of the philosophies of religion. Mr. Greene is unflinching in his respect for Christian ethics, but it is, after all, assumed that most people are. Therefore, while some students are moved by Mr. Greene's approach to his problem and by his patent respect for Christianity, there is a widespread opinion that what he teaches is ethics, not religion.*

---

* I make no apology for defining "religion" in the Christian sense, and eschewing the nebulous, personalized definitions given to that term by so many latter-day psychologists, sociologists, et al. Here and elsewhere, along with Webster, I mean by religion a belief in a Supreme Being, "arousing reverence, love, gratitude, the will to obey and serve, and the like." Other definitions, perhaps more topical and specifically relating to Christianity, are the World Council of Churches' "a belief in Jesus Christ as God and Saviour," and the Federal Council of Churches' "Jesus Christ as Divine Lord and Saviour." In February 1951, Dr. Reinhold Niebuhr, a prominent Protestant spokesman, addressed the Yale University Christian Association, and was unequivocal: "Christian faith stands or falls on the proposition that a character named Jesus, in a particular place at a particular time in history, is more than a man in history, but is a revelation of the mystery of self and of the ultimate mystery of existence."

Much the same can be said of Professor Schroeder's (he is the chairman of the Religion Department) courses on Problems of Religious Thought and the Development of Religious Thought in Western Civilization. Mr. Schroeder, an ordained minister, is emphatically an influence toward the good, but not necessarily through the instrument of his religion. While respecting Christianity and what it represents, Mr. Schroeder does not seek to persuade his students to believe in Christ, largely because he has not, as I understand it, been completely able to persuade himself.*

Next in line is Mr. Goodenough, the renowned scholar of Judaism, who teaches Types of Religious Experience, and Judaism and Jesus. Mr. Goodenough was once a Congregationalist minister, and surprisingly, a number of persons who are, on the face of it, intimately acquainted with the University, have remarked that he "is considered a good Congregationalist."

And yet, I know of at least one occasion on which Mr. Goodenough has classified himself, before his students, as "80 percent atheist and 20 percent agnostic." No wonder that the preponderant influence of a scholar of his persuasion is to drive his students *away* from religion, the subject he "teaches."

There are three or four other instructors in the Religion Department, most notably Mr. Latourette, a staunchly pro-Christian minister who teaches mostly at the Divinity School, but maintains contact with undergraduates by offering a course on the history of Christianity. Unfortunately, the enrolment in this course is very small. Mr. Walton (of the Philosophy Department), a Roman Catholic, teaches a course on scholastic philosophy which is even more lightly subscribed.

---

* It is important to bear in mind that what is relevant to this survey is the teacher's attitude *as it is understood by his students*, even if this be, at times, at variance with personal convictions that the teacher keeps to himself.

Even if we assume, then, that a vigorous Religion Department indicates the prevalence of religion on the campus, we find that at Yale there does not even exist within the Religion Department itself a remarkably pro-religious bias. It is staffed by able scholars, many of whom several universities would be glad to add to their teaching staff. Academically, in other words, it is everything one could wish. But to the student who seeks intellectual and inspirational support for his faith, it is necessarily a keen disappointment.

Let us not forget that even if the courses offered by the Religion Department did lead to a more active faith in Christianity, it would still remain true that less than 10 percent of the student body elect courses in the Department.* We must remember, too, that Yale sets up a number of "required studies" for the students of the liberal arts. Unless he can earn an exemption for this or that exceptional reason, he must take a full year course in each of the following fields: (1) English, Latin, or Greek, (2) Modern Language, (3) Formal Thinking (Mathematics, Logic, or Linguistics), (4) Laboratory Science, (5) Classical Languages, Literature, and Civilization, (6) Modern Literature, the Fine Arts, and Music, (7) Anthropology, Economics, Geography, Political Science, Psychology, Sociology, (8) History, Philosophy, Religion, and (9) Natural or Physical Science.

It is to be noted that the group which includes religion allows the option of a course in history or philosophy. Statistics reveal that the overwhelming majority of students avail themselves of these alternatives. Thus, the University insists that the student take a course in a laboratory science, in a modern language, and in classical civilization, but accepts history and philosophy as alternatives

---

* The figures are for the academic year 1950–51, which list 472 persons as enrolled in the Department. These figures are themselves deceptive since many students take more than one course and are thus counted twice, or three times.

to religion. In so doing, it denies equal status with, say, French or Spanish grammar and pronunciation, to the teaching that has played the most vital role in our civilization and can play the most vital role in our lives.*

THE SOCIAL SCIENCES

> ...the social sciences and humanities are more properly called upon for value-judgments; when these are ignored or are made inimical to religion, the harm is often irreparable.[3]

It should already be clear that the Religion Department is not a source of pervasive Christian influence at Yale, that its impact on the vast majority of students is negligible, and that the University does not recognize religion as an indispensable field of study for an educated man.

To pursue our inquiry, then, it is necessary to turn to other departments at Yale, and to examine the attitudes which prevail where religion is in question. Our attention naturally turns to the social sciences, which year after year attract a majority of undergraduates, and do much to fix the general attitude of the University toward Christianity.

We are, naturally, most interested in those fields of study that treat most often with religion. It seems obvious that the views on Christianity held by a professor of physics are far less influential

---

* There has been serious discussion, at least in undergraduate Yale, of the advisability of a requirement in the field of religion. One student submitted a concrete set of proposals to the Aurelian Honor Society, which voted them down by a narrow margin in the fall of 1949. President Seymour was at least not shocked when the proposal was informally made to him that such a requirement should be instituted if there are to be any requirements at all. But he cited financial difficulties and a number of additional technical obstacles.

than those held by a professor of philosophy or of sociology, since, by the nature of their subjects, the latter must devote a great deal of their time to discussing religion.*

A word, first of all, about Economics and Government. The instructors in these departments often have occasion to refer to Christianity. But religious *values*, as such, are less central to these fields of study than to certain other sciences of human thought and behavior. In history courses there is opportunity to weigh both the validity and the personal value of religion, despite the large numbers of historians who are more prone to chronicle than to generalize. In the Yale History Department, for example, many students are affected by the religious inclinations of Professor Baumer, who teaches the Intellectual History of Europe. Mention ought also to be made of Professor Mack, a straightforward Christian whose attitudes become apparent in his lectures on Shakespeare.

But we narrow down our search primarily to an evaluation of the influences that stem out of the departments of Sociology, Philosophy, and Psychology. Most particularly, of course, we are here concerned with those teachers within these departments who actively disparage or encourage religion. We notice at once that teachers whose bias is conspicuously *pro*-Christian are not easy to find at Yale. For while they undoubtedly exist, they seem reluctant, perhaps in the interest of "objectivity," to proclaim their convictions. We concentrate, therefore, on those instructors and those texts that are overtly or covertly hostile to religion, whether through the "silent treatment," active opposition, or supercilious disparagement.

---

* There is no question that the scientism and ersatz objectivity that characterize the teaching of many courses in natural sciences can lead to doctrinaire secularism; but by and large, the student is less prone to formulate a religious orientation on the basis of attitudes in the pure sciences than he is in those where values are more urgently relevant.

The History Department sponsors a course, as much sociology as history, called the Contemporary World. It is largely the dynamism and color of the instructor, Professor Ralph E. Turner, that bring to his classroom year after year twice as many undergraduates as attend the next largest courses in the History Department (American and European History). Mr. Turner is emphatically and vigorously atheistic. An able scholar, he is nevertheless a professional debunker, a dedicated iconoclast who has little mercy either on God, or on those who believe in Him, and little respect for the values that most undergraduates have been brought up to respect.

Many Yale students laugh off the influence of Mr. Turner and ultimately classify him as a gifted and colorful fanatic. Others, more impressionable, and hence those over whom there is cause to be concerned, are deeply disturbed by Mr. Turner's bigoted atheism and finish the year they spend with him full of suspicions and doubts about religion that they may retain for a lifetime. I shall save until later a discussion of the utility of skepticism. It is enough for the present to acknowledge the presence of Mr. Turner, sponsored by Yale University and addressing a large number of Yale students every year in such fashion as to wean a number of them away from religion by relentless disparagement of the whole fabric of Christianity.

The Department of Sociology presents a special problem for our purposes. It is safe to say that a large majority of its personnel regard religion as nothing more than a cultural "phenomenon" caused by human ingenuity to serve as an opiate to make life seem more meaningful, and to promise—falsely, of course—an after-life.

It must be noted that one need not disbelieve in God in order to gain eminence in the field of sociology. An increasing number of scholarly sociologists and anthropologists believe in a personal

God—without embarrassment of any kind, without violation of the basic principles of their science, and without impediment to objectivity.* But, the atmosphere that seems to predominate in the department at Yale, under the intellectual aegis of renowned scholars like Professor Ralph Linton, is that religion is, at best, a useful superstition. Many instructors believe that it is distinctly harmful benightedness.

Until his tragic murder in Borneo in the spring of 1950, Professor Raymond Kennedy could be singled out as the member of his department who had the greatest effect on the greatest number of students. Teaching Basic Sociology and Anthropology, a course which discharges one of the student requirements at Yale, Mr. Kennedy never left room for doubt as to the contempt in which he held religion, Christianity in particular. His class was consistently one of the largest (I believe the largest) at Yale, and his influence far-reaching. To illustrate different points of view about the propriety of Mr. Kennedy's approach and techniques, it is perhaps worthwhile to review the controversy that raged at Yale for a week in the spring of 1949, and caused Mr. Kennedy's detractors and his disciples to stand up and be counted. It served, too, to give Mr. Kennedy an opportunity to defend himself and his classroom procedure.

The issue was touched off by an editorial I wrote and published in the *Yale Daily News*, on March 9, 1949. Quoted almost fully it read as follows:

For a Fair Approach

Last year, an undergraduate put his beer bottle down on the table and, with an air of finality, said, "Well anyway, it's unscientific to believe in God. You ghost-fearers ought to take Kennedy's course

---

* The relationship of sociology and religion is discussed at greater length in Appendix A.

and find out about these things. You're living way behind the times."

It is of course true that if this student had been more intelligent, less gullible, he could have inquired of any reputable sociologist, "Must a social scientist disbelieve in the existence of God?" The answer would be no. Rather, as a . . . Yale sociologist has remarked, "It is the duty of the anthropologist to deal dispassionately with religion as a societal factor of major importance. There is no more compulsion to assert the non-existence of God than there is to assert the value of one form of government over another. It is the institution of religion, not its validity, that is proper subject matter."

This notwithstanding, Professor Kennedy, who year after year addresses several hundred freshmen and sophomores in Sociology 10, has made a cult of anti-religion. It is a waste of breath to assert the obvious truth that he is entitled to his own beliefs in regard to the existence of God; it is similarly obvious that in undermining religion through bawdy and slapstick humor, through circumspect allusions and emotive innuendoes, he is guilty of an injustice to and an imposition upon his students and the University.

"Jungle Jim"—"good old Jungle Jim"—always teaches an amusing class, and his courses are always oversubscribed. This is partly due to the brilliance of his oratory, to the interest of his field, and to his general competence to deal with it; but it is also due to his constant concern for the entertainment of his students. References to genitalia are as effective in the classroom as they are at a bachelor dinner, and flippant allusions to sacrosanct subjects are as delightful from the podium as from the soapboxes of Hyde Park.

Mr. Kennedy never makes the positive assertion that God does not exist. Instead his beliefs form an inarticulated hypothesis. Ridicule and slant have always been more effective. "This place limbo," he says, "all I know is apparently the flames there aren't as hot as in hell. That's where all the Greek philosophers are, along with unbaptized babies." "All I know about heaven is it must be awfully crowded there!" "Chaplains accompanying modern armies are comparable to witch doctors accompanying tribes." "Religion is a matter of ghosts, spirits and emotion."

"A cleric today is the modern counterpart of the witch doctor." "After many days of argument, I said to these Jesuits (en route to Manila one time) 'I'll tell you how you can convert me and the rest of the world overnight: submit the wine to a chemical analysis after consecration and then see if you've gotten hemoglobin out of grape juice!' " Funny, without a doubt. So are Bob Hope and Bennett Cerf. The question is whether this sort of business, blatantly unintellectual, biased and unobjective, in some cases harmful, is proper business for a University lecturer....

Our complaint has an additional aspect. Disregarding for the moment the question of the existence of God, and the desirability of a Christian code of morality to guide the behavior of man, it seems unjust to employ pernicious techniques to undermine the tenets of Christianity. Most students, it is true, are unaffected. Some on the other hand, impressionable and malleable, lose faith in God after taking Mr. Kennedy's course. If a student comes to Yale believing in God and leaves convinced that all Christians are deluded, the conviction should come from a more intellectual appraisal of theology than he receives from Sociology 10.

A number of students and faculty members rushed to Mr. Kennedy's defense, and others sided with my views. Several members of the faculty and of the administration wrote to me confidentially, approving the censure of Mr. Kennedy and the exposition of his biases. A few sample communications appear in Appendix B.

Finally, Mr. Kennedy spoke in his own defense, insisting that he was not anti-religious, but merely "unbiased," as all sociologists must be. Of other charges, he simply pleaded innocence, while never contradicting any of the quotations attributed to him.

In short, the illustration here serves to point up an approach to religion tolerated by Yale for years and which, when publicly aired, stirred up a great deal of comment. Interestingly enough, excepting Mr. Kennedy's own defense of himself, in which he forswore any bias against religion, those many persons who defended him did so (with a very few exceptions) for many reasons, *but not on the grounds that Mr. Kennedy was falsely charged with making a "cult of anti-religion."* Rather, the arguments of his advocates centered about Mr. Kennedy's privilege to hold his own beliefs, the advantages of "shaking the beliefs" of the students, and so on. These arguments will be faced in time; for the moment, let us rest in the knowledge that Mr. Kennedy held forth at Yale for a great many years, teaching a basic course in one of the most important fields of social science, and revealing an unswerving contempt for religion in general and Christianity in particular. To my personal knowledge, he thus subverted the faith of numbers of students who, guilelessly, entered the course hoping to learn sociology and left with the impression that faith in God and the scientific approach to human problems are mutually exclusive.

Nor was the classroom bias in the basic course redressed by textbooks that deal sympathetically with religion. Almost all of the books assigned dealt with religion wholly as a cultural phenomenon, of no greater or lesser interest than ecology or diet. Professor Margaret Mead, in analyzing college texts and religion in the field of Cultural Anthropology, states that

Two examples of the effects of anthropological handling of religious behavior—when taken as models—upon views of our own

society may be found in *Middletown* and *Plainville, U.S.A.* Both
of these studies treat religion as part of the culture. Neither of
them gives any discussion of the religious beliefs and attitudes of
the peoples of "Middletown" and "Plainville" or shows the slightest feeling for religion.[4]

Both the books she mentions, along with others mostly of
similar character,[5] are used in Yale's Basic Sociology.

While he was more flamboyant than any of his colleagues, Mr.
Kennedy's biases were not out of tune with those of department
members as a whole. Mr. Linton has been mentioned; others, less
influential, to be sure, convey to the student who majors in sociology the definite impression that at best religion is *non grata* to
the department, at worst it is the subject of relentless attack.

DEPARTMENT OF PHILOSOPHY

The chairman of the Department of Philosophy, a distinguished
scholar and a distinguished man, is an earnest and expansive atheist. Mr. Brand Blanshard taught and teaches, among others, basic
courses in philosophy, and he reveals his biases freely and frankly
both in and out of the classroom. One of the most popular and
also one of the most influential teachers in the Philosophy Department, a man whose scholarship, originality, and personality are
highly regarded, is Mr. Paul Weiss, an agnostic. Though sympathetic with, and eminently fair to, religious students, he is a confirmed debunker of the Christian religion: "Christ was a minor
prophet . . . a man of violent temper . . . a man of set ideas to which
he didn't conform . . . he responded to violence where he preached
gentleness."[6] These are extreme but illustrative remarks from the
statements and teachings of Mr. Weiss; for he has created his own,
full-bodied philosophy, in which there is no place for a personal

God, save as a convenience for certain persons who find Him a useful propeller toward the good.

Best equipped to challenge the secularists in the department is Professor Robert L. Calhoun, an ordained minister vastly respected as a scholar, as a lecturer, and as a man. He devotes most of his time to the Yale Divinity School, but teaches one course in the undergraduate school every other year, called the History of Philosophy. Unfortunately, like so many pro-Christian scholars, Mr. Calhoun keeps his convictions largely to himself, and even his treatment of Hebraic-Christian philosophy (which he covers in one lecture) makes it impossible, but for the knowledge that Mr. Calhoun is a "parson," as he sometimes calls himself, for the student to deduce whether or not Mr. Calhoun is himself a Christian. The off-hand treatment of religion may be partially explained by Dr. Calhoun's penchant for cosmology, metaphysics, and epistemology, and his consequent minimization of ethics and politics. But the result is that a potentially powerful, scholarly, pro-Christian philosophical force is lost to undergraduate Yale. He is, to be sure, much appreciated and exploited at the Divinity School; but many undergraduates deem it a tragedy of huge proportions that Mr. Calhoun does not provide the much-needed antitoxin in the undergraduate Philosophy Department.

It is difficult to generalize about the textbooks used in basic philosophy courses at Yale for several reasons. The first is that probably to a greater degree than most colleges Yale encourages wide reading in primary sources. This, of course, means relative neglect in some departments of textbooks in the usual sense. Again, the basic philosophy course has grown from one general course to three, one in logic, one in ethics, and one in "problems of philosophy." Little attention is given to religion in the logic course, which is to be expected where the matters in hand are deduction, induction, the scientific method, language, and symbolism.

The basic ethics course is taught jointly by Mr. Greene, whom I have mentioned above as a religion instructor highly sympathetic to Christianity, and Mr. Hendel, who is also cordial to religion. Yet surprisingly, one of the textbooks these men assign is Philip Wheelwright's *A Critical Introduction to Ethics.*[7]

In his analysis of books in the field of philosophy, Professor Peter A. Bertocci summarizes this text as follows:

> All in all, the student will be fortunate, as he finishes this book, if he realizes that the critical method, in showing that belief in God can neither be proved nor disproved, is indicating its own limitations rather than making significant statements about religion.[8]

Professor Schrader's course in Problems of Philosophy uses largely primary sources of reading, but employs Bertrand Russell's *Problems of Philosophy* as the nearest equivalent to a textbook.

I am not forgetting that no honest or fruitful course in philosophy can be taught without readings from some of the famous and brilliant skeptical philosophers of the post-Enlightenment. The student must be introduced to Hume, Kant, Russell, et al.; but when he reads them in the original, the responsibility of the teacher for guidance and explanation is all the more urgent. I question whether such guidance and explanation is provided in the three courses listed above, which constitute the department's program in "Formal Thought"; rather, there is reason to believe that the instructors in these courses would consider it presumptuous to contradict, or to attempt to refute, a great many of the findings of the skeptics.

Mr. Calhoun's course in History of Philosophy, already referred to, is in a sense a basic course, and it is curious that although he offers a choice among three texts, he has himself written of one of them, while praising its general philosophical worth, that "... [its] treatment [of religion] is vitiated by fundamental misunderstanding...

the author's conception of religion is so simple as to be sheer travesty."[9]

A final note about Mr. Robert Cohen, who has taught both philosophy courses in the Directed Studies Program (devised for especially promising students who elect to follow a prescribed course of study for the first two years). Under the title the Forms of Reason, the course employs, throughout the first year, reading matter that is heavily naturalistic.[10] During the second-year course, Standards of Value, a great deal of religious and biblical literature is used. Mr. Cohen is himself a naturalist and an agnostic, and has described his course as "a fire through which they [i.e., believers] pass." At the same time, he stresses his belief that skepticism cannot itself be an adequate philosophy, and urges this upon his students.

For the rest, there are philosophers of all shades of belief. While the atmosphere is not as universally discouraging to religion as for example in the Department of Sociology, it cannot be in any sense deduced that the spirit of the department is either pro-Christian or even remarkably tolerant of Christianity. My opinion is that taking all the courses in the department into consideration, the bias is notably secular, and, in some cases, straightforwardly antagonistic to religion.

DEPARTMENT OF PSYCHOLOGY

From the students' point of view, the Psychology Department of Yale does not seem to be as vigorous as either the Philosophy or Sociology departments.* Certainly in so far as religion is concerned, there is not nearly so much outspokenness. That is to say,

---

* Although it was classified as among the strongest departments at Yale, academically speaking, by President-emeritus Charles Seymour in his final Report to the Alumni, distributed in December 1950.

more often than not, Yale's psychologists simply do not mention religion. This is the case, for example, with the most popular professor of psychology, Mr. Doob, who makes no reference to religion in his course on Social Psychology. It would appear that this "silent treatment" is in tune with the attitude displayed by many basic textbooks in the field.*

In the basic psychology course (10 ab, General Psychology), texts by Dorcus, Shaffer, Ruch, and Klineberg[11] accounted for four of the seven books used during the period here in question.[12] (The other three were Munn, *Psychology;* Hartley et al., *Outside Readings in Psychology;* and Symonds, *Dynamic Psychology.*)

Neither L. F. Shaffer nor Dorcus and G. W. Shaffer have anything whatever to say about religion, and the student who reads them, Professor Gordon W. Allport points out,[13] *"would obtain . . . no idea that religion plays any significant part among the motives or interests of mankind"* (italics added).

Ruch's *Psychology and Life* makes mention of religion in only one passage, which is unabashedly derisive: "It is interesting to note that when the part of his brain thought by the phrenologists to be the center of religion is stimulated, a man twitches his leg."[14]

Klineberg's *Social Psychology,* in the opinion of Professor Allport, "veers towards an unfriendly position":

> The impression the student gets from this book is ragged in the extreme. Though there are 17 references to religion in the index, the entries concern such matters as the ferocity of the Mayan religion, the eccentricities of shamans, the "artificial schizophrenia of the catatonic type" that characterizes the self-absorption

---

* For a more extended analysis of psychology and religion, and a résumé of Professor Gordon W. Allport's research into religion in psychology texts, see Appendix D.

of mystics in India, the proposition that Buddhists may prevent schizophrenia by their self-induced splitting of personality. Religion is regarded chiefly as withdrawal, and Horney is quoted with approval to the effect that "Religion which offers such a possibility [withdrawal] has lost its power and appeal for the majority." . . . All in all, Klineberg's picture of religious activity is one of quaintness, superstition, escapism, and on the whole, of a prescientific illusion.[15]

I have not analyzed the textbooks offered in the advanced courses, but the basic course in most Yale departments is generally organized with the active help and participation of the department's policy-makers and thus reflects the mood of the more advanced courses. This is certainly the case in the departments of Sociology and History. Whether or not the whole department mirrors the mood of these textbook writers, I cannot say for sure; but I have heard no testimony to understanding or sympathetic treatment of religion in the advanced courses though I have interviewed several students who have majored in the field. Moreover, an inquirer into the religious attitude of a university will never equate courses in importance. The basic course is by all odds the most important, primarily because of the number of students that take it. In evaluating the secular or religious influence on a psychology major, the emphasis given to religion in all the courses he takes must be weighed; but dismissing the psychology major, there are those with a general interest in the broad field, others who seek to discharge curriculum requirements in the way they find least painful, and still others who are inveterate "course tasters." The students in these groups do not, for the most part, persevere in a field after one year; and this year is always spent in the basic course.

Unless the influence of the textbooks is vigorously counteracted from the lecture platform—which it is not—then the student of basic psychology is unlikely to learn that "the historical Christian faith has today and has had throughout the ages a colossal impact upon human personality."[16] Even more, as seems always the case where there is little or no mention of religion, the student assumes that the subject is neither important, nor relevant. And conditioned by the treatment religion receives at the hands of at least one of the textbook writers he studies at Yale, he is more likely to consider religion as a "prescientific illusion."

Before leaving religion in the curriculum, brief reference should be made to the substantial contribution to secularism that is being made at Yale and elsewhere by widespread academic reliance on relativism, pragmatism, and utilitarianism. The teachings of John Dewey and his predecessors have borne fruit. And there is surely not a department at Yale that is uncontaminated with the absolute that there are no absolutes, no intrinsic rights, no ultimate truths. The acceptance of these notions, which emerge in courses in history and economics, in sociology and political science, in psychology and literature, makes impossible any intelligible conception of an omnipotent, purposeful, and benign Supreme Being who has laid down immutable laws, endowed his creatures with inalienable rights, and posited unchangeable rules of human conduct.

EXTRACURRICULAR ACTIVITIES

[Extracurricular activities] cannot go far enough, and the belief that their existence discharges the responsibility of the institution for religion is a major source of weakness.[17]

High in the list of alleged "indications of religious activity at Yale" is the extracurricular work of a more or less Christian nature that is undertaken by undergraduates. It seems that the extracurricular religious program at Yale is far more pronounced than, for example, at Harvard, and those who seek to demonstrate the religious nature of Yale make much of this fact.

First to be cited is Dwight Hall, the headquarters of the Yale University Christian Association. Dwight Hall is, beyond question, a beehive of activity during most of the year. It is supported by revenue from its own endowment and by a small percentage of funds collected from the campus once a year under the auspices of the Community Budget Drive. There are five full-time workers on its staff, including one ordained minister, two graduate secretaries, and two clerical secretaries.

The core of Dwight Hall is the Church of Christ, which was founded in 1757 and has continued ever since as the center church for Protestant students at Yale. The membership of Dwight Hall is large. A straightforward solicitation of freshmen membership is made early in the academic year, and the Association sponsors a "Freshman Cabinet" to which is given various administrative responsibilities and chores in connection with the organization of freshman activities.

Dwight Hall is an organization of some social prestige, and this, as a matter of course at Yale, increases the size of its membership. Its officers are generally religious, and recently, some of them have begun to conduct periodical religious retreats. The institution also offers its members an opportunity to do social work among the poor of New Haven; in recent years, "seminar" groups were launched in the homes of various members of the faculty to discuss books and religious movements with interested students; the building in which the organization is housed contains ample recreational facilities: a snack bar, Coca-Cola machine, phonograph, lounge. It sponsors a body of students who band together as the "Dixwell Group" and dedicate themselves to improving interracial relations; an intellectual magazine called *Et Veritas* springs out of Dwight Hall; occasional projects are undertaken, as for example an inquiry into the possibilities of an honor system; and every day at noon there are twenty-minute chapel services, at which, once a week, an undergraduate speaker occupies the pulpit.

Yet the impartial investigator cannot but conclude that the *religious* influence of Dwight Hall is in no way commensurate with its general importance on the campus. While there is no question that some of its members are primarily concerned with practicing and strengthening their religion, far more of them—and I do not imply that their motives are ignoble—utilize Dwight Hall as a cushion for some of their excess energies. I repeat, most of these energies are well and fruitfully spent. There are no laurels more deserved than those won by students who spend several hours a week administering a recreational program for New Haven children. At the same time, the work need have no bearing whatever on religion. I will be challenged that the motives are irrelevant: charitable work gets done. True in a sense, but the activity cannot be interpreted as indicating religious activity at Yale, unless one would be willing to assert that *all* good activity stems out of religious motivation, and I am certain that this generalization would meet with the disfavor it deserves.

Dwight Hall's magazine, *Et Veritas*, has no clear-cut editorial brief for Christianity. In fact, membership on its staff requires no profession of faith in even the most attenuated dogmas of Christianity. The November 1949 issue of *Et Veritas* did, it is true, contain some sort of a statement of faith by the editors, who "choose the Christian" philosophy, but as a "personal conviction rather than an editorial policy." Later they reminded their readers that they do not forsake their "conviction that the Christian philosophy is the *most adequate*, the *most pervasive*, the *most conducive* to understanding" (italics in the original). Such a utilitarian conception of Christianity, coupled with this brand of self-effacement and steadfast refusal to proclaim Christianity as the true religion (which is what all genuine Christian leaders proclaim it to be, thus committing themselves logically to the proposition that other religions are untrue) is a sample of the adulteration of religion to the point that it becomes nothing more than the basis for "my most favorite way of living." The instincts are fine, and a good life is inevitable for such persons, but so long as what they profess can be subscribed to wholeheartedly by an atheist, we have not, really, got religion at all.

The previous editor of *Et Veritas* does not even classify himself as a Christian, although he saw fit to edit a magazine which is a function of the Yale University Christian Association. The present editor is an avowed agnostic.

Another institution at Yale which is revealing in some respects is called the undergraduate deacons. Every year, twenty-odd juniors are elected by their predecessors, with the advice and consent of the university chaplain, to serve as ushers at Battell Chapel for the Sunday services during the year, to take part periodically in church organizational work, and to speak, once a week, from the pulpit of Dwight Chapel. It would seem that no conceivable job should be more forthright in the requirement that candidates believe in God, since, after all, people assemble at Battell Chapel in order to worship Him.

Formerly, deacons were elected to office by popular vote of the campus, with the result that deaconship soon developed into nothing more than a popularity contest. The situation became unbearable several years ago, and the university chaplain preempted the selection of deacons. And yet, despite the reform, several atheists and agnostics have been chosen as ushers, at least during the past four years.

Commenting on this extraordinary anomaly in an editorial in the *Yale Daily News* for the issue of March 14, 1950, under the title "All God's Chillun Are Shoe,"* 1951, Chairman Garrison N. Ellis wrote:

> When the selection of undergraduate deacons for 1949 was being made, a prominent man in that class was asked whether he wanted to usher in Battell. Actually an atheist, he allowed as how he professed no particular religious beliefs. Assured that the fact was inconsequential, he accepted the post.
>
> Doubtless the occurrence was exceptional. In general, however, the prerequisites for undergraduate deaconship have in the past seemed to lie in the political and social, not religious, distinction of the individual. . . .
>
> When the selection of the 1951 board is announced after spring vacation, we trust it will represent an actively religious group. It's a superfluous consideration whether, when the squads march down the Battell aisle gray-suited and carnationed, they resemble a composite picture of senior societies on the march.

Catholic students at Yale who wish to take part in religious activity can avail themselves of the facilities of the St. Thomas More Club, which presents lectures from time to time, and occasionally publishes a newsletter of sorts. The Jews can join the Hillel Foundation, presided over by their Rabbi, who acts as their counselor. The Foundation conducts religious services, presents lecturers, and conducts classes in the Hebrew language and culture. Neither of these two groups has social prestige of any sort, and the membership is, quite naturally, much smaller than Dwight Hall's, proportionate to the far smaller number of Catholic and Jewish students at Yale. The Baptists, Congregationalists, Episcopalians, Lutherans, Methodists, and Presbyterians carry on denominational work.

---

* I.e. White Shoe, i.e., Long Island polo set.

In addition to the activities sponsored by the established "religious" centers at Yale, there are occasionally special "projects." The most publicized of these in recent years was an "Inter-Faith Conference" held in the spring of 1949. It was more or less subsidized by Dwight Hall, St. Thomas More, and the Hillel Foundation, but was the brainchild of one student, F. Goldthwaite Sherrill, the son of the presiding Bishop of the Episcopal Church in America, who is also a member of the Yale Corporation. A blue-ribbon committee was set up, and three principal speakers were presented on three consecutive evenings. For the Protestants there was Bishop Norman B. Nash of Massachusetts, for the Catholics, George N. Shuster, president of Hunter College, and for the Jews, Lewis L. Strauss, of the Atomic Energy Commission.

Unfortunately, all the speakers were careful not to antagonize any participating faith to the point that they themselves, in my opinion (as co-chairman of the conference), and in the opinion of those members who assembled later for a postmortem, gave little impetus to religion. As a part and parcel of the Conference, however, there were nightly discussion groups presided over by assorted ministers, priests, and rabbis, and these were generally regarded as fruitful.

In my opinion, the Conference did some good, and certainly testified to the enterprise of its organizers. It received generous publicity and a goodly number of students interested themselves in the proceedings. The following year, Dwight Hall sponsored three lectures by Bishop Stephen C. Neill of England. He is a magnificent orator, and gave the community genuine spiritual encouragement.*

---

* In February 1951, Dwight Hall sponsored a series of lectures by Dr. Reinhold Niebuhr as the principal feature of its Religious Emphasis Week. Until something better comes along, the *Yale Daily News*'s

But these conferences are desultory affairs, and while they serve as an occasional stimulus, even combined with extracurricular religious activities, they cannot offset the sustained treatment given to Christianity and religion in the classroom and in the textbook. Distractions of every type and variety stand in the way of a student and his academic chores while he is at college. Athletic and nonathletic enterprises offer up every sort of blandishment, and even at Yale, where there exists a relatively rigorous academic regimen, many students manage to cruise through without learning very much. Even so, the student's basic attitudes are not, in my experience, conditioned by community life, locker-room chatter, debates, conferences, and the like. His disciplines and values will be got from the hours, no matter how few, spent in the classroom and with his books. It is true that many students are not easily susceptible to classroom influences and hence do not change the fundamental opinions that they bring with them to college—sometimes, of course, because the convictions they bring with them from their previous environments, from their preparatory schools or, most likely, from their homes and experience, are

---

editorial comment on the Conference will stick in my mind as the *ne plus ultra* of contemporary liberalism: " 'In these tragic times we are all faced with reevaluating our beliefs.' So reads the Christian Mission's brochure on the Niebuhr talks. But now that they're all over, we fail to see how they have helped in this search. The next time a Religious Emphasis Week rolls around, we would propose the following: let's have a forum in which we'd hear, as well as the Christian, the Taoist point of view, the Buddhist, the Mohammedan, the Jewish, the Hindu, and so on. Here would be some real meat for thought: here would be a real basis for re-evaluation of beliefs. . . ." This was too much even for the Yale student carefully nurtured in tolerance and relativism. Sample reply: "Today's editorial is a bogus and a phony, pretending to the merit of honest criticism but really possessing only the false splendor of irrelevance and condescension. . . ."

emotionally and intellectually deep-rooted, and hence abiding. But I cannot overemphasize the fact that neither religion nor anything else can be taught dynamically or thoroughly in college by off-hours exposure to organizations like Dwight Hall, by attendance at occasional religious conferences, or the like. Even the most frivolous student has respect for *expertise*, and it is to his professors and to his books that he turns for *expertise*. It is to the faculty that he looks for the frank of authority for a field of learning, for a set of values. Writing for *Life* magazine, issue of October 16, 1950, Canon Bernard Iddings Bell, whom I find eloquent on the subject of education, wrote,

> They [our schools and colleges] simply ignore religion. They look on it as a minor amusement to be practiced by those who find it fun, to be neglected if one desires. Obviously this outlook is quickly communicated to the young. If a child is taught in school about a vast number of things—for 25 hours a week, eight or nine months of a year, for ten to sixteen years or more— and if for all this time matters of religion are never seriously treated, the child can only come to view religion as, at best, an innocuous pastime preferred by a few to golf or canasta.

What is more, that extracurricular endeavor is an unsatisfactory substitute for classroom exposition and guidance must be a well-known fact to scores of educational administrators who nevertheless point to undergraduate religious groups and sporadic activity as evidences of "the impetus" that their institutions give religion. Canon Bell's generalization is not altogether applicable to Yale, since it cannot be said of an institution that sponsors a large Religion Department that it "ignores" religion. And yet, considering the total impact of the Religion Department, considering also the small number of students who expose themselves to any course that *teaches* religion, the situation can be said to be worse; for while religion is offered, and the University thereby goes on record as considering it to be an area of study that lays claim to a "body of learning," the University's off-handedness, perhaps unintentionally, reduces religion to approximately the status of a course in Greek mythology. If you're interested, study religion; you'll learn something about the history of the world and something about the traditions of our culture. If you want more, you will find a lot of facilities open to you in extracurricular life.

> Students who come to college with strong religious convictions will take an active part in one or more...undergraduate activities. The majority, however, will unconsciously look to see what the authorities judge to be important. If religion is relegated to the role of a not-too-important sideshow, if its part in our intellectual and emotional tradition is ignored, and if the members of the faculty act with indifference, whether deliberate or unconscious, toward those questions of ultimate import which no discipline can escape and on which religion has had much to say, then it is small wonder that a majority of students will go their way, troubled perhaps and a little uneasy in the absence of answers, upon the assumption that religion does not matter.[18]

This is the attitude toward religion that, in the opinion of sixteen respected scholars, prevails in too many American universities and colleges. Under the sponsorship of three national foundations and councils,* these men, at the invitation of college administrations, held detailed discussions with the faculties of fifty-three colleges and universities. Although the consultants felt

---

* The American Council on Education, the Edward W. Hazen Foundation, and the National Council on Religion in Higher Education.

that "there are signs in many quarters, some of them the most unexpected, that the place of religion is due for reexamination," they concluded that "in many institutions the majority of the faculty with whom they talked are either hostile to or indifferent toward religion":

> As to faculty members, the consultants are surprised more often than they should have been at their naïveté in religious matters. Both those who declared themselves "hostile" or "neutral" to religion revealed the most archaic and regressive notions about the contemporary religious situation and the intellectual temper of modern liberal Christianity and Judaism. Most of them seem to rely on garbled childhood memories to tell them what religion is and their familiarity with the literature and living spokesmen of liberal religion was strangely scant for cultivated and intelligent people. Occasionally faculty members denounced religion as "superstition," "pre-scientific benightedness," and "an emotional crutch," "both useless and dangerous." A larger group were convinced that a humanistic or naturalistic creed was wholly adequate for a modern man.[19]

A comment specifically directed at state universities is equally applicable to other educational institutions, Yale included:

> Not without justice are they regarded as irreligious, when they receive freshmen who are eager for ideal values in which intelligent men and women can believe and four years later send them out naturalized, skeptical, or cynical.... The destruction wrought by professorial intellectuals... far more than offsets the construction accomplished by the university in its decent espousal of university sermons, denominational organizations, discussion groups, and the Y.M.C.A.[20]

What is more, it is not only in the classroom that teachers effectively communicate their biases on religion:

> ... among university faculties there is a widespread tendency to slur religion in and out of the classroom, and the slurring attitude has been inculcated in countless graduates. One has only to discuss religion with undergraduates in any institution ... to find ample verification for this assertion. . . . In the hands of a lecturer, a "recognized authority" in a specialized field, a slur becomes a vicious weapon against which the student has little or no defense. How long will we continue to regard as competent those specialists, however well equipped with their own skills, who carelessly or maliciously scoff at religion?[21]

More than any other one characteristic of the colleges in the last twenty-five years, this problem of the secularism of their faculties and students has represented a stumbling block to religion.

Much has been written about a "revival" of religion that has swept the country since the war's end. Much of this, the analysts insist, has centered about the college campus. Professor Merrimon Cuninggim has written a book called *The College Seeks Religion;*[22] and on the local scene, Professor Clarence P. Shedd of Yale has broadcast under the title "Religious Activities in Increase in the Colleges."[23] We may, indeed, be riding the crest of a wave. The state of religion often tends to be cast about, at the mercy of the times; and the times today, as perhaps never before, conduce to a return to the God that has been so emphatically renounced by the world's troublemakers. I have read that the period of skepticism that followed the Revolutionary War in this country saw a Yale at which, for several years, fewer than 10 percent of the student body (at that time about a hundred) professed religion openly; but it was only a matter of time before

Timothy Dwight "preached . . . and all infidelity skulked and hid its head."

Perhaps we are witnessing a grassroots movement back to religion. But this is highly debatable. After devoting several hundred pages to the encouraging indications of a revival of religious interest in the colleges, Professor Cuninggim concludes sadly, *"Secularism is too widespread for one to be able glibly to conclude that colleges are more Christian in atmosphere than in 1900."*[24]

More explicitly, in a later section, Professor Cuninggim exposes the "religious front" of so many colleges, among which I would number Yale:

> If we center our attention solely upon the collegiate interest in religion and the religious programs of instruction, worship, and activity, we may hopefully conclude that the campus atmosphere is religious in quality and that students breathe clean air. But when we broaden our consideration to include all institutional interests and all aspects of college life, then we must perforce admit that the tone of higher education is secular *and the total impact upon the majority of students is, if not anti-, at least nonreligious*[25] [italics added]. [For a review of Mr. Cuninggim's remarks about religion at Yale, see Appendix E.]

If we are, indeed, witnessing a religious revival, it would seem to be only against the rigid resistance of probably the most influential, and certainly the best publicized, policy-makers in education. The two most widely circularized attempts to analyze the plight of education at the half-century point are revealing. The first of these was sponsored by Harvard; after exhaustive consultations, an expenditure of $60,000, and three years' work, the project appeared in 1945 and under the title *General Education in a Free Society*.

In this exhaustive work, religion is mentioned only a few times, and then merely to note the historic association of Christianity with democracy and humanism. The importance which the educators who drafted this document attached to religion is symbolized by their acknowledgment of the educational value of Harvard's glee club and orchestra, while saying "nothing of the chapel or of Brooks House, long a center of religious and social service."[26] The report is explicit when it states:

> We are not at all unmindful of the importance of religious belief in the completely good life. But, given the American scene with its varieties of faith and even of unfaith, we did not feel justified in proposing religious instruction as a part of the curriculum.[27]

President Lowry of the College of Wooster, in his critique, points out at least one of the fallacies in this statement when he says:

> By the same token, politics might be excluded because there are Democrats and Republicans; physics, because there are divergent views about cosmic rays; or athletics because some like Harvard and some like Yale. On this theory, any matter lively enough to call forth more than one deeply or widely held point of view is a doubtful item in the curriculum.[28]

The report emphatically discards religion as a potential source of the desired "unifying purpose and idea" of education: "Whatever one's views, religion is not now for most colleges a practicable [or desirable, the report urges throughout] source of intellectual unity."[29]

Some comfort is yet to be derived from the report's stipulation of goals: The student should learn *to think effectively, to communicate thought, to make relevant judgments, to discriminate among values"* (italics in the original).[30]

President Lowry acutely points out that

> ...the document is asking for leading ideas and a quality in the
> human life that religion, time out of mind, has notably fostered.
> Therefore, the Christian can hardly be blamed if he sees his own
> faith, not alien to, but actually the forming and completing agent
> of the kind of education Harvard describes....[31]

The second influential document to which I refer is the Report of the [U.S.] President's Commission on Higher Education, *Higher Education for American Democracy*.* While this report is primarily a highly controversial package of political and economic ideas looking to increasing educational benefits, more student subsidies, and tripled college enrolments in the next ten years, the document, by indirection, deals a body blow to religion, whose relevance it does not so much as acknowledge. Pages are spent in a discussion of democratic ideals, and much is made of our cultural heritage. The report, where education is concerned, is one more victory for the secularists. President Lowry comments that

> [This is] no particular surprise.... The Commission was not
> opening the Senate or laying a cornerstone and was therefore
> under no obligation to unite in prayer. It passes on, apparently as
> a rumor, the fact that "religion is held to be a major force in cre-
> ating the system of human values on which democracy is predi-
> cated." It is concerned almost dangerously with the production
> of citizens who can realize certain social goals—dangerous in

---

* Published after vast research and seventeen months of study, in March 1947.

spite of all the Report's talk about the "free citizen, his self-discipline and appreciation of a wide range of values, because the ethical standards the citizen will have, if he follows the implication of the Report, will be the same utilitarian and relative standards that have put mankind in the mess it is now in. The Commission is composed of high-minded men who, obviously, want more than that. But not even in a minority report or in an appendix have they dared say more than that. Again, we should feel no particular surprise. We have become accustomed to writing nobly of American ideals without either the historical accuracy or the common candor of recognizing that these ideals grew largely out of a mind and conscience that believed in God and in some eternal standards. *Almost our subtlest form of self-deception is our amiable habit of talking about our "cultural heritage" with the main inheritance left out* [italics added].[32]

On the sixth of October 1950, A. Whitney Griswold was confirmed as sixteenth president of Yale University in the simple and impressive ritual that has marked presidential inaugurations for 250 years. According to custom, the new president delivers an inaugural address, an oration of some interest since it is customarily interpreted as a fundamental pronouncement of his educational policy.

The incessantly cited Christian "symbols" of Yale were forthright and unambiguous; all was in keeping with the Connecticut Charter of 1701 which conferred upon the president and the Fellows of Yale "liberty to erect a collegiate school wherein youth may be instructed in the arts and sciences and who through the blessings of almighty God may be fitted for public employment both for church and civil state." Indeed, of the four men who raised their voices on that afternoon, three were clergymen, one of them the presiding bishop of the Episcopal Church of America.

Hymns were sung, and a footnote on the program extended an invitation to tea to the members of the "congregation."

The traditions and the atmosphere had no apparent effect on President Griswold's thinking as revealed in his address. He did not cite or pay tribute to the contribution to the good life which for so many generations was regarded as the distinctive attribute of Christian education. He did not mention religion.

It was more than a mere omission, for the president summoned to the attention of his audience three "vital forces" at Yale which are supported by "powerful traditions." *Christianity was not among those he cited*, which makes Mr. Griswold, even considering him exclusively as a historian, guilty of astonishing lapses regarding the relative importance of Yale's traditions.

Failure to mention religion in an educational address can signify preoccupation with other things. Failure to mention religion in a speech of such outstanding importance as an inaugural address is sheer dereliction. Failure to mention religion in an inaugural address at which other cultural inheritances are mentioned is unexplainable.

> ...the statements of college presidents which omit the subject [of religion] might signify merely the incompleteness of their treatment. But one would hardly suppose that such obviously important statements as inaugural addresses would be intentionally incomplete.[33]

Too much significance can, of course, be attributed to an inaugural address. President Seymour had made a clarion call for a return to Christian values in 1937, but that did not exorcise the extreme secularism that characterized Yale at least during the last four years of his administration:

Yale was dedicated to the upraising of spiritual leaders [President Seymour had said]. We betray our trust if we fail to explore the various ways in which the youth who come to us may learn to appreciate spiritual values, whether by the example of our own lives or through the cogency of our philosophical arguments. The simple and direct way is through the maintenance and upbuilding of the Christian religion as a vital part of university life.

For, after all, it is the policies of the university president that count: "No observer of the college scene can take undiluted delight in the mere fact that lots of colleges go through the motions. The motions must be meaningful or they are worse than meaningless."[34]

President Seymour's devotion to Christianity and his scholarly appreciation of religious values are on the record for all to see. What I call a failure to Christianize Yale was not due to any lack of sympathy or understanding of religion on his part. It was due, rather, to the shibboleths of "academic freedom" that have so decisively hamstrung so many educators in the past fifty years. More of this later. Of Mr. Griswold, it was said by the editors of the *Yale Alumni Magazine* on the occasion of his election to the presidency,[35] "... here's to Whitney Griswold. The Lord, in whom he devoutly believes, bless him and this University." Rumor has it that he too is a religious man. It will, in any case, matter little what he said or did not say at his inauguration if he wages an earnest campaign to improve the lot of religion on the campus.

There can be no judgment of President Griswold's policies and no prediction as to his intentions at this early date. We can do no better at this time than to invoke the same prayer of his friends on the alumni magazine: may the Lord, in whom he devoutly believes, bless him and his University—the University which was founded by churchmen, whose trustees for two hundred years were exclusively ministers of the gospel, whose corporation meetings are even today opened by prayer, whose every symbol commits it to furthering God's fight.

∾

Chapter Two

INDIVIDUALISM
AT YALE

In June of 1949, William C. De Vane, dean of Yale College, addressed the graduating class roughly as follows:

> Several periodicals of national circulation have described the graduating classes of 1949 as "primarily interested in seeking security." The journalists tell us that security and the avoidance of risk are ends that loom foremost in your minds.
>
> I would remind you that it was just one hundred years ago that Americans of every type and description invaded the West Coast in search of their fortunes, and formed the vanguard of a vast colonial movement which increased immeasurably the health and strength of this country. I would remind you that it was they and men like them that have brought this country to greatness. It was not men who sought security first, adventure and enterprise next, who built Yale.
>
> I should say that if these periodicals are correct, if it is true that your attitudes lent weight to their conclusions, then Yale has failed. For Yale expects of her graduates something more than a sodden search for security. She would see in you something of the spirit and the drive of the forty-niners.

Perhaps Yale, traditionally, has engendered something of the spirit of the forty-niners. But if the recent Yale graduate, who exposed himself to Yale economics during his undergraduate years, exhibits enterprise, self-reliance, and independence, it is only because he has turned his back upon his teachers and texts. It is because he has not hearkened to those who assiduously disparage the individual, glorify the government, enshrine security, and discourage self-reliance.

Much of the matter that I shall present to substantiate these charges is interpretable. I believe the net influence of Yale economics to be thoroughly collectivistic. If the reader disagrees, that is surely his privilege. I shall make every effort to avoid distortion. I have no interest in painting a picture of a situation that does not exist.

At the same time, no one should be so naïve as to expect that I could conjure up a list of professors and textbooks who advocate the overthrow, violently or otherwise, of all vestiges of capitalism in favor of an ironclad, comprehensive socialist state. There is very little of this at Yale; but this approach is not needed to accomplish, ultimately, the same transformation. Marx himself, in the course of his lifetime, envisaged two broad lines of action that could be adopted to destroy the bourgeoisie: one was violent revolution; the other, a slow increase of state power, through extended social services, taxation, and regulation, to a point where a smooth transition could be effected from an individualist to a collectivist society. The Communists have come to scorn the latter method, but it is nevertheless evident that the prescience of their most systematic and inspiring philosopher has not been thereby vitiated.

It is a revolution of the second type, one that advocates a slow but relentless transfer of power from the individual to the state, that has roots in the Department of Economics at Yale, and unquestionably in similar departments in many colleges throughout the country. The documentation that follows should paint a vivid picture.

Let me add that my remarks in this chapter in no way attempt to rebut the arguments of the collectivist. For the present I shall confine myself to inserting in this section only what is necessary to point up the collectivist nature of the policies that are being propagated, and to expose the bias and innuendo, the impact of which can be fully appreciated only after spending several years at Yale, reading a half dozen of the most frequently used economics textbooks, and listening to the majority of the lecturers on economics.

I cannot repeat too often that I have cause to object to current Yale policies only if there exists a disparity between the values the alumni of Yale *want* taught, and those currently *being* taught in the field of economics. If, after digesting this section or pursuing a personal investigation, the alumnus finds himself in accord with the values that are being fostered at his college, I have nothing more to say to him—unless, of course, I find him, some day, lamenting the collectivist drift of our government.

With economics as with religion, our attention must focus primarily on the basic course—Economics 10, Elementary Economics. Approximately three hundred and fifty students—over one-third of the average class—take this course every year, while only a tenth as many major in economics. Many students not majoring in the field elect one or two additional courses in economics. Even so, it is the elementary course that provides the framework for future studies, and affects the attitudes of the greatest number of economics students.

As many as two or three texts, and usually as many or more articles and pamphlets, are used as standard reading matter in the basic course. However, one or two books dominate the course, and are most reasonably considered the basic texts. These are of primary interest especially in so far as they treat with problems of public policy, for it is in this area that value judgments are brought sharply to bear on the genuinely controversial economic issues of the day. A professional socialist is as competent as a classicist to explain the price system, the laws of supply and demand, the cost curves of the business firm, and the myriad details and background knowledge that must serve as the basis for any well-conceived course in economics. The elementary textbooks selected at Yale do this job well enough. It is when the author begins to talk about *desirable* government action, *appropriate* social policies, *just* economic goals; it is when he discusses the *obsolescence* of individualism and the *waning* of free enterprise and capitalism, that he reveals his biases. And these biases are readily espoused by the average student.

A student who entered Yale in the fall of 1946 and elected Economics 10 (whether out of interest or to discharge a distributional requirement in the Social Sciences) was issued, as a principal textbook, *Economic Analysis and Public Policy*, by Professors Mary Jean Bowman and George Leland Bach (New York: Prentice-Hall, 1946). The following year, Bowman and Bach was replaced by two textbooks, *The Elements of Economics* by Professor Lorie Tarshis (Boston: Houghton Mifflin Company, 1947), and *Income and Employment*, by Theodore Morgan (New York: Prentice-Hall, 1947). During the next two years, the department used Professor Paul A. Samuelson's *Economics, An Introductory Analysis* (New York: McGraw-Hill, 1948).[1]

The bias of these books prevailed in the basic economics course during these four years. Nor has there been a change in the academic year 1950–51: the department has gone back to the text of Bowman and Bach.

All of these textbook authors take some pains to assure the student that they have in mind the "strengthening" of the free enterprise system. Not one of them, I am certain, would call himself a socialist or even a confirmed collectivist. Witness, for example, Morgan's eulogy:

> ...it is our general assumption that government should not do anything which individuals or voluntary associations can more efficiently do for themselves [p. 184].... Capitalist, or dominantly free-enterprise, economies have succeeded very well in the Western World in raising tremendously the volume of production [p. 176].... Obviously, the American public does not want a nationalized economy or a totalitarian unity. We want to give up no segment of our area of freedoms unless there is clear justification [p. 177].... There are both economic and non-economic reasons for preserving a dominantly wide area of free enterprise [p. 193].

Tarshis states that "the pattern made by the individual flows from the millions of firms in our economy is one that broadly reflects our wants" (p. 239), and the others generally agree.

THESE ARE CHANGING TIMES

The authors in question are apparently ready to point up some of the shortcomings of individualism, and to remind us that we must face the fact that these are changing times and that we must fashion our economic thinking accordingly. After all, write Bowman and Bach, "nineteenth century individualism...in its extreme form" is as "impractical of application" as "the philosophy of totalitarianism" (p. 346).

Samuelson tells the student that

> A cynic might say of free competition what Bernard Shaw once said of Christianity: the only trouble with it is that it has never been tried. There never was a golden age of free competition,

and competition is not now perfect in the economist's sense; probably it is becoming less so every day, in large part because of the fundamental nature of large-scale production and technology, consumers' tastes, and business organization [p. 36].

As far as changing times and the welfare state are concerned, he adds that " 'Cradle-to-grave' security has great popularity; if the private economy cannot supply it naturally, people will insist upon getting it artificially from governments."

There is not a word about the *wisdom* of this sort of economics, which is surely something that a professional economist is supposed to pass judgment upon.* Can there be, over the long run, cradle-to-grave security served out by the government? But it is not surprising that Samuelson withholds adverse judgment, for his reliance upon the state is complete.

These changing times—requiring a reorientation of our concept of economics—were brought about by the inadequacies of free enterprise and by the highly dubious humanitarianism of this economic philosophy. Bowman and Bach remind us that

> . . . equality of opportunity in the theory of rugged individualism is not the same as equality of opportunity in fact; and the most expert of consumers is inadequate to protect himself in the complexities of the modern market. The rugged individualism of

---

* It is seen here, and throughout, that I look upon economics as a science of adjustment between the appetites of man, which are limitless, and the resources of nature, which are limited. I am, further, committed to the classical doctrine that the optimum adjustment—private property, production for profit and by private ownership, and regulation by a free competitive economy—brings not only maximum prosperity, but also maximum freedom. I therefore consider any infringement upon the component parts of the free economy to be unsound economics. It goes without saying that I consider such infringements as militating against maximum freedom.

a pioneer country is giving way to changing concepts of what is meant by true equality of opportunity in economic affairs.... Government is viewed as playing a far more positive role today than formerly. Democracy as expressed in current American ideologies appears to be taking on a more collective character.... American ideology and the American economy itself appear to be moving along a path towards a middle ground.... [In short], *the direction of movement in recent decades in America is clearly further away from the extreme of atomistic individualism and in the direction of increased central planning of the economic life of the country* [pp. 346–47, italics added].

It may be interjected that after all it is a historical fact that we are moving away from individualism and toward central planning, and that Bowman and Bach have done nothing more than to chronicle this changing emphasis. This is all true, but the balance of their book will amply demonstrate that the changing emphasis is taking place with the hearty support of the authors. And besides, let me repeat, is the changing emphasis sound economics? Is it *economically* desirable? Is it not the duty of the economist to reveal that a political trend may not be a wise economic trend? Has economics become nothing more than a subsidiary branch of political science?

Bowman and Bach's palliatives are mild by comparison with some of their brethren textbook writers who have molded the attitudes of so many students. Professor Tarshis, for one, comes right out and says it:

We must be prepared to accept new ways of doing things as well as old, for the problems we face are new and alarming [p. 686].... As the nature of our economy has changed and as the problems that it has been compelled to face have altered and grown in gravity, *we have been compelled to call upon the government* [p. 54, italics added].

For the government, we are told, is the new protector against the excesses of an antiquated system.

> As individualism found expression in the nineteenth-century American economy, it was a philosophy for the strong man, rewarding strength. It was ruthless in its destruction of the weak [p. 345].... The story of American "big business" over the last century is a dramatic one. It is a story of the growth of great business empires, of ruthless cut-throat tactics, and of "gentlemen's agreements," of a shifting pattern of organization arrangements and business policies to meet changing legal and market conditions, and of a repeated use of political pressures by large business groups [Bowman and Bach, p. 351].

This is in part true. But it is special pleading nevertheless—heavily slanted and unbalanced. It is as though a political scientist were to condemn Lincoln as "that man who put his feet up on the desk and told coarse stories." It is nowhere recorded that the nineteenth century was one of unparalleled production of goods and services; we are not told of the mammoth increases of the capital structure of the country and how it was built out of wilderness; nothing is said of the growth of a world of little capitalists, the grocer, the dress manufacturer, the newspaper owner, the farmer—all the millions who attained ratings in Dun and Bradstreet; nothing of the log cabin that blossomed out into a seven-room house with hot-and-cold running water and a garage. No tribute is paid to the *support of the weak that is an automatic result of the free enterprise system* because no one can bring prosperity to himself without bringing it to others (except where prosperity is due to government subvention).

By no means all the serious criticisms of individualism that one hears about at Yale are historical: the effectiveness of free enterprise is today substantially vitiated by inequalities of income, and because of the prevalence of noncompetitive conditions (Tarshis, pp. 240, 243).

> Does our economy provide the ideal output judging it by its correspondence with consumers' wants?...We have developed... reasons for thinking not...income inequality...is as though we gave some people 100 votes, others 50, and still others only 1, and in addition permitted some tampering with the ballot-boxes [Tarshis, p. 246].

In other words, optimum output is impossible under individualism, because of income inequality. But there is a remedy: the state, of course:

> In short, we, acting through our government, have not been disposed to accept as perfect the composition of output that would have been produced in a completely *laissez-faire* economy. By various kinds of government regulation, we have interfered with that result in an effort to make the pattern of our output conform more closely to our wants [p. 249].

The coldness and self-interest of business, which we are not to forget is essentially antihumanitarian, may be seen in a study of the role of an accountant, who after all, says Samuelson, "... is a practical man who must make a living without concerning himself unduly over social welfare" (p. 149).

Thus it is that redistribution of income becomes a major goal of the economist. Although an economic justification for such a redistribution is occasionally supplied (the Keynesian insistence that more money go to that group which has a higher propensity to consume, that is, the lower middle and lower income groups), the principal argument for redistribution seems to be in terms of *ethics*, which these economists have embraced as their province.

UNFAIR DISTRIBUTION OF INCOME

"The division of the output among members of the society must be compatible with the society's standards of justice," Tarshis tells us in his Introduction (p. 3). And as far as the United States is concerned, "The distribution of income is very uneven, and it is questionable whether the maximum social well-being is achieved with this unequal division" (p. 157).

For Morgan, the redistribution of income is a sacred goal:

A spirit of general good will is likely to exist if, as a result of measures like those we are suggesting, the society attains [among other goals] the diminishing inequality of income and wealth [p. 194].... greater equality of wealth brings non-economic advantage in greater social and political democracy [p. 187].... [Our] guiding principles... are to move in the direction of lessening inequalities of wealth and income... [which] are generally accepted objectives [p. 183].

In short, "avoidance of great inequality of wealth and income" is a "goal which a healthy democratic society must keep in view" (p. 198).

Bowman and Bach have no quarrel, economic or ethical, with the distribution of wealth as it is carried on in a socialist society (p. 575), although they concede that some economists offer up two arguments against complete equality of income, namely:

(1) that some income inequality is a necessary incentive to get goods produced efficiently, and (2) that unless some people have

very high incomes there will be insufficient saving and a society will tend to use up resources without accumulation and possibly even without replacement [p. 566].

They go on to say that,

Experiments in Russia seem to prove the truth of the first of these arguments against income equalization . . . the Russians have been forced to introduce income differentials. . . . How great these differentials would need to be to get efficient productive activity remains an open question, *though it is clear that they need not be as great as the inequalities currently existing in the United States* [p. 567, italics added].*

And how to bring about "just" redistribution? The answer is obvious:

. . . the government can go far towards achieving this end through the public economy. . . . The obvious method of approach is through heavy taxes on the high income groups with the funds transferred directly or indirectly (through free or subsidized services) to the low income groups [p. 714].

There is no disagreement among these economists as they condemn the present distribution of income. For reasons "economic, political, and social" something must, they say, be done about it. It is

---

* No mention is made of the fact that in many activities in Russia today, the realities of economics have prevailed upon the classless society, to the extent that the disparity in incomes is far more accentuated than in the United States. Twenty years of failure have brought about almost total desertion of the Marxian motto, "From each according to his ability, to each according to his need."

not enough that *they* believe something must be done about it: we are assured that "most Americans insist on it." No proof of any kind is given to support the contention that "Americans insist" on greater redistribution. But even if such proof were available, the authors of these textbooks in basic economics refuse to address themselves to the question: *Is what most Americans want sound economics?* Obviously, there is no limit to what everyone wants for himself. Since no society can escape the dilemma of an insatiability of human wants on the one hand and a scarcity of economic resources on the other, an adjustment has always been made. The individualist tips his hat to the notion that man should enjoy the fruits of his labor; and since free enterprise displaced mercantilism, he has presented incontrovertible empirical evidence that no other adjustment in the history of the world has brought so much to so many.

But no mention is here made of the inescapable dilemma. Nothing is said about the *insatiability* of human wants.

It is clear that these economists believe that it is good economic (to say nothing of political and social) policy to redistribute income to a far greater degree than is already being done in the United States. Not one of them mentions contrary observations by highly reputable economists. Not one of them so much as pays lip-service to the highly respectable doctrine that it is anti-democratic to take from someone what *the people* in the first instance decide to give him. If several hundred thousand people, acting without coercion of any description, elect to pay Joe DiMaggio $100,000 a year for the privilege of seeing him at bat (and of course in a free economy it is the *people* who, in their role as ultimate employers, pay the wages), and the government promptly turns around and absorbs the greater part of this sum, who is thwarting the most directly expressed will of the people? I can understand these economists' entertaining their own points of view about redistribution of income even if such points of view are, in the opinion of a formi-

dable array of economists, unsound economics; but it is more difficult to excuse them for assuming further redistribution of income
to be an unassailable goal of modern economics.

THE INCOME TAX

As to specific measures to bring about this income equality, the
best of all possible ways is, of course, the income tax. Bowman
and Bach write:

> Many economists believe it would be desirable to place almost
> complete reliance on income taxes as the source of federal rev-
> enue. [As it now stands], the personal income tax, equitable as
> it is, presents to the wary taxpayer several avenues for escaping
> the rates apparently applicable to his income, . . . [and] as long as
> such invitations to tax avoidance exist, serious inequities as
> between individuals, to say nothing of tax revenue losses to the
> government, are certain to result [pp. 766–67].

As to "the extent to which high income tax rates reduce the
incentive to work and to assume investment risks in periods of
relatively dull employment,"

> Much evidence indicates that as long as any substantial portion
> of increased earnings remains after taxes, little reduction in
> productive activity results, since relative incomes apparently are
> at least as important in providing the incentives as are absolute
> dollar levels [p. 768].

This is an important argument of the socialist, and it is seen
applied in Russia, where Stakhanovite medals, decorations, extra
ration cards, and the like have been presented to deserving workers

in lieu of additional income—with diminishing success, as the increasing income differentials of the past few years would indicate.

At any rate, in spite of some avenues of escape in the present law,

> general agreement among economists remains that the personal income tax is the best of all taxes [p. 768]. . . . A "model" tax system might have four major revenue sources. *First, and of major quantitative* importance, there would be a progressive personal income tax plus progressive death and gift taxes. . . [p. 788, italics in original].

The other economists mentioned are of the same general persuasion. Morgan advocates, generally, that 60 percent of federal revenue ought to come from income taxes (p. 188), that exemption for capital gains ought to be eliminated (p. 197), and that a tax of 42–49 percent on incomes between $20,000 and $100,000, and a tax of 75–99 percent on incomes over $100,000, would seem equitable (p. 197).

It is significant that all these tax suggestions are not made in consideration of extraordinary government expenses such as defense or war-waging. They are intended to apply to the normal peacetime situation.

THE INHERITANCE TAX

Inheritances come in for a broadside. Samuelson introduces the matter with his typical glibness and rank, soap-opera appeal, by comparing Barbara Hutton to a Woolworth salesgirl:

> A naïve and uninspired physician in examining the two women in question might find little to choose from with respect to

physique, I.Q., or temperament. But, although each was equally endowed by her parents as far as arms and legs, one was not so generously treated with respect to lockboxes and property. Under our common and statute law, any owner of private property has the right to give, bequeath, or sell it to whomever he pleases (subject only to taxation), and few will criticize père Hutton if he felt that "blood is thicker than water." *But everyone will be curious about the workings of an economic society which enables a few individuals to amass such large accumulations of wealth and power and to perpetuate them by inheritance* [p. 72, italics added].

Morgan is unequivocal about the viciousness of inheritances:

With respect to the subject of inequality, we should note that it is no part of the logic of private enterprise that family dynasties should exist and continue parasitically over the generations to draw tribute from the flow of production [p. 175].

"The prescription is plain," he concludes:

Estate taxes (on the entire property of the deceased) and inheritance taxes (on the amount bequeathed to individual heirs) should be consciously aimed at the goal of ending transmissions of hereditary fortunes. Beyond the modest aims of securing to the widow and dependents unable to work a sum adequate to maintain them and of completing the full education of all children, the justification for bequests tapers off rapidly. *It is not allowable in a democracy* to set up the goal of establishing a family dynasty [p. 198, italics added].

There follows a list of recommendations as to how to eliminate the "notorious loopholes" which allow some families to salvage money for their heirs. With the implementation of his program, Morgan assures us that "there is no reason why we should not achieve at least the level of success of the British in increasing the productivity of death taxes" [p. 199]. A possible alternative to immediate first generation confiscation is that,

> the first inheritor might be taxed at the rate of 50 per cent; at his death the tax might be at the rate of 80 per cent on the portion he inherited; the next death tax on the remainder of the original estate might be 100 per cent [p. 199].

And Morgan adds a remarkable observation:

> [Death and inheritance taxes] are unimportant as revenue producers, *having as justification only our desire for less inequality of income and wealth* [p. 199, italics added].

Bowman and Bach make the same comment:

> Death taxes are obviously of little significance for fiscal stabilization purposes because their yield is so slow and uncertain. . . . *For their justification death duties must rest primarily on the desire for the redistribution of wealth and income* [p. 771, italics added].

In other words, *there is little or no economic value attached to such confiscation. It simply advances the "social welfare"* as these "economists" define social welfare. That social welfare, for them as for all collectivists, is egalitarianism.

PRIVATE PROPERTY RIGHTS

What has happened to the doctrine of private property rights which emerged during the Enlightenment as an indispensable element of personal freedom? What about the right to go into business for one's self? Scarcely any reference is made to these rights even though these economists anxiously embrace morality and justice as proper subject matter of their investigation. Morgan, alone, breaks silence when he tells us:

> Probably, majority opinion agrees with our own national policy that the right of a man to engage in business for himself is not a basic freedom, like freedom from fear, want, freedom of speech and of worship. It is a right which only about one in five of our working force finds himself able, or finds it worth while, to accept [p. 175].

It seems, then, that the volume of indulgence in any given freedom is a relevant factor in determining whether or not it is, properly, a "basic freedom." If, that is to say, only one of five persons goes into business for himself, then the right of man to engage in business for himself is not basic. One out of tens of thousands of men chooses to get up in public and make a speech. Therefore freedom to address assemblies is not basic. Only one out of a hundred thousand decides to start a newspaper. What happens to freedom of the press? And one out of a million will write an economic textbook. Ought Mr. Morgan to have been allowed this privilege?

Besides, Mr. Morgan, *who* says our "national policy" does not admit as basic the freedom to go into business for one's self? Does the Constitution say it? Does the Republican national platform so declare? Or the Democratic National Committee? Has the ex–small business man, Mr. Truman, ever said anything of the sort? And by what authority do you offer yourself as a spokesman for "majority opinion" in this matter?

Morgan's pragmatic attitude is easily extended to include free enterprise itself:

If free enterprise is not a basic freedom, then it must be justified as a central principle of organizing production, or fail to be justified, primarily on the ground of whether it has "delivered the goods" [p. 175].

PRODUCTION AND EMPLOYMENT— RESPONSIBILITIES OF THE STATE

It is apparent by now that these economists invariably have recourse to the state to resolve economic and social difficulties. All of these authors, whose economic texts have been and are being used in the basic course at Yale, are slavish disciples of the late Lord Keynes, and follow his basic program religiously. They do not so much as acknowledge the existence of economists who violently dispute Keynes's conclusions, and *who warn against them alike in consideration of national prosperity, individual freedom, and public morality.*

The basic problem of the free enterprise economy, the Keynesians agree, is periodic unemployment. This comes about as a result of insufficient private consumption or private investment, the latter a hallmark of an advanced, mature economy. The only methods by which stability at full employment may be achieved are through the transfer of money to that group which has the highest "propensity to consume," and through government "investment" (spending) to make up whatever difference is needed in order to maintain national income at the full employment level. The individualist, counter-Keynesian theory that an untrammeled free market, mobile wage rates, and decentralized, non-political credit policies, can in the long run cope with economic fluctuations far more efficaciously than can the government and with far fewer ill effects, if mentioned at all, is scorned. For economics has become a matter of *public policy*, not individual action (witness the title of Bowman and Bach's book, *Economic Analysis and Public Policy*), and, after all, "To set the responsibility for attaining and maintaining full employment on the shoulders of individual consumers or individual businessmen, is absurd" (Morgan, p. 169).

Times, we must remember, have changed, and

Unfortunately, there is no reason to suppose that the economy is a self-adjusting mechanism, that it has a governor which insures stability at full prosperity [Tarshis, p. 507].

So far as total investment or purchasing power is concerned, ours is a system without a steering wheel.... As far as total investment is concerned, the system is in the lap of the gods.... The private economy is not unlike a machine without an effective steering wheel or governor [Samuelson, pp. 256, 412].

We are thus introduced to the necessity of accepting "drastic action" by the government, for without it we must face the fact "that it is as hard for wealthy nations to avoid unemployment... as it is for a camel to pass through the eye of a needle" (Samuelson, p. 17).

Let us bear in mind that unemployment is a *public* problem, and the inadequacies of individual action to cope with such problems are best understood by contrasting

the situation in our economy with that in a *socialist economy*, such as the Russian or Czechoslovakian. In the Russian economy *the decision to produce*, let us say 20 million tons of pig iron, *is made by the Central Planning Board, which presumably takes into account the needs and resources of the Russian economy before it comes to a decision.* The same board determines how many automobiles to produce, how many pairs of socks to manufacture, and how many acres to put into wheat. In our economy, no such institution exists. No one group or person determines how much steel to produce, how many tractors to make, or how much land to plant in cotton. The United States Steel Corporation determines how much steel it will produce, the Bethlehem Steel Corporation determines how much steel it will produce, and the other steel companies make their decisions independently. . . . In a socialist economy, important questions of output, price, employment, and so on are planned collectively. In a capitalist economy, these decisions are made separately by individual firms. . . . *How does the business firm determine the amount it will produce?* The answer to this question is to be found in the fact that the business firm in this country is privately owned. No matter what its form, whether a partnership, a proprietorship, or a corporation, the firm is owned by private individuals. *The determination of how much to produce, or of the price to be charged for the product, is made with one interest in mind—that of the owner. The owner's interest is to secure as large a profit as possible* [Tarshis, p. 29, italics added].

But the individual firm, the individual himself, is powerless to cope with the complexities of the economy in times of stress. The government must step in. For the government, as Bowman and Bach point out (pp. 715–16), has four unique powers which render it capable to discharge responsibilities that the private economy cannot assume. First, the state has the power of compulsion, "which is necessary for regulatory action, for effective redistribution of income (by taking from some and using the funds to aid others), for restricting production and consumption of particular commodities, and so on." Second, the state can undertake to provide "many goods and services that are generally desired but not marketable under a price system in the private economy." Third, because of its long life and great resources, "the state is able to undertake long-run, expensive projects, which, though desirable, would not be feasible for private enterprise." Finally, "the state, being free from the 'profit motive' and having the power of compulsion, is able to make its revenues fit its expenditures (within limits) rather than the reverse."

With such an introduction, the wisdom and indispensability of government action to regulate the economy becomes the inexorable next step. Thus, in all four of the textbooks under discussion, we are launched into a doctrinaire collectivist program. Government-directed "compensatory fiscal policy" must harmonize the economy. "High taxes for redistribution. . . . Public spending to close the gap between consumption and private investment and full production. . . . Regulation of production. . . . Social service. . . . If necessary, let the government guarantee full employment" (Morgan, p. 189).

During depressions, government spending of any sort is wise because, in the long run, "wise domestic investment is no more powerful than ultimately foolish investment . . . because of the favorable respending effects on those who receive government expenditures" (Samuelson, pp. 371, 434). Morgan tells us that "it is better to employ men in digging holes and filling them up than not to employ them at all; it is better to employ men to make products which we thereupon dump in the middle of the ocean than to leave them idle" (p. 182). He quotes Keynes: "Pyramid-building, earthquakes, even wars may serve to increase wealth. . . ."

Why did not "compensatory fiscal policy" work during the '30s? Because it was "too little and too late" (Bowman and Bach).*

---

* I am careful not to imply that large-scale government spending will not relieve unemployment. It is indisputable that it will—for the short run. "All I know about the long run," Keynes once quipped, "is that we are all dead." One of Keynes's most distinguished critics,

NO LIMIT TO
GOVERNMENT SPENDING

What about the perils of deficit financing? Prior to understanding this subject, certain superstitions about money must be overcome. First to be dispelled is any untoward faith in gold or the gold standard, which Tarshis compares, by no means favorably, to a limburger cheese standard (pp. 332–33, 635). It is a good thing that gold certificates no longer exist, Samuelson tells us (p. 286), because the gold standard "made each country a slave rather than a

---

Professor Ludwig von Mises, retorted that this was "the only correct declaration of the neo-British Cambridge school." But it must be realized that unemployment is never a problem if freedom is to be the sacrificial offering; unemployment is unknown to the Soviet Union. We can, then, distinguish more clearly the line that divides the individualist and the collectivist, for the latter sets full employment as the first goal of any society, and its realization is not to be obstructed by any consideration of private property, freedom of production, freedom of investment, or freedom of job selection. The former recognizes that some fluctuations in employment are inevitable in the free, expanding economy. It is the price one has to pay for a secular trend toward maximum freedom and greater and greater prosperity. The individualist insists that drastic depressions are the results of credit inflation (not excessive savings, as the Keynesians have it), which at all times in history has been caused by direct government action or by government influence. As for *aggravated* unemployment, the individualist insists that it is exclusively the result of government intervention through inflation, wage rigidities, burdensome taxes, and restrictions on trade and production such as price controls and tariffs. The inflation that comes inevitably with government pump-priming soon catches up with the laborer, wipes away any real increase in his wages, discourages private investment, and sets off a new deflationary spiral which can in turn only be counteracted by more coercive and paternalistic government policies. And so it is that the "long run" is very soon a-coming, and the harmful effects of government intervention are far more durable than those that are sustained by encouraging the unhampered free market to work out its own destiny.

master of its own economic destiny" (p. 380). And in support of "compensatory fiscal policy," deficit financing, and welfarism, Morgan italicizes "the basic truth that money is the servant and tool of the economy and not its master" (p. 244).

Let the student constantly bear in mind that there is no practical limit to government debt:

> The government may be said to exhaust its credit only if it is unable to borrow; and, as we have just seen, its ability to do so can never be seriously in question.... The only question, then, is whether the government can always find a lender or someone who will accept government bonds. In the final analysis this is no problem, for the simple reason that the government controls the Federal Reserve Banks and can always compel them to buy government bonds.... There is no sign that a high debt exhausts the credit of the government of the United States. And since as a last resource "it can borrow from itself," there need be no fear on this account.... *There are no grounds for believing that a high public debt destroys the nation's credit or leads to a marked fall in the value of the dollar* [Tarshis, pp. 535, 541, italics added].

Samuelson underscores this, as he concludes his analysis with the statement: "In short, there is no technical financial reason why a nation fanatically addicted to deficit spending should not pursue such a policy for the rest of our lives, and even beyond" (p. 433).

There is no disagreement from Bowman and Bach, who assert: "The fear that increasing the public debt will make the nation go bankrupt is almost completely fallacious" (p. 697).

But is a high national debt desirable? It is of course an inevitable by-product of Keynesian policy, and as such, acceptable to the economic textbook authors at Yale. Tarshis asserts unequivocally that deficit spending is the best means of coping with modern economic problems (p. 534 et seq.), and asks, "Why should it be better to increase the private than the public debt?..." Can anyone find a "clear answer" to this problem, he asks rhetorically?*

The policy of government deficits and government credit is extended, without difficulty, into the realm of international loans. In fact, considering the desirability of increased foreign investment, we ought to encourage foreign nations *not* to repay us what they owe us, for *"the only cost [our economy really sustains] is that which we face when the loan is repaid"* (Tarshis, p. 632, italics added). In fact, once money becomes the slave not the master of the people, many of our economic problems could easily disappear. For one thing, "If we could only export one of the printing presses used for the manufacture of Federal Reserve Notes to, let us say, China, our foreign investment would be enormously higher" (Tarshis, p. 391).

As for the bugaboo that an element of internal debt is being passed on to future generations, it is "unmistakably false." "Can it truthfully be said that 'internal borrowing shifts the war burden to future generations while taxing places it on the present generation'? A thousand times no!" (Samuelson, p. 427).

Bowman and Bach (pp. 798–99) and the rest agree—as does the individualist, but only if he agrees to look upon the American people as an indivisible entity, instead of as one hundred and fifty million individuals. Note the interesting reservation that appears both in the Tarshis and in the Bowman and Bach analyses of passing debt on to future generations. Bowman and Bach include a

---

* "Here is one clear answer, Professor Tarshis," wrote Rose Wilder Lane in her review of the Tarshis book for the National Economic Council, August 1947. "There is a limit to debt, fixed by the debtor's ability to pay it. This limit operates on private debt, because private borrowers have no means of compelling lenders to lend them money...."

footnote (p. 799) to the effect that "if the war generation borrows funds *outside* the United States, and the future generation has to pay foreign bondholders, then it is justifiable to speak of a burden of payment being placed on the future generation in the United States." Tarshis makes the same observation (p. 427).

Herein, it seems, lie the differences:

If, after a generation has gone by, a million Americans who hold $50 billion in war bonds wish to cash them in, the government must indeed honor their decision. Now, if the government were to tax nonbondholders $50 billion to retire these bonds, it could surely be said that the nonbondholding citizens of the country were forced to shoulder a tax burden that would never have existed but for a war that was waged before they were born.

But such a direct manner of discharging government debt is never seriously considered. How much easier to refund the debt, thereby satisfying not only the war-bond holders who wish to sell their government securities but also other elements of the population who may wish to buy government bonds. And a final ace in the government's hole: if a substantial number of bondholders should simultaneously determine to cash in their bonds, the government could formulate special tax legislation aimed at such persons, thereby, in effect, taxing all or most of the funds derived from the sale of their bonds. Thus, if the individual cashed his bond, the money would flow from the Treasury to him and immediately back to the Treasury in payment of new taxes. If he decided not to cash the bond, we are back where we started, with only the small interest on the bond to concern us.

So it is that "we owe it to ourselves," and "any given generation owes the money to the contemporaneous generation."

But the government cannot play this game with foreigners. The state must be prepared to redeem foreign-held bonds and has no recourse to any of the stratagems that can render internally held bonds valueless.

Thus, the government can forswear or circumvent bona fide obligations *to its own citizens*, but must deal honestly with foreigners.

It is through this sort of logic that the collectivist shrugs off as naïve any concern about financial burdens imposed on future generations. And it is not surprising that he should do so, for to the collectivist, *individual* ownership of bonds, which represent claims to future production on the part of other persons, poses no problem whatever. For to him the individual means nothing; he pauses only to consider society as a whole, and thus he can generalize that internal debt is no burden, for "we owe it to ourselves."

What about the danger of a large national debt? This, we are assured on all sides, is simply not a very grave problem. ". . . there is never any possibility that the government—which has complete powers to issue new currency—would ever be unable to pay off the holders of government bonds in full" (Tarshis, p. 164).

That is one way to do it—simply run the printing presses a few hours more every day. Alternative methods of coping with the debt are described by Morgan (pp. 242–44). First, "The debt might be reduced by achieving an excess of taxes over government expenditures."

But this plan has limitations, not to speak of grave deflationary drawbacks. Therefore a second method could be examined.

The debt might be repudiated.

From this alternative, however, Morgan recoils—not so much out of moral indignation as out of sheer funk: the commercial banking system would collapse, and government credit would be destroyed. A much better alternative looms:

> The debt is expressed in terms of dollars. Hence, monetary and other policies aimed at higher price levels in the economy would

diminish its relative size. If average prices rise by 25 percent, then the holder of a bond (or other obligation expressed in dollars) can buy only four fifths as much as he could if prices had not risen. The *real* debt, in terms of goods and services, has obviously diminished in size. There is much to be said in favor of a gradually rising price level, say 1 to 2 percent a year.*

In other words, whereas it may be immoral and otherwise unwise for the government to repudiate the debt, there remains the completely honorable alternative of simply reducing the value of the debt through government-caused inflation.

A final alternative is listed: let the government "borrow" directly from the Reserve Banks, and let the interest be "only a service fee to cover the expense of the banks." Or, for that matter, let the government "issue new currency itself."

There appears to be no cause for concern over government debt—or over a stable currency.†

---

* It is ironic that this debonair attitude about inflation has come home to roost. The purchasing power of the 1932 dollar now wavers at forty cents. If Yale's capital funds, a substantial portion of which are invested in fixed income-bearing securities, had kept pace with inflation, they would today be worth well over $275 million, and yield, at prevailing returns, $12,375,000 yearly. Instead, the University must struggle along with a $141 million endowment with its $5,038,000 return. This has necessitated drastic educational curtailments and, *ça va sans dire*, desperate appeals to the alumni, who are, it seems, to make up the difference, and to continue to support Yale's economic professors and texts in their cries for more and more inflation.

† These economists might well have quoted Lord Keynes in one of his more sober moments. Fifteen years before he published his *General Theory* he wrote, in his book *The Economic Consequences of the Peace*, "There is no subtler, no surer means of overturning the existing bases of society than to debauch the currency. The process engages all the hidden forces of economic law on the side of destruction and does it in a manner which not one man in a million is able to diagnose."

BIG BUSINESS AND MONOPOLY

A major scapegoat of the collectivist is the business firm—and most particularly the big business firm, to whose policies are attributed some of the major evils of our economy. The monopolist (in most respects, properly) receives a great share of the blame for the vicissitudes of the free enterprise system; but at the same time, these writers convey an utterly distorted impression as to the power and the predominance of monopolies in the United States.

In our matured economy, "Giant industries have grown up, and in most sectors of the economy small firms are no longer very important" (Tarshis, p. 53).

In this connection, it is important to understand just what a monopolist is. He is not, indeed,

> . . . a fat, greedy man with a big moustache and cigar who goes around violating the law. If he were, we could put him in jail. He is anyone important enough to affect the prices of the things that he sells and buys. *To some degree that means almost every businessman* . . . [Samuelson, p. 39, italics added].

As a reputable figure in public life, the businessman suffered a great deal during and after the depression. In fact,

> The businessman has never returned to his previous position of prestige. Shaken of self-confidence by a decade of considerable losses, harassed by government and labor, pounced upon by the courts for violation of antitrust laws he had forgotten existed, it is little wonder that he was dyspeptic before the war. But like the unemployed, he experienced during the emergency a feeling of being wanted and needed. With the return of strength, humility and inarticulateness are ebbing away [Samuelson, p. 91].

These economists' exaggerated notions about the pervasiveness of monopoly darken even their lighter moments, as, for example:

> For good or evil, American labor has declared itself in as a silent partner in every business. With the acquiescence of the public and the government, workers ask for, and usually succeed in getting, some fraction of corporation profits. The moral for the self-interested laborer is to apprentice himself to a profitable quasi-monopolistic industry which has plenty of gravy to share [Samuelson, p. 531].

The authors' animosity toward big business is outspoken, and indications are abundant that large business and free enterprise are irreconcilable:

> We want to attain them [our economic goals] through the means of free enterprise, by which we mean an economy whose dominant tone is set by numerous small enterprises. It is not reasonable to include under the term firms with much monopolistic power, including huge businesses: these furnish a field for the application of sophisticated public policy [Morgan, p. 179–80].

We are to face the fact that

> The policies which are needed for maintaining high production and employment are those which affect the environment in which business decisions are made [Morgan, p. 179].

As also, we must recognize that

> Huge private enterprises are obviously on trial. They have lost their case in the current general opinion of Europe and of England [Morgan, p. 179].

And, of course, nationalization:

> If there is an extension of public ownership...it may often be
> more economic to own "monopolies" than to carry on a running
> warfare of regulation and suits [Morgan, p. 194].

THRIFT AND WELFARISM

It is a basic plank of the Keynesians that ours is a "low consumption" economy that cannot sustain itself at a level of full employment without recourse to the state. A major concern of government, then, must be policies aimed at increased consumption. It follows that *saving* (except in periods of inflation) is evil, and ought to be discouraged by government action. Tarshis announces: "Since, as consumers, we are willing to purchase only five-eighths of our full-employment output, we have a low-consumption economy. And that, from one point of view at any rate, is one of the main sources of our difficulty" (p. 521).

It follows that Tarshis should announce as one of the goals of government "reducing incentives to thrift" (p. 522).

Since the people are not to be encouraged to attend to their own future security, the government, naturally, must take over this function. Morgan laments the inadequacy of present government welfare policies, and calls for extending them substantially in several directions:

> Evidently, we have made only a good start toward the obvious
> target of protecting everyone against all the hazards that might
> leave him without minimum necessities and comforts....The
> social-security program, with the cooperation of state and local
> governments, should, therefore, be made universal in coverage,
> and its benefits increased to the end of assuring at least the new
> higher minimum standard of living [p. 190].

Morgan goes on to recommend obligatory separation wages—
"a lump payment made to anyone who is discharged." As has been
previously indicated, he also believes that "A simple and direct
measure for increasing private consumption is *a guarantee by the
Federal government*, in cooperation with the states, *to employ anyone who cannot get a job elsewhere*" (p. 189, italics added).

Samuelson adds family allowances to the responsibilities of
government:

> Canada, England, France, Sweden, and other governments have
> begun to give "family allowances" every month, the amount
> varying with the number of children in the family. This is done
> both for humanitarian reasons and to try to stimulate population
> growth. It is not hard to see why the government, rather than
> private industry must make these payments; for if corporations
> had to pay higher wages to men with large families, they would
> soon begin to discriminate in their hiring in favor of ancient
> bachelors and against the heads of large families [p. 206].

In dispatching the entire subject of government welfarism,
Samuelson deals with the opposition by simply stating that "if the
private economy cannot supply cradle-to-grave security," which
throughout his book he maintains it cannot, why then the "people
will insist upon getting it artificially from governments" (p. 76).

It would require many additional pages to transmit with any
fullness the collectivist character of these four textbooks. All the
society's ills—the economic, the social, the ethical—can be ame-
liorated by Bigger and Bigger Government. No consideration of
private property or individual economic freedom is to deter the
government from spending "up to the point where the marginal
loss of satisfaction to those providing the revenue is just equal to
the marginal gain in satisfaction derived by those benefiting from
the expenditures" (Bowman and Bach, p. 720); and no doubts are

expressed as to whether even the wisest government can know where this point is. The government, it seems, is to weigh numerical losses and gains in satisfaction; and just so long as there is a net gain (an intangible which the government is to interpret), any government policy is justified. Individual rights of the sort that for generations were never supposed to be prey to government action are cheerily disregarded as unjustifiable *impedimenta* in the way of purposive and enlightened state policies.

The reader's attention is always fixed upon the "social good" (as though this could be anything but the sum of individual goods), and even here the private enterprise system breaks down because social costs don't tally with money costs (Bowman and Bach, p. 714); the individual cannot protect himself, given the complexities of our economic system; hence the government (against whose tyrannies the individual is presumed always to be able to protect himself) is invariably called to the rescue (Bowman and Bach, p. 346).

The point of inquiry for the economist, then, is not whether the government should control the economy, but to what extent (Bowman and Bach, p. 705). Certainly the scope of government is to lie well "beyond regulatory duties," "somewhere between 19th century liberalism and Karl Marx" (Bowman and Bach, p. 705). There is no longer any question that "some of the mistakes that a flock of independent competitors make...would be lessened in an economy characterized by planning" (Samuelson, p. 39). Since "the contributions of government have come to be regarded as more and more necessary, even aside from such emergencies as war" (Bowman and Bach, p. 716), "freedom in the choice of a job or business," whatever this means, "must rest largely on government regulation of the private economy" (Bowman and Bach, p. 714).

State action alone can decrease friction and bring more of everything to everybody; and, up against the unique powers of the government, the individualist is to satisfy himself with the knowledge that "the remarkable fact is not how much the government does to control economic activity... but how much it does *not* do" (Samuelson, p. 35, italics in the original).

A remarkable and appalling aspect of all four of the books under consideration is their treatment of the opposition, which they do not so much as call "loyal." Only Bowman and Bach make any reference to individualist notions on economics. But these are always framed in the nineteenth century—with the implication that they are of purely historical interest. For the rest, neither Morgan nor Tarshis nor Samuelson ever intimates that some reputable economists have read Keynes *and disagreed with him!* Opposition to their brand of collectivism is simply untenable, and what little recognition is given to that barely noticeable corps of economists and individuals who repudiate the collectivists' program is sometimes forthrightly savage. *"No longer is modern man able to believe 'that government governs best which governs least,'"* Samuelson states (p. 152); or, to put it the other way around, one cannot believe in minimum government and be a "modern man," to which, it is to be assumed, we all aspire.

Samuelson is more explicit in the following page as he states that "where the complex economic conditions of life necessitate social coordination and planning, there can *sensible men of good will be expected to invoke the government*" (italics added). And so we are not only to contemn the superficiality of the treatment of economics of such men as Jewkes, F. A. Hayek, Röpke, Anderson, Watt, and von Mises, we are also to doubt their motives.

As for these men, and the hundreds and thousands of others who disapprove of Keynes's "compensatory fiscal policies," we are told that "the real opposition is to certain characteristics of prosperity itself rather than to a particular way of securing it" (Tarshis, p. 507). Had the New Deal engaged more thoroughly and on a

larger scale in applying the remedies of Keynes, says Tarshis, corporation profits during the period would have been more than
three times what they were. It seems, then, that those businessmen who disapprove of large-scale deficit financing, the welfare
state, and the planned society are actually opposed to maximizing
their own profits, which they could readily do by sanctioning the
Keynesian formula.

Although the businessman is painted in so many passages as a
blind and ignoble profit-seeker, it is never quite explained why it
is that this same businessman, as a general rule, opposes measures
that Tarshis assures will bring him greater profits.

Throughout, we are assured that the measures necessary to
government-directed economic stability constitute no violation of
freedom or democracy (e.g., Morgan, p. 172). No credit is given—
not even a footnote—to the serious works of serious students who
insist that abridgement of freedom is an inescapable by-product of
government planning. And when Morgan assures us that his central policies "are compatible with democracy," we must remember
that he does not consider private property or private enterprise
essential to democracy or even to freedom. And neither he nor his
colleagues acknowledge that a democracy can itself be as tyranni-
cal as a dictatorship, since it is the *extent*, not the *source*, of government power that impinges on freedom.

And so the story goes in the basic economics texts at Yale.
Ours is a mixed economy. "The word *capitalism* has become
increasingly useless" (Morgan, p. 172), since all modern economies
have come to recognize that increasing elements of socialism
serve the public welfare. All nations now have mixed economies—
even Great Britain, for *"When the British Labor Government com-
pletes the socialization program underway...some 80 percent of
national production will still be in private hands, only 20 percent in
the hands of the government"* (Morgan, p. 172). In other words in

Great Britain, where the government owns outright coal, steel, transportation, and the utilities, where the government controls credit, travel, agriculture, construction, and employment, we still see a nation that is 80 percent free enterprise; thus the United States can go a *long* way before it ceases to be basically a capitalist country.

What is the net effect of the textbook treatment of Elementary Economics on the thinking of the average young graduate of Yale and of the scores of colleges and universities that utilize one or more of the books in question?*

The college graduate is a potential entrepreneur. If he decides to start a business of his own, he must bear in mind the warnings of the economists at Yale. The first of these is that to enter business is not a basic right. Whatever business he contemplates must be justified in terms of the "social good." He reasons that the social good, as seen through the price system, is determined by whether or not consumers will buy his products; and this seems reasonable, since if no one buys his products—if he isn't, therefore, working for the social good—he'll go broke anyway.

But this is not good enough, for he must remember that money costs do not tally with social costs, and that therefore it is quite possible that the enterprise he is considering, regardless of its financial success, will militate against the social welfare. Since he already knows that private property and entrepreneurship, not being individual rights, must be justified in terms of the "social good," and the social good cannot be affirmed by the existence of satisfied consumers, he must proceed cautiously. For some planner, better equipped than the consumers to evaluate the social

---

* See Appendix G for a partial list of American colleges and universities that have adopted the texts of Samuelson, Tarshis, Morgan, and Bowman and Bach.

good, may order him to desist from his business, even though he may have invested time, thought, and money in the enterprise.

Assuming, however, that he is an inveterate, dauntless gambler and decides to run all these risks and launch his business anyway, there are further considerations that his economists have enjoined him to keep in mind. There is the matter of profit. For reasons of justice and general social harmony, he cannot allow the consumers to set his profits in accordance with their desire for his product and their satisfaction with it. This decision is for a third party to make, with an eye to something called the social good.

Those persons who are going to determine his profit are aware that absolute dollar income is not the only incentive to offer up to the entrepreneur. High *relative* income will do. That is, just so he makes more money than his neighbors *before* taxes, he will enjoy his prestige and continue to work hard, exploit his ingenuity, and take risks. So he must determine, before he goes any further, whether or not this fits him. It may become a question of whether he will be satisfied with the knowledge that the money he *might* earn would be enough to buy a Cadillac *before* taxes. In other words, will he be satisfied with the knowledge that he *earned* enough to buy a Cadillac, even though the government won't actually let him go out and buy a Cadillac? Will the knowledge make his Ford any the less a Ford?

A major incentive might be that he wants to leave his children a sizable nest-egg when he dies, perhaps so that they can enjoy opportunities he never had, perhaps so that they may enjoy the opportunities he himself had. But this is out of the question. The economists stated unequivocally that there is no justification for sizable inheritances. Whatever incentive this sort of thing has provided for men in the past must now be written off. Assuming then, that he is successful in the swing of middle age, his major concern will not be to maintain or increase his productivity, but rather to call in the actuaries, pore over their statistics, and attempt to calculate just exactly when he could stop working and die just about broke. Because it's a cinch he is not going to work to amass a sizable legacy for the government.

There is something else that as a civilized and educated human being he should realize; and that is that entrepreneurship is only dubiously humanitarian. He has read about the excesses of business, about the coldness of money costs, about the friction that arises out of unequal incomes. He must decide whether or not, if he decides to start a business, he can escape the conscience which was so delicately refined at Yale. . . .

So he finally decides to go down to Washington and get a job with some government bureau. Or maybe tie in with AT & T. (His first question to the personnel officer of either place will be about pension provisions.)

And Dean DeVane was astounded, puzzled, and shocked in 1949 when he read that the graduating class seemed more interested in security than in enterprise.

THE TEACHERS OF ELEMENTARY ECONOMICS

To an important degree, the textbook is only the tool of the teacher. It is true that in some classes lecturers do not treat the material covered in textbook reading assignments, but this is not the case in Economics 10 at Yale, where classroom sessions follow closely the assigned textbook reading material. Therefore the collectivist inclinations of the textbook writers can be either encouraged or discouraged by the teacher. It is clear from the unanimously collectivistic attitude of the textbooks, though, that even if the teacher were inclined to question the conclusions of the Keynesians, this would be awkward in that it would demand constant

repudiation of the conclusions arrived at in the texts. It is nevertheless interesting to ask whether the teachers of the basic economics course are inclined to agree with the statists or not.

It is difficult to generalize about this because the basic course
is split into a great number of sections (eleven in 1950–51), each
of which, while subscribing to departmental schedules, examina-
tions, and texts, is otherwise conducted independently. Moreover,
in the past four years in particular, there has been a tremendous
turnover in instructors of the basic course. Most of the teachers
have been young men, in large part graduate and law students.

I am best equipped, of course, to relay my personal experiences with Economics 10, which I studied in the academic year
1947–48. During this period our class had three teachers, all of
whom were students at the Yale Law School. One of these
(Alexander Brooks) was an outspoken socialist; in fact, he energetically promoted Wallace's Communist-dominated Progressive
Party in the spring of 1948. He never lost an opportunity to disparage the free enterprise system.

The other two instructors were doctrinaire Keynesians. At
least in this class, and in the other classes taught by these instructors, there was no disparity between the attitudes of the teacher
and those of the textbook writers in regard to public policy.

There have been too many teachers of Economics 10, as I have
already conceded, to admit of facile generalizations about them.

But it is safe to say that at least at the basic level, the department is Keynesian. If there are graduates of the elementary course
who were taught by teachers who sought to deflate the Keynesian
brand of collectivism, I have not met any of them. This is not surprising, as a glance at the staff members of the Department of
Economics will reveal later.

I did attempt, over a period of several weeks, to collect sample examination papers written by students in Economics 10. For

by matching questions and average answers, significant generalizations can be made as to the dominant values promulgated in the basic course. I knew that to satisfy my own teachers, I was expected to regurgitate the Keynesian formulas; and I am fairly certain that similar answers are expected in other divisions.

But I was totally unsuccessful in my search for papers. Several people whose help I enlisted in collecting the examination books ran into a stone wall no matter what avenue they followed. One was finally told that examination books were not to be released without the special permission of the department chairman, since "too many people are trying to get hold of them." I cannot understand why the department should be reluctant to withhold these papers from anyone. But since it is not feasible for me to ask why, I shall keep to myself my guess as to its motives.

THE DEPARTMENT

A large number of economics courses are available to the student who wishes to pursue his studies beyond the elementary course. As I have already stated, conversance with economics is to a substantial degree a matter of mastering noncontroversial subject matter—technique, historical methods, and the like. For the purposes of this survey, our interest is with those courses that engage heavily in discussions of public policy, and that attract—and presumably influence—a sizable number of students. Thus, I shall omit discussion of any of the courses that deal with statistics, accounting, or marketing, or with international or regional finance. It is, needless to say, impossible to review all the textbooks used by the department during a given year.

Except for Economics 10, the course which attracts most students (in large part because it is required of majors in Applied Economics) is entitled the Economics of the Business Firm. It is heavily subscribed to by engineering students and deals to a great extent with technical and financial theory and detail. It is described in the official *Course of Studies Bulletin* as follows:

> The nature, functions, and forms of the business firm; its acquisition and management of capital funds; relations between owners, creditors, employees, and management; and the economic and social implications of the large corporation.

It should be noted that no student is admitted to this course unless he has taken an elementary course in the principles of accounting; a large number of students whose interest in economics is nontechnical are thereby excluded.

But the course is nevertheless of interest because its teachers, Mr. Hastings and Mr. Saxon, are individualists in the classic tradition. Mr. Saxon is particularly vocal in his defense of the free marketplace.*

Aside from Elementary Economics, I believe that the most influential course in the undergraduate department is Professor Lindblom's combined Comparative Economic Systems and Economic Security and Labor Legislation, which attracts approximately two hundred students. I believe it to be indisputable that

---

* The Course Critique of 1950, published by the *Yale Daily News* as a consensus of undergraduate opinion on the various courses in the curriculum, says of the Economics of the Business Firm: "...Mr. Saxon was criticized [by his students] for his very opinionated point of view. His ideas represent those of the last century and are generally considered out-dated.... Mr. Hastings also is very conservative and his interpretation of the material covered reflects his biased thinking. Most of his ideas are considered out-dated." I know of no more eloquent testimony to the success of the collectivists and the thoroughness of the basic course in economics than this bland dismissal of individualism as "out-dated."

Mr. Lindblom is, in undergraduate circles, the best known and most frequently quoted economist on the Yale faculty, despite his relatively junior rank (associate professor). Professor Saxon's name is probably bandied about as often, but he is not taken seriously because, of course, as an individualist, his ideas are "generally considered out-dated." But there is nothing dated about Mr. Lindblom, that is, if we are willing to forget that collectivism is as old as tyranny.

It is difficult to categorize Mr. Lindblom's values. He himself repeatedly discourages the use of general classifications to label either his own economic philosophy or that of most other people. Like Morgan he finds the descriptive terms "capitalist" and "socialist" quite useless, since, let it be remembered, we are living in an age of mixed economies.

Mr. Lindblom dislikes a doctrinaire attitude toward anything. He incessantly encourages the pragmatic approach to economics (and, for that matter, to everything else). It naturally follows that any reliance on absolutes, or any reference to indefeasible "rights," is unwarranted and anachronistic. Early in the year, Mr. Lindblom initiates his classes in his pragmatism with respect to both ends and means.

It was in his second or third lecture in the fall of 1948, when I was enrolled in his class, that Mr. Lindblom stated that one of his foremost ambitions in teaching the course was "to disabuse as many of you as possible of 15th century [sic] notions about capitalism." The first subject of his assault was the concept of the right of private property, which, he stated, no enlightened society, no reputable philosopher, can uphold.

My abbreviated lecture notes read somewhat as follows:

"After all, let's take the Ford Motor Company. What sort of success would Henry Ford have had if he had built his plant in the middle of the Sahara Desert? None, of course. It is seen, therefore, that his wealth is only partly attributable to his own enterprise and ingenuity. These qualities would have availed him nothing had it not been for the community—whose services and labor he enlisted, whose materials he used, and whose citizens gave him his profits. It is easy to see from this that it is not the community that is indebted to Mr. Ford for his contributions to their standard of living, but rather Mr. Ford who is indebted to the community for making possible his success. Hence, the rewards that he reaped properly belong to the community, which must now determine, through *legislative* policy, to what extent Mr. Ford should be rewarded."

From this illustration, it is a short step to the subservience of the individual to the society, whose wishes are, of course, uniquely expressed through the mechanisms of the state.

I have material for page upon page of discussion of Mr. Lindblom's philosophy which is, manifestly, collectivist in the extreme. But for lack of space, I shall limit myself to a few additional illustrations.

Mr. Lindblom recognizes as indispensable to a successful economy a price system of one sort or another, and thus he devotes several weeks to discussions of alternative price systems. He uses as the basis of discussion a pamphlet on the price system written by Karl de Schweinitz Jr. and published by the Yale Department of Economics (1948). Mr. de Schweinitz describes at some length the competitive price system and the socialist price system. In comparing the two, he arrives at a decision as to their relative merits:

> If we assume that consumers can compel their representatives through observances of the rules to allocate resources for maximum want satisfaction, *the socialist price system becomes less vulnerable to criticism than other price systems* [p. 41, italics added].

Mr. Lindblom does not dispute this conclusion, although he stresses the fact that reliance on "discretionary political control" is a gamble.

At one time or another during his course, Mr. Lindblom advocated progressively higher income and inheritance taxes, and nationalization of all noncompetitive industry; in discussing social security, he investigates sympathetically some of the "social dividend" theories (one version: everyone in America to relinquish to the government all or practically all of his income, and to receive, from the state, annual stipends). In the field of labor relations, he suggests that "collective bargaining" cannot be fair unless plants are forbidden by law to operate when a union calls a strike. In reply to the suggestion, often heard during the depression, that workers on public relief be denied the franchise, he asserts it as far more reasonable that the unemployed workers be allowed a double vote, and the industrialists none at all, because, after all, "who caused the unemployment?"

The reading material assigned during this year is also revealing. Edmund Wilson *(To the Finland Station)* discusses the historical inadequacies of the Marxian movement, but does not conceal his own sympathy with the socialist ideal; Schumpeter *(Capitalism, Socialism, and Democracy)* believes that capitalism gives birth to political developments and public attitudes that must spell its own destruction; Loucks and Hoot *(Comparative Economic Systems)* discuss various economic systems without revealing any particular bias; Pritchett *(T.V.A.)* extols the accomplishments of the mammoth government enterprise; Childs *(Sweden, the Middle Way)* enthusiastically surveys the socialist experiments in Sweden; Golden and Ruttenberg *(Dynamics of Industrial Democracy)* are two union leaders who plead earnestly for closed shops, the Wagner Act, profit sharing and egalitarianism; Gregory's *(Labor and the Law)* is a fairly impartial review of the judicial history of labor disputes; Kaltenborn *(Government Adjustment of Labor Disputes)* analyzes, dispassionately, the history of mediation and arbitration; Mills *(New Men of Power)* explains the dynamic opportunities that beckon to union leaders, and disparages conservatism and free enterprise.

One item from the reading prospectus is omitted from the foregoing list: a 37-page pamphlet by the late Professor Henry C. Simons, of the University of Chicago, entitled *A Positive Program for Laissez Faire*, which is introduced by Mr. Lindblom as presenting the "only intelligent conservative position." I find this pamphlet an extraordinary document, for perhaps to a greater extent than anyone else has done in so few pages, Mr. Simons indicts the state as bearing heavy responsibility for the evils that led to the great depression (the pamphlet was written in 1934, probably in a fit of pique), but promptly outlines a program which would give to the state unprecedented power. He equates freedom with free enterprise, and proceeds to outline a sure program for the destruction of the free economy. Mr. Simons's specific proposals include (1) reduction of inequality by heavy taxation, (2) nationalization of all railroads and utilities and "other industries in which it is impossible to maintain effectively competitive conditions," (3) abolition of private deposit banking on the basis of fractional reserves, (4) legal limitations to advertising and selling activities, (5) limitation upon the total amount of property which any single corporation may own (suggested: no more than 5 percent of the total output of that product), (6) enactment of laws to prohibit any person's serving as an officer in any two corporations engaged in the same line of business, (7) outright federal ownership of the Federal Reserve Banks, (8) elimination of all special tax treatment for capital gains, and (9) increased government welfarism.

This, we are led to believe, is the conservative alternative to even greater statism and socialization.*

It is true that Mr. Lindblom is not doctrinaire, and some of his asides (as witness his recent book, *Unions and Capitalism*, New Haven: Yale University Press, 1949), are unorthodox from the point of view of doctrinaire collectivism. But it is enough for our purposes to stress that Mr. Lindblom strongly supports the socialist government of Great Britain, and that his teachings are consistent with such support. His influence and popularity are also in point. His personal appeal is brought to light by the enrolment in his course this year. Mr. Lindblom is on leave of absence and a substitute took over. Enrolment plummeted down from 195 to 26 students.

Economics 36, Private Enterprise and Public Policy, does not seem to be a very influential course. Its attendance is small (approximately 55) by comparison with the courses previously mentioned. Its instructors have not excited undergraduate attention in the manner of Mr. Lindblom or Mr. Saxon.

Taught by Professors Miller and Tennant, Economics 36 is a frontal assault upon monopoly, as also against big business. The textbooks that have been used over the past few years[†] insist that monopoly looms as a serious problem because it is destructive of free enterprise. Some of the volumes attack monopoly and bigness

---

* Simons's pamphlet is now (1950–51) also being used in the basic economics course.

[†] L. S. Lyon et al., *Government and Economic Life* (Brookings, 1939); Arthur R. Burns, *Decline of Competition* (McGraw-Hill, 1936); H. Leslie Purdy, *Corporate Concentration and Public Policy* (Prentice-Hall, 1942); John M. Clark, *Social Control of Business* (McGraw-Hill, 1939); Corwin D. Edwards, *Maintaining Competition* (McGraw-Hill, 1949).

indiscriminately. Both the textbook authors and the class instructors call upon the government to regulate free market violators.

Professor Bakke's courses on labor unions are well attended. There is a great deal of variety in reading assignments from year to year. Mr. Bakke at one time found himself well to the left of his present position, which is now more or less middle of the road, although retaining a heavy pro-labor union bias (e.g., his opening statement to his classes: "You sons of rich capitalistic fathers aren't going to like this course...").

The alumnus is entitled to wonder what's going on.

How is it that a Department of Economics that once upheld individual self-reliance and limited government is—but for a few exceptions—now dedicated to collectivism in various degrees? The answer is not easy, but a great deal of evidence points to the influence and policies of one man, Edgar S. Furniss, provost of Yale University.

The duties and powers of the provost are vast and were enlarged as recently as in 1950. The *Yale Corporation By-Laws* describe him as follows:

> The Provost is the chief educational officer of the University after the President. He shall be elected by the Corporation for a definite term on nomination by the President. In the event of the death, disability, or prolonged absence of the President, the Provost shall perform the functions of the President until some other appointment or arrangement is made by the Corporation.
>
> Subject to the authority of the President, the Provost shall direct educational policies and activities throughout the University. He shall prepare the educational budgets of the University on the basis of the estimated income furnished by the Treasurer, and shall present such budgets to the President. The Provost shall be *ex officio* a member of every Faculty and Governing

Board, and of all committees or other bodies concerned with educational policy or with appointments or promotions in the teaching staff. All Deans, Directors, Division and Committee Chairmen, and other educational officers, other than the President, shall report to the Provost. The Provost shall attend the meetings of the Corporation and of its Prudential Committee. He shall serve as Secretary of the Committee on Educational Policy.

Although he is listed in the Yale faculty directory as "Pelatiah Professor of Political Science," Mr. Furniss is a professor of economics and is a member of the Department of Economics.

When the Lorie Tarshis textbook, *The Elements of Economics* (analyzed at length in connection with the basic course in economics), was published in 1947, it was under the editorship of Mr. Furniss, who said of it in the Introduction, *"This book contains the best that the expert economist has to offer regarding the economic problems of our times."** *

This is the book that places total reliance for economic welfare on government. This is the book that decries "inequities" in wealth, that mocks individualist philosophy, that discourages thrift, deplores the gold standard, and encourages deficit spending on the part of government, whose credit is inexhaustible.

When this book, generally classified as "the most frankly Keynesian of all full-length elementary textbooks,"[†] was published, it was immediately put to use as the basic textbook in Economics 10. It

---

* This marked a dramatic departure from notions about economics that Mr. Furniss once held, as witness the textbook, *Economics* (New York: Macmillan Co., rev. ed., 1940), which he coauthored, and its adherence to the classical line.

† See, for example, *Economic Council Review of Books,* August 1950.

was withdrawn after a year due in large part, I am certain, to the ire its use evoked in so many alumni.*

But Mr. Furniss's influence did not lapse with the displacement of Tarshis. He remains the "chief educational officer of Yale after the President"; and, what is of crucial importance, the man who passes on "educational budgets." This, of course, allows him decisive power to exercise his discretion in faculty appointments and promotions. With his supplementary role as a professor in the Department of Economics, his vise-like grip on Yale economics becomes clear.

Since the outset of Mr. Seymour's administration (1937), and Mr. Furniss's appointment as provost, the chairman of the Department of Economics has been appointed by the president. Formerly, he was elected by vote of the full professors of the department. The switch consolidates the domination of the administration.

Today, of the nine full professors in the department, only four are forthright defenders of individualism. Of these four, one (Mr. Westerfield) is about to retire; another (Mr. Hastings) has been transferred to the School of Engineering (where, due to the more technical nature of the subject matter, personal attitudes toward economic philosophy have less sway); and a third (Mr. Saxon), who is himself nearing the retirement age, has been urged to transfer to the School of Engineering. A fourth (Mr. Buck) is hale and hearty and seems likely to survive for some time. Recently, after prolonged absence from the classroom as a result of his duties as Dean of Freshman Year, he decided to teach one section of the basic course. Apparently he refused to adopt the department-prescribed textbooks. Instead, he uses the text that for many years,

---

* In answer to one critic of the use of the Tarshis text, President Seymour wrote, incredibly, "I do not understand that it is advocating the doctrines of Keynes as desirable for the American economy." In his book, Tarshis admits himself to be a disciple of Keynes in so many words (p. 346).

and in a happier age, was used by the entire department, *Economics*—a book which he coauthored with Professor Fairchild and, *mirabile dictu*, Professor Furniss.

The Department of Economics is not alone in deifying collectivism. A complete survey would take us into the departments of political science, history, sociology, and others. But to canvass these fields here, even lightly, is a practical impossibility—for all that the job should be done, and soon. Should anyone undertake such a project, he might start with a textbook that was used by the Department of Political Science in the academic year 1949–50—again, in the basic course.

I refer to the infamous *A Grammar of American Politics—The National Government* (New York: Alfred A. Knopf, 1949), by Wilfred E. Binkley, of the Ohio Northern University, and Malcolm C. Moos, of Johns Hopkins. This "grammar" is a plea for basic changes in the political and economic structure of this nation which, the authors contend, are "inescapable." The planned economy is a must and is not to be obstructed by bigoted "constitution worship." "It is time to square off and take another look at our governmental system and in that way attempt to free ourselves from some of the generalizations, abstractions, and conventional fictions that so often obscure a clear view of the realities of American Government" (p. vii, Preface). The student is enjoined to beware of "the whole elaborate system of fictions with which the realities of government have long been obscured." The chief objects of criticism are the present constitutional limitations on the power and functions of the federal government, the remaining vestiges of states rights, and our traditional separation of power.

Increased government control of the economy is both inevitable and desirable. Indeed, "with the possible exception of military preparedness, the most important functions of the Federal government are those which lie in the field of economic activity"

(p. 573). Effusive enthusiasm is shown for the Tennessee Valley Authority, the expansion of presidential power ("the president is in fact more representative of the people as a whole than is Congress"), and the like; sympathy is extended to the British in their "mild nationalization program."

On the other side of the ledger, the Taft-Hartley Law has, we are told, "restricted some and abolished other labor *prerogatives*" (p. 4, italics added); the Republican Party, as the spokesman for entrenched big business, is "on the side of wealth" (pp. 177, 193) (the Democratic Party is "pronouncedly the party of the underdog"); and the nation must think twice about the man it elects as president, for

> It is of importance whether a Coolidge or a Roosevelt occupies the White House.... One man may be obsessed with an obstinate faith in an outmoded economic or social ideology while another is a crusader for the good life by increasing the social services of the government [p. 309].

The Economics Department is by no means the only pleader for statism in the United States.

A half-hearted effort has been made to pass off Yale's American Studies Program as a concerted effort by the administration to restore the balance, to imbue students with respect for the free enterprise system. The program is heavily subsidized by Mr. William Rogers Coe, who donated to Yale first his unique collection of Western Americana and then, in the spring of 1950, a capital gift of $500,000 which, in the words of ex-president Seymour, "now puts us in a position to launch our whole program of American studies."

Mr. Coe is an unflinching individualist, and demanded of Yale that the "Professor to head the Program of American Studies shall always be one who firmly believes in the preservation of our System of Free Enterprise and is opposed to a system of State Socialism, Communism and Totalitarianism, and that the portion of the income of the fund which is set aside for the Program of American Studies shall be used for the furtherance of the System above referred to."

Mr. Coe was satisfied that the administration would so orient the program. In fact, the preamble to the program, as it appears in correspondence from the administration to Mr. Coe (November 14, 1949), reads: "A program based on the conviction that the best safeguards against totalitarian developments in our economy are an understanding of our cultural heritage and an affirmative belief in the validity of our institutions of free enterprise and individual liberty."

However, the program, now in operation, serves no such purpose. The *official* description of American Studies, as listed in the *Bulletin of Undergraduate Courses of Study*, reads as follows:

> The aim . . . in American Studies is to assist the student to gain an understanding of the civilization of his own country. The principal institutions of American political, economic, and social life, the ideas and policies surrounding them, and the achievements of American literary and artistic expression are studied both historically and in terms of the present in an effort to present the total cultural picture.

Thus, on the face of it, the Program is no more committed to upholding the virtues of individualism vis-à-vis the current struggle between free enterprise and collectivism than a course in British Studies would imply a commitment to mercantilism.

And this is not a theoretical analysis. The major course in the American Studies Program is taught by Ralph H. Gabriel. The catalogue describes it as follows:

Lectures and readings on religious, social, political, and constitutional thought. Folk literature and music of the frontier and
the importance of American thought to the rise of science are
considered.

—and this is an accurate picture of the course, which has been
taught a good many years, and which I took in my junior year. Mr.
Gabriel is a fine scholar and his course is of vital scholarly interest. But in no way does it attempt to persuade the student to line
up on one side or the other of the collectivist issue. In fact, Mr.
Gabriel lectures so dispassionately as to make highly reckless, on
the basis of this course, any guess about his personal convictions
on current issues.

Other courses in the program deal with American art, philosophy, and prose. There is clearly no bias—for or against free enterprise—in these courses. As with Mr. Gabriel, the instructors
examine various fields of American culture. The catalogue requires
prospective majors to study the basic course in American History,
and advises them to enroll in the basic course in European History
and in the basic course in economics.

Mr. Coe's generous gift to Yale has made possible highly interesting studies in American cultural history. But it is nonsense to
assume that the instructors of the courses dedicate themselves to
affirming a "belief in the validity of our institutions of free enterprise and individual liberty."

It may be asked why it is that the current situation in Yale has
not already been exposed by some of the professors listed above,
or by others recently retired, who are relentless enemies of collectivism? This question baffles me as much as it does the man who
asks it. In the course of collecting data for this section, I found that
although there has been much moaning in recent years over the
ascendancy of collectivism in the classroom, the professors who

might have helped me chose instead to pass me on the other side of the road. They offered a variety of reasons for doing so; most often, they satisfied themselves with the explanation that this book was not the "proper channel" for criticism. It remains to be asked, what do these professors consider the proper channels to be? And how long are they willing to wait before a decorous opportunity presents itself for exposing the steady drive in the direction of collectivism that has gathered so much momentum at Yale over the past dozen years?

There is a ray of hope: the small group of individualist-minded professors in the Economics Department presented their complaints forcefully (I understand), in the fall of 1950, to Mr. Frank Altschul, chairman of the University Council Committee on Social Sciences.* Whether or not something will come of this I do not know. But I am certain that these professors were able to paint a far more vivid, convincing, and complete picture of the fate of individualism at Yale than I have been able to do without their help.

EVIDENCES OF COLLECTIVISM IN EXTRACURRICULAR LIFE

It is interesting to note that the dominant ideological attitudes of the Department of Economics, and other departments also, bear some fruit even in undergraduate extracurricular life. Though a brief survey of those activities that lend themselves to student expression of ideas is relevant and significant, rigid generalizations about student opinion are impossible, as the great majority of Yale undergraduates do not take part in organizations of this kind. At the same time, it is likely that those who are articulate

---

* The University Council is discussed later in this book.

as undergraduates will also be articulate as citizens, and thus their attitudes are of some interest.

THE YALE DAILY NEWS

The *Yale Daily News*, the oldest college daily in America, is unquestionably the most influential student organization at Yale. As such, it commands an almost 100 percent reading audience, and active reader participation through its "Communications" column.

The editorial policy of the *News* is created by the chairman of the board (whose duties are also those of editor in chief). In the circumstances, the editorial page is an exact impression of the chairman's philosophies, which, as those of one man, are not important except for the fact that they elicit in the Communications column campus-wide reactions to his editorials on international, national, and community issues.

The chairmen of the 1948 and 1949 boards of the *News* were, roughly speaking, noncommittal, neoconservatives. As chairman of the 1950 board, I was classified as a good number of things, the most charitable being "conservative." The chairman of the 1951 board, Garrison Ellis, is a pronounced, emphatic, undeviating left-winger.

With recourse to these extremes, then, some generalizations as to the political temperament of the articulate members of the student body can be made by comparing reader sentiment to my year of editorial writing with that during Ellis's year. For Ellis (as also his successor) sits, broadly speaking, as far to the left of "center" as I do to the right. We are, in a manner of speaking, roughly equivalent. That is to say, if we should single out a dozen or more controversial figures or issues that serve, generally, to separate the "conservative" from the "left-winger," a fairly clear line would divide Ellis and me. Where he sympathized with Truman, Acheson, Hiss, Humphrey, and Bowles, I contemned them. Where I backed the McCarran Act, the Taft-Hartley Law, the Committee on Un-American Activities, the autonomy of private clubs and associations, and restriction of government activity, he deplored them. On the issues of a Fair Employment and Fair Educational Practices Laws, on the Brannan plan, and on the Labor government in England, we again parted company.

Now: for every letter that appeared in the Communications column of the *Yale News* berating Ellis, I was excoriated many times. And the attacks directed at me were far more splenetic. To a score of correspondents I was a "black reactionary." To one professor, I was possessed of "twisted morality." Not so with Ellis. No one—and rightly so—called him a Communist. "Idiot" was about as far as anyone went. In a word, Ellis's collectivism elicited far less protest than my individualism.

This is of some importance, it strikes me. For where public criticism is vocal and intense, it is because *the minority has offended the majority*. Even discounting the disproportionate addiction of the collectivists to propagandize their doctrines at every opportunity, I am forced to conclude from my experience with the *Yale Daily News* through several years, and from other evidence also, that at least at this college level, the great transformation has actually taken place. The conservatives, as a minority, are the new radicals. The evidence is overwhelming.

THE POLITICAL UNION

The largest undergraduate organization at Yale, with a membership of about two hundred students, is the Political Union. Its purpose is organized debate of public issues, and it is currently divided into four political parties—from left to right, Labor, Liberal, Bull Moose, and Conservative. With the exception of the Labor Party, which is composed of a small, militant group of doctrinaire leftists and socialists, the other party labels reflect only marginally the political persuasions of their members. The Liberal Party is the most numerous and, politically, the most heterogeneous. It attracts its members in part because of the noncommittal and pleasant connotations of its title, as also because its sprawling membership is uncannily mobilized come election time. The Liberal Party is thus the most important ally of the ambitious office-seeker.

I must here repeat that no effort is being made to pass off the Union as a rigidly representative political sample of undergraduate Yale. Such a generalization would not stand up under examination for several reasons, not the least important being that the student body as a whole seems to be apathetic to politics. Moreover, the inordinate emphasis the Union places on its own politics, which are heavy with deals, coalitions, stuffed ballot boxes, and haggling of the most fruitless and extravagant sort, has discouraged from membership a number of students who are politically articulate but unwilling to cast their lot with an organization that devotes so much of its effort to time-consuming and frivolous politicking.

Nevertheless, the Union is composed of vociferous and politically interested students who run the ideological gamut. As such, while the attitudes of its members are not conclusive, they are to some degree indicative of those of the interested and articulate members of undergraduate Yale.

The routine of the Union is fairly consistent. Each party, meeting in caucus, debates a proposed issue and determines, by majority vote, a party stand, though individual members are always free to oppose their party and vote as they will. Each party selects one of its members to represent its stand by delivering a short speech when the resolution faces the Union.

Each meeting of the Union features a guest speaker who upholds one or the other side of the resolution before the house (a few who spoke between 1946 and 1950 are: Robert Taft, Norman

Thomas, Henry Wallace, Eleanor Roosevelt, Irving Olds, Lee Press-man, Tom Clark, Warren Austin). He is followed by the party speakers, and the question is then turned over to the house for floor debate. It is interesting to note that the principal speaker seldom seriously affects the outcome of the Union vote. Students have generally made up their minds before arriving at the meeting.

There are few individualists in the Political Union. The voting is by and large in consonance with the orientation of Yale's teaching. Reliance for all that is good is on government. At only one meeting during the years 1946–50 at which the welfare state was argued did the house stand against it. On the basis of previous and following meetings, it is safe to generalize that during those years the Political Union was heavily collectivist. In October 1946, the house voted overwhelmingly for "a greater degree of socialism in the United States." In April 1947 and March 1950, the Union called for socialized medicine. In October 1947, over one-third of the house voted to approve "the domestic policies of Henry Wallace." (This was several weeks after Wallace had endorsed the resolution of the Progressive Citizens of America calling for the nationalization of basic industries.) By more than 2–1 the Political Union encouraged, in October 1948, the "development and distribution of our major hydro-electric power resources by a system of Federal Authority." The Fair Deal was ratified again, both in December 1949 and in March 1950. In October 1949, only five votes (79–74) stood in the way of passing a resolution that "the British Labor government should be returned to power."

These resolutions are significant, but they are not nearly so revealing as the arguments that are leveled in their behalf on the floor of the Union, arguments that in some cases patently stem from such textbooks as those used in the course in basic economics, arguments that are sometimes clearly recognizable as personal favorites of this or that Yale professor. It is true that much of what is said and thought is traceable to newspapers, magazines, national political speeches, and even, on occasion, original thought. But, from time to time, observing the heated debate that takes place in the Political Union, a spectator can get a vivid, dramatic picture of the short, short path between the classroom and the national legislature.

The National Students Association

A fairly inconspicuous organization which operates at Yale, as it does in 289 American colleges and universities, is not an inconspicuous case in point. The National Students Association was founded in the summer of 1947 largely as a "service organization for all college students."

Primarily, it promised such services as would facilitate exchange students, curriculum comparisons, textbook-discount plans, foreign travel at reduced rates, and the like. Its highly political constitution was given little publicity, and a last-minute effort on the part of a few students to alert the Yale campus to the full implications of this body was of no avail. Yale joined up with it in December 1947, after a close, campus-wide vote. Even today, the vast majority of Yale students are unaware that they are being spoken for as constituent members of the NSA by an alert pressure group and on behalf of leftist policies.

I reprint here a communication received by the *Yale News* in May 1949, which inquired into the political machinations of the NSA:

To the Chairman of the *NEWS*:

A letter in last week's *News* referring to the NSA as "nonpolitical" has revived a question that has been bothering me for a couple of weeks.

The *Daily Worker* of April 5 included an article saying: "The executive committee of the National Students Association yesterday took a firm stand against the dismissal of college professors for alleged membership in the Communist Party.

"The Committee, representing 730,000 students in 289 American colleges, empowered its national staff to investigate... (three cases of dismissal or expulsion listed)."

Granted, the *Daily Worker* is not above editorializing, but the statement seems to imply that the NSA is political in nature, and that Yale students are among those "represented" as upholding this point of view.

I would appreciate it if someone would clarify the political stand of the NSA, since I, for one, have no desire to be represented politically by any group which I did not personally desire to join.

GORDON MILLIKEN, 1949E

Mr. Milliken's concern is well founded. Early in its career, the NSA set up a subcommission on legislation which is bent on applying political pressure for the furtherance of NSA "goals." Because these goals are so loosely described in the NSA Constitution, the National Executive Committee has been able to pass resolutions, and press for legislation—always, of course, in the name of 730,000 students, a figure which includes every student of every member college—which have little or no relevance to the "service functions" of the organization. For example, as of 1949, the NSA had, to mention a few of its stands, (1) supported the entire Merchant Marine Bill (because a minor provision of the multimillion-dollar bill would have allocated several ships for student travel to Europe), (2) called for the repeal of the DP immigration bill on the grounds that it was discriminatory against Catholics and Jews (no apparent connection with students), (3) opposed pending state bills forbidding the hiring by state educational institutions of Communist teachers, (4) advocated Fair Educational Practices Laws, (5) pleaded for passage of the Federal Aid to Education Bill, and more besides.

My prediction is that it will be a long time before the Yale student body disaffiliates from the National Students Association. We have, again, testimony either to a majority sanction of left-wing national policies, or else evidence of deft, left-wing manipulation of an insensate and tractable student body. Either spells the same thing: the predominance of leftism in undergraduate Yale.

MISCELLANEOUS

Of other politically minded undergraduate clubs, nothing very conclusive can be said. The Young Republican Club was vigorous and energetic during the Republican jag in the spring, summer, and fall of 1948. It collapsed as emphatically as Thomas Dewey on November 2. That summer saw, also, a Young Democratic Club and a Young Progressive Club. Since the election, sporadic activity has been maintained by these groups. In addition, the small but vigorous chapter of the Americans for Democratic Action has retained an energetic cadre. The Young Progressives also continue their activity, but are suffering from the increasing antipathy to Communism in this country.

Of the undisguised Communist groups, only the semi-intellectual John Reed Club maintained its existence over the years. It commands little attention and loyalty only from the fanatic fringe. An attempt in 1946 to establish a Yale Chapter of the American Youth for Democracy, a straight-forward Communist group, listed on the attorney-general's subversive list, met with so little enthusiasm that it disbanded several meetings after its inception.

Other groups marginally or directly interested in politics include the American Veterans Committee, which was extremely vigorous during the academic year 1946–47, but fizzled shortly thereafter. A similar fate befell the World Federalists, who succumbed to apathy by the middle of the year 1948–49. An organization known as the Dixwell Group, which operates under the aegis of Dwight Hall and was referred to above, in connection with religion at Yale, maintains activities which are dedicated to "bettering interracial relations." It becomes interested in politics only when legislative measures to curb discrimination of various sorts are under consideration.

Individualism is dying at Yale, and without a fight.

~豫~

Chapter Three

YALE AND
HER ALUMNI

President Griswold, as an alumnus himself, is known to feel strongly that alumni interest in Yale is dependent upon full understanding of the university as a great educational center; that the alumni are adults and should be treated as such.

—Yale Alumni Magazine,
March 1950

I f the alumni wish secular and collectivist influences to prevail at Yale, that is their privilege. What is more, if that is what they want, they need bestir themselves very little. The task has been done for them. There remains only a mopping-up operation to eliminate the few outspoken and influential figures who stand in the way of real unity in Yale's intellectual drive toward agnosticism and collectivism.

Let me add something else: if the present generation of Yale graduates does not check the University's ideological drive, the next generation most probably will not *want* to. I should be disrespectful of Yale if I did not credit her with molding the values and thinking processes of the majority of her students. Many of these, of course, withstand Yale's influence even while living in her cloistered halls for four years; and many more, in the course of future experience, learn to be first skeptical and then antagonistic to the teachings of some of the college professors they once revered.

But my contention that the values and biases of the University linger with the majority of graduates is surely not controversial. It is basic to education and to human experience that this be so, and I have no reason to doubt that it is so. If Yale alumni come to be dissatisfied with the international, national, and community influence of the forthcoming generation of Yale graduates, they can only do so with the irrationality of the Scotsman who complained that his new Dictaphone had the worst Aberdeen accent he had ever heard.

And so I repeat: unless something is done now, or soon, by collective or individual alumni action, nothing in all probability will be done in the future about Yale's predominant biases, because these will be in full accord with the wishes of the next generation of alumni.

The question arises, of course, whether or not the alumni have the power or the right to interfere if they are in disagreement with Yale's educational policy. My contention on both points is yes, they have the power and they have the right to "interfere." But I go one step farther than some people; for I maintain they also have the *duty* to "interfere."

It seems logical, before analyzing the almost universally accepted decalogue of "academic freedom," to examine the relationship of the private university to its alumni—specifically, to analyze Yale's relationship to her alumni, which, as I understand it, follows the general pattern. For after all, if Yale's alumni are not her governing body, then this thesis would be inexcusably academic.

But the administration is the first to concede and italicize her ultimate responsibility to her alumni (and hence, conversely, the responsibility of the alumni to support Yale). There don't seem to be two points of view about this. The official pamphlet, *Yale*

Alumni Organizations, which is distributed to graduating classes, states in part: "The alumni of Yale, although widely scattered, maintain close ties with the university. All have a place and a responsibility in shaping the future of Yale."

Again, under the heading "Yale Corporation," the pamphlet goes on to say, "The final authority in the 'government, care and management' of the university is the corporation, a body of nineteen trustees. . . ." Of these nineteen, all are, as a matter of course, alumni, with the exception of the governor and the lieutenant-governor of Connecticut, who serve *ex officio,* and are sometimes not Yale graduates. It has happened that the third *ex officio* member of the Corporation, the president of Yale, was not a graduate.*

For the rest, of Yale's sixteen Fellows, ten are "successors of the original trustees" and serve until they retire, and six are elected by graduates, one every year to serve for a period of six years. Although it would seem that the majority could perpetuate their interests through the appointment of successors to the original trustees, further analysis and familiarity with the realities of the situation make it clear that, assuming that there is wide public knowledge of candidates under consideration, no graduate who is generally distrusted by the alumni could be appointed to fill the ranks of the original ten. In other words, the ultimate sovereignty of the alumni is not only a symbol. It is fact.

The extent to which the alumni exercise a directional power is quite another thing as is also the extent to which Yale encourages them actually to assume top-level responsibility for educational policy.

This is not surprising in view of the general thought and procedure that underlie the selection of members of the Corporation.

---

* Governor John Davis Lodge, for example, is a Harvard man. Yale president James Rowland Angell, 1921–37, was not a Yale graduate.

Each year Yale's Alumni Board nominates a Standing Committee for the Nomination of Alumni Fellows. This committee consists of six alumni and one member of the Corporation. Through the Executive Secretary of the Alumni Board, local alumni associations are canvassed for nominees to the Corporation. Names and biographical material are sent in, and the Nominating Committee screens applicants, writes to some to ascertain whether they would be willing to run, and finally presents for publication a list of "not less than two* and not more than five nominees for each vacancy." These may or may not be selected from the names advanced by the local associations, though a petition signed by one hundred fifty alumni automatically certifies a candidate. The Yale Corporation By-Laws and Regulations stipulate that

> The Standing Committee shall secure the consent of each nominee and shall prepare brief impartial statements of the qualifications of each. The statement shall include a short biography of the nominee, giving his class, department, residence, occupation, public record, and other information which may be of value in assisting voters to make a choice.

But, for some reason, it has never been considered relevant to ask a potential member of the Yale Corporation what are his feelings about *education*. A typical description of a candidate (successful in his bid) is here taken in its entirety from the *Yale Alumni Magazine*, issue of March 1950. It represents the total information given to the voters:

---

* In the past, the Nominating Committee occasionally came forth with only one nominee. This blatant imposition on the alumni aroused so much criticism that the rules were changed to forbid fewer than two nominees.

ROBERT TEN BROECK STEVENS, '21*

Stevens was born July 31, 1899, in Fanwood, New Jersey, the son of John Peters and Edna (Ten Broeck) Stevens, and is the brother of John P. Stevens Jr., '19. He was prepared for college at Andover and was graduated from Yale College in 1921. He was a 2nd Lieutenant, Field Artillery, during World War I.

Since graduation he has been with J. P. Stevens & Co., Inc., New York City, manufacturers and distributors of textiles. The plants of the Company are located in New Hampshire, Massachusetts, Rhode Island, Connecticut, Virginia, North Carolina, South Carolina, and Georgia. He was elected director and assistant treasurer of the company in 1924 and was president from 1929 until 1942, when he resigned to enter the army.

In June 1940, at the request of the late E. R. Stettinius Jr., he became head of the Textile Section of the National Defense Advisory Commission. He attended the Command and General Staff School, Fort Leavenworth, Kansas, in 1941 and joined the Quartermaster Corps in January 1942. From 1943 to 1945 he was Deputy Director of Purchases of clothing, textiles, and general supplies for the Armed Services. He was awarded the Legion of Merit and the Distinguished Service Medal and was released from active duty October 1945, with the rank of Colonel.

He resumed his connections with J. P. Stevens & Co., Inc., and was elected chairman of the board, which position he now holds. He served as director of the Federal Reserve Bank of New York from 1934 to 1942. He was elected a director of the Guaranty Trust Co. in 1945, but resigned in 1948 to become again a director of the Federal Reserve Bank of New York. He is currently

---

* I picked Mr. Stevens's name at random. The *Magazine's* biographical sketch of any other member of the Corporation would have served as well.

chairman of the board of this Federal Reserve Bank, and also serves as chairman of the Conference consisting of the chairmen of the twelve Federal Reserve Banks.

Stevens is a director of General Electric Company; General Foods Corp.; New York Telephone Company; Alexander Smith & Sons Carpet Co.; Whitney-Hanson Industries, Inc., Hartford, Conn.; and Owens-Corning Fiberglass Corp., Toledo, Ohio. He is a trustee of the Mutual Life Insurance Company of New York. He is a member of the Executive Committee, Business Advisory Council of the Department of Commerce, and Vice-President of the Association of Cotton Textile Merchants. Stevens operates a cattle ranch at Two Dot, Montana, where he and his family spend summers. In 1938 he received the honorary degree of LL.D. from Presbyterian College, Clinton, South Carolina. He is a member of the Crescent Avenue Presbyterian Church in Plainfield, New Jersey, and a trustee of the Roosevelt Hospital in New York.

He was married on October 6, 1923, to Dorothy Goodwin Whitney and has four sons; Robert Ten Broeck Jr. 45S.; Whitney; William G.; Thomas E.; and a daughter Joan Peters. He has a nephew, John P. Stevens 3d, in the class of 1951. Stevens lives on R.F.D. No. 1, Woodland Avenue, South Plainfield, New Jersey.

A member of the Nominating Committee told me that the committee "never asks" about the political, economic, or educational views of a candidate. "The alumni vote for the most prominent man. It's as simple as that."

Brushing aside those alumni who know Mr. Stevens personally, and for whose enlightenment the foregoing description was obviously not written, it is of interest to analyze, for the average voter, what information can be got about this alumnus from the Standing Committee's description.

We can see that Mr. Stevens has had extensive experience in business management, but so has Chester Bowles. He has also had experience in government, as has Henry Wallace. He is a director of a good many business concerns, as is Frederick Vanderbilt Field, and he had a good war record, like Marshall Field. He is a member of the Presbyterian church, like Norman Thomas.

But we must be realistic, and acknowledge the heavy presumption that Mr. Stevens is pro-capitalist, and has great business and managerial talent.

But what else can the alumnus who takes some interest in education at Yale weigh in considering Mr. Stevens's qualifications? What does Mr. Stevens know about what goes on at Yale? How much time is he willing to devote to the study of Yale's problems? How does he feel about the wisdom of the private university's accepting government money? Does he believe Communists on the faculty ought to be fired? Does he believe socialists or atheists should be allowed to teach at Yale? Does he believe Yale ought to take its stand on the great value questions that face American society?

The answer, of course, is that the average voter has not the slightest idea what Mr. Stevens or his running-mates think about these questions, and the situation seems to be much the same in most American universities.[1]

It is my opinion that the administration of Yale does not encourage this sort of interest. In fact, I believe that because of her violent, all-consuming search for money, Yale finds herself in the twilight zone of hypocrisy with respect to her alumni.

I have put it this way to a number of prominent and shrewd men on the Yale faculty: "It seems clear to me that the administration of Yale has virtually no interest in sharing her educational problems with her alumni. There is only one problem for the solution of which they turn readily and openly to their graduates, and this is Yale's constant *financial* problem. The administration feels that it can best cope with educational policy without inter- ference of any sort. At the same time it must continue to foster the illusion that the alumni are in fact the 'governing body of Yale.' To this end, the Alumni Board, the *Alumni Magazine*, the University Council, meetings of the Yale Club, and so on."

I have never heard this analysis challenged by anyone on the Yale scene who has observed Yale's activities and has been willing to discuss them candidly. Several faculty members, while affirm- ing the soundness of my analysis, hasten to add that on the other hand they support Yale's public relations policy: "After all," some said, in essence, "the alumni don't really know anything about education, and their advice on this matter would probably be superficial. Besides, if they are encouraged to be too active, and their proposals become too concrete, it might lead to constraint and possibly to violations of academic freedom."

One man, a senior officer of the alumni organization, added his own analysis in the course of a conversation: "I'll admit," he said, "the alumni haven't the slightest idea of what is going on. They get their information primarily from three sources: the members of the administration on speaking tours, the *Alumni Magazine*, and the members of the Corporation.

"And what does this mean? It means that they get their infor- mation exclusively from the administration. The administration dominates the Alumni Board,* the administration molds the poli- cies and the personality of the *Alumni Magazine*, and the adminis- tration tells the Corporation just what it wants the Corporation to

---

* In point of fact, although to my knowledge this is unusual, the pres- ident of the Alumni Board, Edwin Blair, is also a member of the Corporation.

know.* The Yale University News Bureau is controlled by the Office of University Development, which is in turn controlled by the administration. In other words, the administration is the source of all the organized news that alumni receive about Yale. The new University Council *may* change the situation somewhat, but it hasn't yet."

This analysis tallies very closely with the facts as I see them. The Yale Corporation By-Laws (Article 57) describe the Alumni Board as,

> designed to secure careful discussion of University interests by a group of accredited representatives of the alumni.... The President, Provost, Secretary, and Treasurer of the University, the Director of the Student Appointment Bureau, the Assistant to the President, and the Chairman of the Board of Control of the Athletic Association shall be *ex officiis* members of the Board.... Communications from this Board shall be regarded by the Corporation as privileged business to be considered without delay.

The Board is the central alumni agency, and its Executive Secretary supervises the welter of administrative details that attend

---

* In the circumstances, it is not difficult to understand the incredible ignorance of Corporation members themselves about the Yale scene. As an example, one member of the Corporation, who has sat with that body for thirteen years, and, as a "successor to an original trustee," will do so until retirement age, assuming good behavior; a man whose curiosity and knowledge are well above the Corporation mean, told me in February 1951 that Professor Blanshard, chairman of the Yale Department of Philosophy, was a "good Quaker." I am sure he found it hard to believe me when I told him Mr. Blanshard was an atheist, though the professor has never made any secret of this, even from the Corporation members.

reunions, visiting speakers, and the like. The weighty list of members *ex officiis* from the administration can attest to the close relationship between the Board and the University, but it can also signify, as I believe it does, the hegemony of the administration over the Board.

The *Yale Alumni Magazine*, which reaches almost all graduates, is officially described as "the chief connecting link between the alumni and the University." If this is the case, as it seems to be, it is no wonder that Yale alumni are egregiously misinformed.

I am not aware of the issues that the Yale Corporation faced between 1946 and 1950, but I am fairly confident that with the exception of those which involved money, no word about them reached the columns of that extraordinarily arid, persistently dull journal, the *Yale Alumni Magazine*. I do know that during that period there were perhaps a half dozen major issues which split at least undergraduate Yale and, in some cases, involved the faculty. They were questions of a widely different nature and, for the most part, unquestionably of interest to the alumni. And yet they were never described in the *Magazine;* not so much as a line was devoted to them. The editor has made it clear that *controversy is out*, that he has no intention of printing material that, as he once told me, "would bring all sorts of alumni letters of comment to the President's desk."

It is clear that the editor, Mr. F. W. Bronson, has been signally successful in the fulfillment of this goal. For the *Magazine* presents very little grist for opinion or discussion. It is true that the *Magazine* is severely hampered by a shoestring budget, but it is nevertheless tragic in the first degree that due largely to its own lethargy, only a half dozen or so letters from alumni appear in each issue of the *Magazine;* and these, for the most part, discuss athletics, Yale traditions, or personal reminiscences.

As every Yale graduate knows, several times the amount of space the *Magazine* devotes to nonathletic undergraduate activities goes to sports. It is commonly pointed out that the average alumnus is more interested in athletic than in intellectual contests, and that, therefore, he should be given what he wants. After all, aren't football movies most in demand at Yale Club functions throughout the country? Don't most Bulldogs put Herman Hickman first on their list of preferred speakers?

They probably do. And the probable reason why is the devastating dullness of the nonathletic diet that Yale prescribes for her alumni. The feature articles in an average issue of the *Magazine* might deal with alcoholic studies, or the School of Nursing, or the Science Laboratory's new cyclotron, or (and this is to be found somewhere in every issue) the frightening implications of Yale's financial deficit. These are often well presented and of some interest, but they leave most readers hungry for the relative excitement of the Harvard hockey game.

The column "The Undergraduate Month," written by a carefully selected senior, is mostly subjective banter about the seasons, Yale's "mood," Phi Beta Kappa awards, and the like. Occasionally there emerge the mildest, most temperate rebukes of this or that University edict.*

It is true, as I have indicated, that the *Alumni Magazine* suffers from a shortage of funds which precludes comprehensive coverage of University activities. But it is what it selects to write about that makes the journal all but useless as a basis of an intimate

---

* 1951's columnist, Henry B. Hager, made his first appearance in the December issue of *Y.A.M.* He confessed disappointment with President Griswold's inaugural address and with a freshman rally. He lasted one issue. His successor appears to be better disciplined.

knowledge of Yale affairs. The pulse of Yale is never bared. Fundamental issues of immediate and future interest to Yale (again unless they concern money) never reach the ears of the alumni, for whom are reserved all the dramatic details of Levi Jackson's 80-yard run and endless statistics to demonstrate Yale's imminent bankruptcy.

But lo and behold, in the May issue of the *Alumni Magazine* what should appear but a reprint of a speech delivered at Yale by William C. Bullitt, close friend of President Charles Seymour, laying it on the line about the threat of Communism. It wasn't, in the real sense, a controversy that involved Yale, but since the stand was provocative, the consensus is that Mr. Bronson must have been out getting a haircut when that one slipped into the issue.

One letter of protest appeared in the following issue, from a Yale alumnus, enjoining the staff to stop printing such controversial items immediately. The next issue carried thirteen letters of comment advertised in the editor's foreword as "representative of alumni opinion" on the *Magazine*'s bold venture, and *all but two* congratulated the editor on his decision to reprint the Bullitt speech. Some letters carried emphatic encouragement to do more of this sort of thing, but nothing has come of it to date; the *Magazine* seems still to be in a state of minor exhaustion from having handled fourteen letters of varied opinion.

The University Council, organized in February 1948, is described as,

> designed to promote and strengthen Yale resources. Its primary function is to study the major constituent parts and activities of the university at close range, to offer recommendations for their support. The Council functions through a group of committees composed mainly of Yale alumni.[2]

The Council could grow to serve a great purpose. Much tribute has already been paid it. President Seymour, for example, wrote in his report to the alumni, 1948–49,* that

> All Yale is deeply grateful... for the devoted service which they [the personnel of the Council] have given to the study of university educational problems and for the recommendations which they have formulated. The active interest of the visiting committees set up by the Council has been manifest in their gatherings here in New Haven and in the quality of their reports.

President Seymour added that

> The deliberations of the Council have resulted in a critical appreciation of the educational aspects of Yale which has already proved of the greatest service to the administration.

In his final report to the alumni (1949–50), Mr. Seymour wrote that

> The reports of the visiting committees of the Council have cast fresh light on our educational problems and pointed a path to their solution. Never before has so large a group of friends come to know Yale with such intimacy.[3]

---

* I refer here, and in succeeding chapters, more often to the policies and pronouncements of President-emeritus Charles Seymour than to those few that President A. Whitney Griswold has made during the short period since he went into office. It is impossible to make significant generalizations about Mr. Griswold's policies at this early date, or to assume that they will differ substantially from that of his predecessor.

It is too early to weigh the effectiveness of the Council. Not much evidence is immediately available as to the exhaustiveness of their investigations. But hallmarks of danger are available already. The personnel who serve are carefully selected, with perhaps a disproportionate emphasis on complacency. It seems to be altogether too likely that their preeminent function will be, as the University states, to "promote and strengthen Yale resources," by which Yale means to raise money. There is a little bit too much of the Potemkin-tour in the visit of some of the committees to the University. Appointments are set up for them, and they are put in touch, primarily, with administration and faculty stalwarts. The reports they submit are legion and, undoubtedly, as President Seymour has said, "of great value."

But my present diagnosis, and certainly my prognosis, is that the committees are not, in the most meaningful sense, representative alumni investigating or policy-making bodies. They are too clearly intertwined with the administration and with the faculty; they report to the administration,* not to the alumni; no publicity (that I have seen, at least) is given to highly controversial elements of their reports; if there are no controversial elements in their reports, it is certain, considering the present situation at Yale, that they are not performing their jobs exhaustively.

To cite two examples which illuminate the role of the Council and something more besides, I shall draw upon a personal experience. In December 1949, I was selected as the undergraduate speaker for the annual February Alumni Day. I submitted my

---

* The Yale Corporation By-Laws (Article 56) stipulate that "Committees of the Council shall study the aims and needs of particular areas in the University; they shall submit their findings and recommendations to the Council as a whole, where the reports of all committees shall be coordinated and presented to the President and Corporation for action."

address,* which raised the question of *laissez-faire* education at Yale, to the University News Bureau forty-eight hours before it was to be delivered. I shall not soon forget the comment of the director of the Bureau as I handed the speech to him: "What are you saying in it?—nothing, I hope!"

Not two hours had elapsed before I was unearthed by a senior officer of the alumni hierarchy who had come from Woodbridge Hall to report, on his own initiative, he insisted, that the president was "deeply disappointed" with my address, that the secretary of the University regarded it as an "indictment of the administration," and wouldn't I please change it?

Our discussion lasted some time, during which I was told that "the alumni simply wouldn't *understand* it . . . they'll leave the place thinking Yale is communistic . . . the alumni can't grasp your point . . ."—and so on.

The upshot was interesting. After consideration, I offered to alter a few specific passages in my address—to obviate "alumni misunderstanding." But beyond this, I insisted that the substance would remain unchanged. I did, however, volunteer to withdraw from the program, readily admitting that in the last analysis Yale could not be required to sponsor a speaker whom it considered inflammatory or pernicious.

At first, my offers to withdraw were met with hurt feelings and with astonishment at my even having considered this solution. The University had conferred upon me an honor, and it would certainly not be revoked—besides which, it was too late to get a substitute. I offered not only to secure a substitute, but to write him a speech of the "good old Yale" variety, but this offer was also spurned.

It was the next day, upon receipt of a personal letter outlining my thoughts on the matter, that President Seymour called

---

* The address appears in full in Appendix F.

me over and told me that because of the specific nature of this particular Alumni Day (the lunch was to be followed by a dedication of the World War II Memorial in Woolsey Hall), he was regretfully accepting my offer to withdraw from the program since he was afraid that the visitors would be "upset" by the speech.

It is of some interest that the decision that I was not to speak was, to my knowledge, reached upon the administration's initiative, and this despite the fact that great pains were taken throughout Alumni Day proceedings, and throughout similar proceedings, to convey the impression that "the alumni are running the whole show." At the lunch itself, attended by some twelve hundred alumni, my name was still listed on the program, but no explanation was offered when my turn came to speak. The whole thing ran off smoothly,* and Chairman Edwin Blair, of the Alumni Board, told the guests, in praise of President Seymour:

> He has recognized the function of Yale's alumni in all phases of Yale's administrative and educational work . . . his policies have allowed Yale alumni more than ever before to participate in the affairs of Yale. . . .

and Mr. Symington, in the course of his address, was heard to say: "In a democracy, it is important that everybody know the truth. Given this truth they will meet the problem."

The *Alumni Magazine*, naturally, was silent about the missing speech.

---

* Although it was ironic that the principal alumni speaker, W. Stuart Symington, then secretary of the air force, must have done his share of "upsetting" the guests who were to attend the War Memorial Dedication Services. Mr. Symington painted a stark picture of Russian might, and indicated that a world struggle might not be indefinitely postponed.

In the course of discussing my address before Alumni Day, I had been told that it was improper to give my message to the alumni at large, that I should be far better off addressing the University Council; I was encouraged to do this at an early moment. Instead, I was invited to address the Executive Committee, "preliminary to addressing the entire Council."

This I did on April 12, 1950. In addition to the Executive Committee,* President Charles Seymour and Mr. Carlos F. Stoddard, director of the Office of University Development, were present by invitation—a minor, but indicative, factor of my suspicion that the administration dominates the Council.

I hasten to add that I was received with marked courtesy and interest, and that I was heard through. The minutes of the meeting, in their entirety, read:

> Mr. William F. Buckley, Jr., chairman of the 1950 Board of the *Yale Daily News*, was invited to present a speech which he had prepared for Alumni Day, and which had not been given. Following detailed discussion of his point of view, it was agreed that a student or recent graduate representing a contrary opinion would be invited to attend a subsequent meeting of the executive committee.

Let me add that I found only one unflinching ally in the entire company; one or two others, while in general disagreement, thought I had something to say.

On the other hand, the invitation to present my analysis of Yale education to the entire Council was repeated. But it was

---

* This committee consisted of Mr. Lucius F. Robinson, president of the Council, Mr. Frank Ashburn, Mr. William Sheffield Cowles, Mr. John Hay Whitney, and Mr. R. S. Holden, secretary (and assistant to the president).

suggested that I do it the following fall, after the Council had interviewed a student of "contrary opinion." This last, incidentally, was my suggestion.

I do not know whether a student of "contrary opinion" has been interviewed. I do know that he would not be hard to find. I also know that as of April 12, 1950, when this hearing took place, advertising itself as only a preliminary to a series of hearings, I have not heard a word from the Council about this matter. Nor have the alumni at large.

This is item number one among my reservations about the present-day effectiveness of the Council in so far as its accountability to the alumni, the "ultimate governing body," is concerned.*

During that same spring, a venerable scholar and fine gentleman, long associated with Yale and a member of the University Council's Committee on Religion, spoke with me and requested copies of two speeches I had recently written, both of which lamented the plight of religious training at Yale.

A month later, he wrote me a letter in which he took me to task—amiably, to be sure—for gross exaggerations. His letter, among other things, stated (1) that there were "almost a thousand students" attending courses on the Bible and the Christian religion at Yale. This is an error. There are fewer than four hundred. (2) Professor Goodenough "has always been considered a good Congregationalist."

---

* I do not mean to imply that simply because my viewpoint was not energetically circularized, the Council proved itself *ipso facto* ineffective. The Council clearly must screen out patently absurd ideas and recommendations. But I believe there are enough people interested in the ideas I presented to have warranted some public examination of their merits. If not this, I should think that the Council would at least itself have pursued these ideas, which could not possibly have been adequately discussed in the course of one afternoon. And anyway, what issue have they considered of sufficient general interest to refer to the alumni at large?

Mr. Goodenough as we have seen, describes himself as 80 percent atheist and 20 percent agnostic.

The Council member implied strongly, what is more, that the religious symbols at Yale were strongly pervasive; all in all, while saddened by the "few" anti-religious members of the faculty, he suggested that there was little cause for uneasiness about the state of religion at Yale. He completely ignored my analysis of the status of religion within the Religion Department itself and made no mention of religion and its treatment in the social sciences. In short, this member of the University Council's Committee on Religion knows next to nothing about religion at Yale.

Such a situation must lead to skepticism about the Council's intimacy with the Yale scene. It follows that while there may be hope for the future, there are doubts at the present about the effectiveness of the Council.

I have charged Yale with duplicity in her treatment of her alumni, but I must add two comments: The administration of Yale is, in its fashion, proud and very fond of her alumni. It would reflect no credit on her if she were not at least proud of them, for Yale, after all, screened them as teen-age applicants and then processed them for four years. And there is no question that the administration, for the most part made up of Yale men, lavishes great affection upon the spirited, courteous, generous, and influential company of men that form the corps of Yale graduates.

And where contributions to Yale are in question, elaborate solicitude is displayed. In 1949, President Seymour advised me that a potential contributor to Yale wanted some sort of evidence "that the place wasn't swarming with New Dealers." Would I, then, clip out a half dozen or so of my editorials in the *Yale Daily News* to be forwarded to him? I did this willingly, but have since wondered to what extent my editorials, freakishly conservative, affected Mr. X's opinions about the political temperament of the Yale scene.

I know examples of Yale's money-raising techniques that would appear shocking to many persons except for the fact that latitude must be given those men who devote their lives to furthering the cause, as they understand it, of education. It could be said in fairness that all the money thus solicited goes straight to the student in one form or another. In the last analysis, it is being solicited for altruistic purposes.

At the same time, once the chips are down, the alumni either are or are not the ultimate overseers of Yale's educational policy. Everybody seems to agree that they are. In the circumstances, they are abdicating their responsibilities. And administrative Yale is not making it easy for them to fulfill their obligations for the simple reason that, sound and fury notwithstanding, she is glad to settle for their money and to eschew their counsel. She shapes her alumni policy accordingly.

At a plenipotentiary "Convocation of Alumni," held in New Haven on the weekend of October 14–15, 1949, and described by its chairman as a "Constitutional Convention of alumni to determine and share the part that Yale alumni shall play in the future of Yale," Mr. Otis L. Hubbard of Chicago addressed the assembly:

> We are invited to a "Convocation." Now, out in the Middle West, where culture isn't quite so prevalent . . . we are not familiar with words like that. I counselled with some of my erudite friends, and they shook their heads and said, "That is an ivy-covered word for a sales convention."

This jocular description more accurately describes the sum and substance of the relationship of Yale and her alumni than Mr. Hubbard or the audience realized at the time.

Chapter Four

THE SUPERSTITIONS OF "ACADEMIC FREEDOM"

O n April 26, 1949, Mr. Frank B. Ober, a Baltimore attorney and a graduate of the Harvard Law School, sat down and wrote a letter to President Conant of his alma mater. Mr. Ober was sore. He had been working as chairman of a Maryland Commission charged with drafting laws to cope with Communist influences in that state. A Harvard professor had come down to Baltimore to address a rally sponsored by the Progressive Party and designed both to excite opposition to the anticommunist laws and to solicit funds with which to combat them.

Mr. Ober was also upset at the fact that another Harvard professor, Harlow Shapley, had just a month before chaired the Communist-inspired, Russian-dominated Cultural and Scientific Conference for World Peace at the Waldorf-Astoria. He told Mr. Conant—in a letter not intended for publication and manifestly inadequate as a well-rounded statement of his position—that he could no longer, in good conscience, contribute money to a university that harbored within its halls faculty members who were giving aid and assistance to "agents of a foreign, hostile power which is engaged in efforts to subvert this country by conspiratorial methods."

I have seen several letters of this general disposition which have been addressed to Yale, and I know of many more. Only the personalities are different, for while Harvard has her Harlow Shapley, president of the Communist Cultural and Scientific Conference for World Peace, Yale can counter with her Thomas I. Emerson, president of the National Lawyers' Guild, and so on. I have also seen a variety of official answers to correspondents of Mr. Ober's general persuasion. Replies are, by and large, mollifying in tone, but firm, and abundant in phrases like "freedom of speech," "the free area of ideas," "the value of skepticism," "the great traditions of academic freedom"; and the letters end, more often than not, with some such dismissal as, "we regret exceedingly your decision to discontinue your contributions, but we are sure that you will respect and appreciate the reasons that impel us to refuse to compromise our traditions of freedom. . . ."

But Mr. Ober was scheduled to receive the full treatment. We can only guess why: the volume of mail of this nature must have increased to a point at which form-letter answers could no longer do the job. The big guns were, therefore, leveled at Mr. Ober and his kind, and they fired in the *Harvard Alumni Bulletin*, issue of June 25, 1949.

Mr. Ober's original letter was about a thousand words long. The *Bulletin* carried it—along with a short letter by President Conant, a quotation from President Lowell's annual report of 1916–17, and a lengthy, erudite statement signed by Grenville Clark, a senior member of the Harvard Corporation. The sum of these rebuttals totaled six thousand words. For his own rebuttal, Mr. Ober was allowed an additional thousand words; a last rebuttal, of some three hundred words, was given to Mr. Clark. The total space devoted in the text of the *Bulletin* to Mr. Ober's point of view, then, was two thousand words. To his adversaries', six thousand three hundred and fifty.

But that wasn't all. In the "Letters to the Editor" section of the same issue, the two professors Mr. Ober had criticized were given space to speak for themselves. They took it, for a total of three thousand words. A resounding slip-up then occurred. The magazine's editor, in his foreword to the communications section, announced that after hearing from the professors, "Dean Griswold, of the Law School, and John D. Marsh, Chairman of the Law School Fund Drive, take opposite sides on the question of freedom of expression at Harvard."

By "slip-up" I do not mean the use of that loaded phrase, "opposite sides on the *question of freedom of expression*"; nor do I have reference to the fact that the statements giving the "opposite sides" occupied one-fifth as much space as the professors', or even to the fact that Mr. Marsh's letter only marginally supported Mr. Ober (it was primarily dedicated to expounding the greatness of Harvard and its need of funds). I was, though, stunned when I reached Dean Griswold's letter. Introduced by the editor as an ally of Mr. Ober, the Dean simply stated in his letter, "You [Mr. Ober] will not be surprised at my own conclusion. It is not in accord with yours." From here he went on about the Harvard Law School needing money.

And so, the total count: 9,350 words vs. 2,600 words. The combatants: President Lowell, President Conant, Corporation Member Clarke, Professor Ciardi, Professor Shapley, and Dean Griswold vs. Mr. Ober.

Sic Semper Tyrannis.

I have taken the time to describe the Ober controversy because it indicates to me the power of the machine and the techniques that are so readily available to the academic "liberals" for immediate use against anyone meddlesome enough to find fault with existing policy. Up against such a machine, the Obers are relatively helpless, for they have no similar weapons, no organization. Yale has not yet made an example of an Ober in the *Alumni Magazine*, probably because the *Magazine* would not officially concede that there are any Obers among the Yale alumni.

But the administration of Yale, and the president in particular, dwell from time to time in speeches and in articles on the merits of *laissez-faire* education, hinting that there exist some alumni with contrary notions—notions which are, of course, demonstrably fallacious.

Here as with an increasing number of the issues that confront the democratic community, the "liberals" have it—without so much as a gesture of obeisance to the toleration and open-mindedness they so ostentatiously enshrine—that there is a Right Side and a Wrong Side. Mr. Ober was on the Wrong Side. He was treated not as an alumnus offering a tenable policy alternative for Harvard, but as a recalcitrant Main Streeter who didn't *understand* "academic freedom,"* the implication of education, or the mission of the university. For this reason, Mr. Ober got no proper hearing, and his allies no hearing at all.

For similar reasons, it is not unlikely that this book, upon its appearance, will be branded as the product of an aberrant who takes the Wrong Side, i.e., the side that disagrees with the "liberals'." I expect to be Yale's Ober. But I ask reasonable observers to look out for evasive and irrelevant answers, for rebuttal by epithet, for flowery anathemas; and I ask the educators to whom I address myself in so large a part to demonstrate their touted receptivity, to practice the open-mindedness to which they lay claim, and to face up—more honestly than did the administration of Harvard—to the reservations about current educational policy that continue to trouble so sorely so many alumni.

No exhaustive exposition of the arguments advanced by the liberals on behalf of their notions of academic freedom and the university's mission is necessary. The principal tenets are well

---

* The reader is no doubt weary of seeing quotation marks around "academic freedom." Hereafter, I shall mostly dispense with them, except occasionally, so that they may serve as a reminder that I am at sword's point with the common usage of the term, as I shall explain later.

known. This side of the question is well advertised, and the reasoning (if that is the right word) behind it indelibly imprinted in the minds of the majority of the "intelligentsia." In most communities, to kill a proposed measure is, with appropriate incantations, to label it as in violation of academic freedom. It has become a matter of reflex action, something like the behavior of a friend of mine, who, when drunk, no matter where he is, or how he got there, stumbles to the nearest telephone and calls a taxi. He is confident that this is all he need do. Many citizens, intoxicated by liberal propaganda, are confident that to get home all right they need only align themselves with the defenders of "academic freedom."

Notwithstanding, some recapitulation of the arguments behind modern ideas of academic freedom is in order, and I shall attempt to deal fairly with them. I shall quote, in some detail, President Seymour, who in his final Baccalaureate Address in June 1950 sought to dismember, with eloquence and evident relish, some of the arguments I shall present here. I shall also quote Professor Edward C. Kirkland's "Academic Freedom and the Community," a part of a symposium on *America's Freedom and Responsibility in the Contemporary Crisis*[1] which took place at Cornell University in the spring of 1949. Professor Kirkland, himself in the ranks of the extremists,* adequately and enthusiastically expresses the academic freedom point of view. Naturally enough, the participants in the

---

* Professor Kirkland excoriates General Eisenhower for stating in his inaugural address as president of Columbia, that universities should teach "the American Way of Life." His patience is also short with the President's Commission on Higher Education for drawing up specific educational objectives for American colleges and universities. With regard to the non-Communist oaths that are increasingly required in so many educational institutions, Kirkland waxes wrathful and echoes Emerson on the Fugitive Slave Act: "This filthy enactment was made in the nineteenth century by men who can read and write. By God, I will not obey it!" "Personally," Kirkland adds hastily, "I recoil from this alternative."

symposium were of a single mind. The foreword to the book asserts that:

> ...from these discussions some general points of agreement seem to emerge: [one of these being] that it was [*sic*] not the proper function of the University to indoctrinate its students in any specific political or social formula....[2]

Finally, I shall quote at random from various other commentators who deem it a violation of freedom, a denial of justice, and a travesty of education for the educational overseer to insist upon some value orthodoxy.

While it is possible to point to some minor differences in emphasis among these commentators, agreement on fundamentals makes of them all, along with the overwhelming majority of the academic profession, contented bedfellows.

1. THE TEACHER'S QUALIFICATIONS

The academic freedomites believe that there ought to be a minimum number of criteria exercised in screening applicants for a teaching position. They agree that professional competence is the first and indispensable qualification. Beyond this, there is agreement slightly less monolithic on "character." Some universities apply more stringent character qualifications than others. To some, "character" means one thing; to others it means something else—which is to say, experience reveals that some scholars will be refused a teaching post in some colleges because of character or even personality traits, but will find the doors open to them in other equally reputable institutions.

Once we leave behind professional competence and character, there is again some variety of opinion. Professor Kirkland does not believe that academic freedom ought to protect the pedant, the dilettante, or the exhibitionist. Yet many colleges that operate on a philosophy of academic freedom almost identical to Professor Kirkland's nevertheless retain an occasional pedant, dilettante, or exhibitionist.

On the negative side, there is real unanimity where the scholar-applicant's convictions are concerned. Incessantly quoted on behalf of *laissez-faire* education is a passage from the inaugural address of President Charles W. Eliot of Harvard, who said in 1869,

> A university must . . . above all . . . be free; the winnowing breeze of freedom must blow through all its chambers. . . . The corporation demands of all its teachers that they be grave, reverent, and high-minded; but it leaves them, like their pupils, free.

What does this mean? It is generally interpreted to mean that the "free" university does not inquire into the personal convictions and values of its staff members, and that the university that does so is *not* "free." Professor Kirkland writes,

> An academic institution is an arena. Into it ride different contestants. They may uphold different causes, some perhaps wholly or partially wrong. They may be differently armed. But all must meet the test of conflict, of argument, and of performance. We believe that in this free and open contest truth will be victorious and error defeated over the long time.[3]

President Seymour, in answering the criticisms of certain alumni in his 1948–49 report, said,

> The fact must . . . be faced that when . . . the faculty of the School give expression to their convictions in fields and upon topics which are inevitably contentious, we must expect strong criticism from those who do not agree with them. This is part and

parcel, it seems to me, of the University's obligation to foster the search for truth. The free expression of a conviction resting upon honest intellectual effort is not merely consonant with university purpose but an essential concomitant of that purpose.

Both these scholars, and innumerable others, in defense of the inviolability of the faculty, advance one and the same set of arguments: "truth will emerge victorious," "error will suffer ignominy," "the scholar's freedom is essential to the country's freedom," etc. All these quotations are taken at random from the writings of various exponents of "academic freedom"; and the historical documents they most frequently refer to, in support of the "truth will out" theory, are Milton's *Areopagitica*, Jefferson's "First Inaugural Address," and Mill's *Essay on Liberty*.

An evaluation and analysis of truth and the proper attitude toward it, of course, figure. Professor Kirkland reminds us that

Colleges and universities, in the nature of things, cannot teach only the truth, though they should strive to do so. They must in the nature of things teach error, though they should strive not to do so. [There follows a description of bacteriological discoveries that came to invalidate the teachings of many nineteenth century doctors who, nevertheless, at the time they held forth, acted in good faith.] ... Colleges and universities do not possess or teach the whole truth. They are engaged in the quest for truth. For that reason their scholars must be free to examine and test all facts and ideas, the unpleasant, the distasteful, and dangerous, and even those regarded as erroneous by a majority of their learned colleagues.[4]

With the stage thus set, the college student enters as a spectator in the arena in which the multifarious forces fight it out. Using the tools that his academic training has provided him, he is to pick out truth and to shovel aside error. It is important that his choice be his own, for it is all the more valuable to him if there has been no exterior suasion on behalf of one or the other protagonist. So trained and so armed, the student leaves school and enters community life. The educational institution has done its duty by the student and, through him, by the community.

This, as I understand it, is the backbone of the case behind "academic freedom" as it is so widely upheld today. The implications of the position are evident, and many of them will emerge in the course of this discussion.

2. DOES YALE PRACTICE "ACADEMIC FREEDOM"?

I believe it to be an indisputable fact that most colleges and universities, and certainly Yale, the protests and pretensions of their educators and theorists notwithstanding, do not practice, cannot practice, and cannot even believe what they say about education and academic freedom. I am not saying that they do not utilize the rationale of academic freedom to obtain license when and where they desire it. This they most certainly do, for their policy is one of expedience.

To take first things first, and to continue to use Yale as a case in point, I shall examine the existing situation in the light of the following plank of the academic freedom platform:

Scholars must be selected to staff the faculty without consideration of their personal convictions, "even those regarded as erroneous by a majority of their learned colleagues."

Let us begin with the field of English literature and poetry, a field about which controversy is largely confined to the academic world itself. It is naturally an area in which values are heavily involved, and, since this entire discussion deals with value inculcation in schools, comes naturally to mind.

Now the term "professionally competent," as it is used by the academic freedomites to describe a legitimate criterion of employment, can, under their credo, be meaningfully applied only to the "fact" aspect of teaching. The mathematician who advances the theory that two and two are five, or that it is possible to take the square root of a minus number, is *demonstrably* in error, and hence not professionally competent.

But the English teacher, the man of letters, is dealing with issues that are by no means this neat. He deals, for the most part, in values. Some scholars, for example, think Gertrude Stein is a momentous literary figure, while others believe her to be a charlatan. I am confident that the scholar who holds her in esteem and the scholar who does not could both make their way into Yale. Does this mean that Yale, true to the strictures of academic freedom, is unconcerned about the teacher's values?

The answer is: only if not pushed too far. What about the scholar who thinks that Joyce Kilmer is a good poet? The cynic will find in that last sentence a paradox. He will say that one cannot be both a scholar and an admirer of Joyce Kilmer. But by definition, since we are dealing in values, this clearly will not do. Stranger things have happened than a scholar's convincing himself that Joyce Kilmer is an admirable poet. Time was when only one critic of distinction believed that Johann Sebastian Bach composed good music. Eventually his opinion won out. Again, stranger things have happened than a possible proliferation of Kilmer enthusiasts. And so what the cynic *really* means is that the scholar shows poor *judgment* when he speaks well of Kilmer's verse.

No one will question the fact that the scholar who has gone on record as admiring the output of Joyce Kilmer would never get an appointment at Yale. He could never pass the departmental screening all candidates must successfully withstand. In justification, the department head would no doubt point out that the textbook used in the basic classes in English at Yale uses a poem by Joyce Kilmer to illustrate everything that is bad about bad poetry, and that an English teacher who thinks Kilmer a good poet could only bring chaos to that department.

The personal convictions of our imaginary applicant are, in short, regarded as "erroneous by a majority of his learned colleagues." And he is not invited to Yale to undermine the carefully inculcated do's and don'ts of "good" poetry.

Let us move to the field of sociology. I should be interested to know how long a person who revealed himself as a racist, who lectured about the anthropological superiority of the Aryan, would last at Yale? My prediction is that the next full moon would see him looking elsewhere for a job. Yale looks upon anti-Semitic, anti-negroid prejudices as false values, though of course they are value judgments just the same and have been upheld by various scholars not only in the past but in the present day as well. But they are value judgments which are not going to be defended in any Yale classroom.

How about political science? Would Yale hire, or, if hired, would Yale retain, a man who openly scorned democracy as a weary, unintelligent, untenable, pernicious political system? It is inconceivable to me that Yale would long tolerate his presence. "A major obligation [of the educator]," President Seymour has said, "is to train our youth in the understanding and practice of American democracy whether in the classroom or in our campus life."

And yet there have been scores of distinguished scholars, dating back to the time Alcibiades said of democracy, "Why discuss such acknowledged madness?", who have regarded the principles of our form of government with unleavened contempt. But Yale feels otherwise, and professional competence notwithstanding, the political totalitarian must go elsewhere for employment.

In early April 1949, shortly after the Communist Cultural and Scientific Conference for World Peace was held at the Waldorf-Astoria, Shostakovitch and his troubadours accepted an invitation by the local Progressive Party to stage an "educational rally for peace" at New Haven. Permission was sought to use Yale buildings. In a terse note, the secretary of Yale announced that since the administration saw "no educational value" in the proposed meeting of the Soviet delegation, the permission was being denied. In short, the administration of Yale said, in practically as many words, "We don't approve of Soviet values, and by God they're not going to be trumpeted from *our* auditoriums." It was not the first time official Yale had pronounced in such a manner against values she considered to be false. In 1933, the auditoriums were refused to Ferdinand Pecora, and in 1936, though less directly, to Gerald P. Nye.

In 1937, Yale University refused to reappoint Jerome Davis, associate professor at the Divinity School, and as a result brought down upon herself the furious wrath of academic freedomites. For despite protestations that Professor Davis had failed to qualify for promotion, and had not otherwise displayed adequate academic competence, it was plain for all to see that he had been eased out because of his outspoken criticism of capitalism, his espousal of numerous left-wing causes, and his attacks on several large financial trusts and holding companies with which various members of the Yale Corporation were affiliated.

An exhaustive investigation into his dismissal was conducted by the American Federation of Teachers which published its findings and came to the unequivocal conclusion that "Professor Davis' dismissal from the Divinity School represents a clear case of the violation of academic freedom."[5]

Again, Yale had decided that Professor Davis had stepped outside the bounds of her orthodoxy. Mr. Angell, who was president at the time, had in effect warned his faculty members to respect those bounds.

> ... If university men [he had written in the *Yale Alumni Weekly*[6]] are to claim freedom of teaching and freedom of thought and speech, they must in turn justify the claim not only by a decent respect for the opinions of mankind but also by sobriety of utterance on acutely controversial issues. They must be sensitive to the dictates of good sense and good taste.

In his baccalaureate address in June of 1949, President Seymour announced that he would not "knowingly hire a Communist to the teaching faculty." This statement coincided in point of time with a resolution of the Educational Policy Commission of the National Education Association, signed by a number of college presidents, including General Eisenhower and Dr. Conant, condemning the hiring of Communist teachers. There followed, as was to be expected, a rationalization of sorts expressed in terms of "academic freedom." Nevertheless, the resolution represented an overt departure from the principles of academic freedom as these same men have often upheld them. Professor Kirkland, himself a former president of the American Association of University Professors, recognized this, and ripped into this boycott of Communist teachers.*

This move was certainly one of expedience. After all, Communists are, in all relevant respects, the same now as they were in 1925, and little previous academic action against them had been

---

* "This test might have validity if the individual were compelled to sign the subscription [the Communist Party oath] and forbidden to depart from it. By and large these conditions do not prevail in a democratic society. Men give allegiance to creeds because their reason convinces them these creeds are sound; they are equally free, at the same dictate, to withdraw from them" (*Freedom and the University*, p. 10).

taken. For twenty-five years, Communists were inviolate under academic freedom. But the temper of the American people, as of 1950, has changed, and the lid goes on. *The Communists hadn't changed, so the theories that protected them for so many years had to be somewhat altered for the occasion.*

In short, I maintain that sonorous pretensions notwithstanding, Yale (and my guess is most other colleges and universities) *does subscribe to an orthodoxy:* there are limits within which its faculty members must keep their opinions if they wish to be "tolerated."

Now these limits are very wide indeed, and they are limits prescribed by expediency, not by principle. My task becomes, then, not so much to argue that limits should be *imposed*, but that existing limits should be *narrowed*.

It is true that the fact that limits already exist does not warrant the conclusion that this is itself good. Perhaps Yale, and her sister universities, ought to go back in the other direction, and tolerate Kilmerites, racists, totalitarians, and Stalinists. I shall consider this possibility later. I ask, so far, only that we recognize some discrepancy between what is preached and what is practiced; because it means that most university administrations are acting on the principles argued in this essay, not on theirs as they state them. This is of course comforting. I must proceed to persuade them to narrow an orthodoxy to which they already subscribe.

3. TRUTH AND VALUE

Truth is probably not apprehendable. Since it is not, it is folly to try to indoctrinate the student in any specific formula. Rather, the teaching community must be left free to approach truth as best it can.

This statement, however else expressed, features prominently in the platform of academic freedom. Many of the problems that confront us at any given time leave us perplexed as to what is truth and what is error. It is inevitable, then, that we shall occasionally teach error. We once taught that certain contagious diseases stemmed from the presence of filth or the proximity of stagnant waters, when in fact it was later discovered that they were caused by disease-carrying mosquitoes and fleas, and by drinking infected water or milk.

Of course the illustration above, though used by Professor Kirkland in his paper on academic freedom, is only marginally relevant and not revealing in the least. The tip-off comes when Kirkland states that scientists *"discovered and demonstrated"* that the previous theories about contagious diseases were *"falsehoods."* In other words, in this field truth has been arrived at, and any scientist who still insists that filth and stagnant waters are the source of the trouble would be regarded as a quack. He would be wrong, just as wrong as a post-Galilean astronomer who taught Copernicus, as wrong as the twentieth-century physicist who teaches the atom as the basic unit of substance. In other words, this example, and others akin to it, deal with the demonstrable. As such they are matters of fact, not of value.

Note well that Professor Kirkland raised no objection to the fact that what later was demonstrated to be a specious biological generalization was taught to several generations of students. It was the best theory that medical research could devise at the time; and most teachers, at the time they taught it, believed it to be an accurate account of the spread of various diseases. We can assume, then, that the academic freedomites admit to the wisdom and inevitability that, at any given time, the best available theory be taught—even though it may in time prove to be false. Their anxiety comes down to a concern for the scholar's freedom to *explore* different theories. This is something else again, and such a concern does not entail denial of the right of educational institutions to advance the best theory that is known at a given moment.

Our problem is whether or not there is justification in embracing one of several value alternatives and indoctrinating with it students for whose education the university is responsible. Furthermore, are we willing to do this in view of the fact that future "discoveries" or "demonstrations" may show that our value system was based on data that were falsely interpreted or improperly generalized upon?

Let us revert to the two sets of values the treatment of which was discussed in the first sections of this book: Christianity and individualism. A complication, though not insuperable, lies in dealing with Christianity. For Christians (I speak, of course, in the religious, not the ethical sense of the term) by definition believe that Christianity is truth. The administration and Corporation of Yale is composed, by and large, of Christians. As such, they cannot believe that Christianity is a transient, environmentally convenient code of living; they believe it is ultimate, irrefutable truth.

But at the same time, Christianity—or even the existence of God—in the opinion of some people, is not demonstrable. Better still, it is arguable whether or not it is demonstrable, and, therefore, the dissenter is entitled to take the line that since there is conflicting opinion as to its demonstrability, it must be regarded as not demonstrable.

Let us not pursue the point. Let us say that Christianity *may not be truth*, but that in the eyes of Christians it is at least the *nearest thing to unrevealed* and *perhaps inapprehensible ultimate truth*.

As for individualism (as expressed in economic, political, and social policy), it is not regarded as truth (as we have been using the term), even by the majority of its most ardent supporters. Even so, we are entitled, if we believe in it, to classify it as the best available philosophy to guide the legislator, the executive, and the judge. Individualism, we are entitled to say, is, if not truth, the nearest thing we have to truth, no closer thing to truth in the field of social relations having appeared on the horizon.

The implications of this analysis are, I believe, of some importance. For the question becomes whether or not educational overseers, acting collectively, can embrace one value system and seek to inculcate this value in their students even while hazarding the possibility that, in some future day, they may themselves throw it to one side in favor of another value.

Again, I maintain that most universities have espoused—and continue to do so—collectively, one value as opposed to another. Democracy, as opposed to totalitarianism, is an example. Both are values. Democracy may not be truth, but so far as at least Yale University is concerned, it is the nearest thing to truth that we possess, so that while a faculty member is perfectly free to point out the limitations, defects, and weaknesses of democracy, as is right and proper, he is not privileged, at the margin, to advocate the abolition of democracy in favor of totalitarianism.

It follows from all this that the average university administration does indeed rule out some values as legitimate bidders for student consumption. President Seymour, for example, has been unequivocal about Communism, which he considers evil and foolish. If he considered atheism evil and foolish, he would have needed only to utilize the same logic and the same powers he invoked against Communism to banish it from the classroom. If he deemed socialism as evil or as foolish as Communism, he could have done the same.

But, it may strike you, suppose he doesn't consider atheism or socialism to be *as bad* as Communism? Suppose he feels that only the worst values should be banned?

This would be an intelligible position. But I would remind President Seymour, and his successor also, that the moral code to which they subscribe exhorts man to abhor *all* that is bad. Murder is a more grievous wrong than theft; but we discourage both, and we invoke divine, social, and legal sanctions against the two. If Mr. Seymour considers socialism to be in any degree wrong, he has, as the first educational officer of Yale, a duty to pass on his convictions, through a faculty of similar convictions, to the student.

Once again, we find that in the absence of demonstrable truth, the best we can do is to exercise the greatest diligence, humility, insight, intelligence, and industry in trying to arrive at the nearest values to truth. I hope, of course, to argue convincingly that having done this, we have an inescapable duty to seek to inculcate others with these values.

4. TRUTH WILL OUT

Let truth and error do battle in the arena of ideas. Truth will vanquish. Let the student and the citizen witness the struggle; let the struggle take place in their minds, and they will ally themselves with truth.

These are unquestionably contentions upon which the case for democracy in part rests. But in their application, they are in large part misunderstood. They are unquestionably misappropriated when they are made to justify *laissez-faire* education.

The school is conceived as an extension of the arena in which battle is done, whereas, more properly, the teaching part of a college is the practice field on which the gladiators of the future are taught to use their weapons, are briefed in the wiles and stratagems of the enemy, and are inspired with the virtue of their cause in anticipation of the day when they will step forward and join in the struggle against error.

This is important since the most casual student of history knows that, as a matter of fact, truth does *not* necessarily vanquish. What is more, truth can *never* win unless it is promulgated. Truth does not carry within itself an antitoxin to falsehood. The cause of truth must be championed, and it must be championed dynamically. Moreover, as President Howard Lowry of Wooster College points out,[7] truth can win only where people are temperamentally and intellectually disposed to side with it, for the mere act of recognizing it as such does not entail the willful act of attaching allegiance to it.

We need go no further back than to the close of World War I to see that this is the case. Since that time, at least three coarse, barbaric, starkly wicked dictatorships have displaced existing, and in two cases democratic, governments. The transition in Russia was, it is true, one from an inefficient and desultory dictatorship to a highly efficient and systematic dictatorship. Truth, it can fairly be said, never had much of a chance to assert itself under either regime.

But the people of Italy, in 1922, did have the opportunity to learn better than to allow Mussolini and his blackshirts to march upon Rome and preempt the power of the people's government. The people of Germany had had what seems like ample opportunity to embrace truth and scorn error when they nevertheless gave the Nazis the largest party vote in an election.*

Both of these "revolutions," to be sure, were wrought by complex forces acting in complex ways; but it is nevertheless a tragic

---

* I recognize that having classified democracy and totalitarianism as values rather than as truth and error I am taking a liberty in saying that truth did not vanquish in Italy or in Germany. But I am assuming that the relativism that guides most of our academic freedomites is not so rigid as to impel them to state that truth did indeed vanquish in Germany and Italy. I recognize also that truth is supposed to emerge "over the long turn." But aside from the pragmatic refutation of this theory, revealed by historical persistence of error at so many times and in so many places, "the triumph of truth over the long turn" is logically indefensible, as a series of "short turns" can be of indefinite length.

fact that truth did *not* triumph, and that this was *not* because the truth had not been made known. It was rather because (a) not enough people recognized the truth, (b) those who did recognize it did not exert themselves sufficiently in its behalf, and (c) many people saw the truth, but were indifferent to it.

The denial of truth in Italy and Germany, coupled with the refusal of Japan to ally herself with truth, resulted in a devastating world war. The continued refusal of Russia to scorn error bids fair to bring an end to truth everywhere in the world.

These examples are perhaps gaudy; but, still and all, they are certainly historical instances of the way in which contempt for truth can lose the battle, if not the war, to the idolatry of falsehood. It would seem that the will of man has never been confronted more dramatically between a choice of black and white, and yet how explain the loyalty that Stalinism commands among millions of people all over the free world?

It is of some interest that the occupation authorities in Germany (and incidentally I have heard no hoots and cries leveled at them for it) unequivocally forbade the use in schools of texts on Nazi philosophy.* In effect, Americans, British, and Frenchmen, all of whom can be presumed to harbor profound respect for democracy and hence for the vitality of truth, gave clear-cut evidence that this time they did not, for the nonce, wish to bank too heavily on the emergence of truth in the free arena of ideas. Instead, the children of Germany are being *taught* the evils of Nazism, and forcefully warned against succumbing to the blandishments of Fascism, in the hope, presumably, that this approach to truth will prove more efficacious.

It is unquestionably the case that the people of America, with a dynamic tradition of freedom, are less easily deceived. But it does not follow that there should be a total abdication of respon-

---

* I am in hearty disagreement with this type of suppression, as will be made clear later when I seek to analyze the function of education and the function of the teacher.

sibility, a lapse into complacency, in giving impetus to values that we consider to be good, that we consider most closely to approximate truth, or perhaps, even, to be truth itself. The communication of values is, after all, the raw stuff of democracy. One political party advances one set of principles, the other advances a different set. Both work hard to propagandize their ideas and to attract consumers to their platform. The people, periodically, exercise their choice between the available alternatives.

At their noblest, politicians are fighting for a cause. The success of such a cause, if the cause is righteous, can, ultimately, bring freedom and justice to the world. For the educator, complacent in his ivory tower, to scorn affiliation with a cause he considers to be noble, to refuse to attempt to win disciples from the ranks of students he is in a position to influence, is unmistakably to forswear a democratic responsibility, and to earn for himself the contemptible title of dilettante and solipsist.*

---

* The extent to which relativism has conquered the thinking processes of the academic freedomites would, on reflection, I believe, astound even the most emphatic of their number. For they proceed on the proposition that the more education, the more visible the truth. This itself gives one pause. The philosophical issues that divided the Greeks in their quest for truth were far simpler and less divergent than those that divide us today after twenty-five hundred years of education. And as a corollary, described above, they believe that the more education, especially of the sort which pleads the cases of all values, the more certain it is that man will be induced to embrace the truth. But the implications of this theory are nothing short of anarchistic. Two students, with equal equipment and training, will often graduate with markedly divergent opinions about what is truth. If they continue with their studies, one may become a Dewey, the other a Maritain. Or one may affirm democracy, the other totalitarianism. Which of the two is in fact closer to the truth? The academic freedomite finds himself hard put to commit himself here if his propositions are to stand up. Truth, their argument on behalf of *laissez-faire* education compels them to admit, is whatever each individual considers truth to be. Otherwise, the educational overseer would be privileged to arrive at conclusions

My concern is primarily with the private university. Its overseers are relatively few and certainly more closely united than the citizenry at large. Yet I am constantly astounded at the fact that the states and the federal government are in some cases far ahead of them in recognizing the nature of academic responsibility. It was as recently as in 1925 that the Supreme Court[8] unanimously ruled that the state has the power, among others, over all schools, to require that "teachers shall be of good moral character and patriotic disposition," that "certain studies plainly essential to good citizenship be taught," and that "nothing be taught which is manifestly inimical to the public welfare."

This decision collides resoundingly with modern notions of academic freedom. Very obviously there can be several points of view about what is "good moral character," and what is "patriotic disposition," and what is "essential to good citizenship," and what is "inimical to the public welfare." These are all value questions, and clearly the Supreme Court left it to the legislatures to decide which were the proper values to encourage. I believe the principles guiding the court were proper, though I should bitterly contest a preemption by the state of the duties and privileges of the alumni of the private institutions themselves to guide the destinies of the schools they support.*

At any rate, our Supreme Court, like many of our legislatures, has shown greater discernment than the majority of our blue-ribbon educators by acknowledging that the most esteemed val-

---

as to what is truth (or the nearest available thing to it) and what is error. And having done this, he would surely feel compelled to instruct his faculty to discourage the one and encourage the other.

* As I should bitterly contest an effort by the court or by the legislatures to outlaw any school that sought any change whatever in national policy, provided such change were to be brought about by constitutional process.

ues, if they are to triumph, must have a helping hand at the educational level.

5. DOES YALE OBSERVE "ACADEMIC FREEDOM" IN SELECTING AN ADMINISTRATION?

Let us trace the thinking that underlies the selection of a president of a private university and some of the steps involved in that process. As usual Yale is our *corpus vile*. The Yale Corporation, which we have already described as responsible to the alumni, selects a presidential nominating committee, which undertakes much of the necessary spade work and serves as a preliminary screening body.

When President Seymour announced his impending retirement, the Corporation appointed three of its members as the Nominating Committee. These were the Right Reverend Henry K. Sherrill, presiding bishop of the Episcopal Church of America, Wilmarth S. Lewis, wit, scholar, and bibliophile *par excellence*,* and Irving S. Olds, chairman of the board of United States Steel.

---

* While still in search for a president to succeed Charles Seymour, Mr. Lewis recited the requisite qualifications: "He must be a leader—not too far to the right, not too far to the left, and of course not too much in the middle. He must be a magnificent speaker and a great writer. He must be a good public relations man and an experienced fund raiser. He must be a man of iron health and stamina, a young man— but also mature and full of wisdom. He must be married to a paragon, a combination of Queen Victoria, Florence Nightingale, and the best dressed woman of the year. He must be a man of the world, and yet he must also have spiritual qualities—a great administrator who can delegate authority. He must be a Yale man and a great scholar—also a social philosopher who has at his fingertips a solution to all world problems, from birth control to Formosa." Added Mr. Lewis: "I don't doubt you have realized that there is only one who has

I choose to believe there was significance attached to one member's lifetime preoccupation with the service of God, another's devotion to pure scholarship, and the third's lifelong championship of individualism.

I am equally certain that no avowed agnostic or atheist, no outspoken socialist, would have been so much as considered for the post of president of Yale.

What is my proof? Largely the makeup of the Corporation, six of whom are directly elected by the alumni, and the rest appointed—with due consideration to the temper of the alumni. I am careful not to imply thorough familiarity on the part of the alumni with the qualifications of nominees to the Corporation, but I do believe that militant atheism or anti-capitalism would serve to disqualify an individual for membership in the Corporation, and hence, certainly, for the presidency.

Evidence of the values esteemed by the majority of the alumni is derived from an analysis of the Corporation today. Its members are: one doctor, two scholars, three ordained ministers, and ten lawyers, politicians, and businessmen.* These last are overwhelmingly favorable to free enterprise; and, to my knowledge, they are all professed Christians. This is not an extraordinary coincidence, for Article I of the Yale Corporation By-Laws goes as

---

most of these qualifications, but—is God a Yale man?" An impious friend remarked to me that this would have been impossible: "God couldn't have graduated from Yale. His moral code is far too corny."

* Corporation members are the Rev. Arthur H. Bradford, Irving S. Olds, Lewis H. Weed, the Rt. Rev. Henry K. Sherrill, George Van Santvoord, the Rev. Morgan P. Noyes, Dean G. Acheson, Charles D. Dickey, Morris Hadley, Wilmarth S. Lewis, Robert A. Taft (1954), F. Trubee Davison (1953), Juan T. Trippe (1955), Robert T. B. Stevens (1956), Edwin F. Blair (1952), and Jonathan B. Bingham (1951). The year when the term of each Alumni Fellow expires is printed after his name.

far as to decree that "Meetings of the Corporation shall be opened
with prayer." And the chairman of the Corporation Committee
on Educational Policy is a bishop.*

Now comes the question that the advocate of *laissez-faire*
education *ought* to ask: What difference does it make what are
the values of the president? To go further, is it not a *violation* of
the spirit of academic freedom even to inquire into the values of
a candidate, assuming him to be a man of "high moral purpose
and integrity"? If in the course of his administration the president is not to allow his values to influence in any way the educational policies of the university over which he is to preside,
then they ought logically to be a matter of supreme indifference
to the Corporation.

Now: if the Corporation insists that the president share, in
greater or less degree, its values, it must do so for some reason.
Since the Corporation is composed of responsible men, we can
assume that their insistence that the president share certain values arises not out of caprice or unreasoned willfulness, but, rather,
out of earnest conviction that the occupant of so responsible a
post *ought to hold* a given set of values.

Why ought he to hold them?

To derive personal comfort from them? Surely not. An individual is himself the best judge of what contributes to his own
comfort and equanimity, and many a socialist and atheist will lay

---

* The Yale Corporation By-Laws (Article 16) outline as follows the
  activities of this Committee: "The Committee on Educational Policy
  shall consist of not less than five members of the Corporation. It
  shall deal with educational policies and plans; it shall inform itself
  as to conditions in the different Schools and Departments and as to
  measures needed to make the most effective use of the resources of
  the University for educational purposes. It shall advise and assist the
  President and his associates in the development and carrying forward of the educational program of the University."

claim to complete peace of mind. Well, then, it must be that the Corporation wishes these values to affect the president's policies. If the Corporation believes that allegiance to Christianity and the philosophy of individualism impel a man to act in behalf of his own good and that of the community, then the Corporation must certainly be anxious that students, for whose education they hold great responsibility, also be persuaded, in so far as is possible, to espouse similar values. Spokesmen of Yale, time out of mind, have described as the *desideratum* of education a dedication of their graduates to the good.

We can assume, then, that the composition of the Corporation, together with the value prerequisites of the president of the University, align the governing body of Yale behind a given set of values. We can assume that the term "educator" is meaningful beyond the function of raising money, supervising spending, confirming appointments, stabilizing the curriculum, addressing the alumni, and maintaining general order. Certainly President Seymour had more to say than the foregoing functions alone would warrant. Yet most of the time, what he stood for was in direct contradiction to what the student was being taught.

For example: in his inaugural address in October of 1937, President Seymour said:

> *I call on all members of the faculty*, as members of a thinking body, freely to recognize the tremendous validity and power of the teachings of Christ. . . . Yale was dedicated to the upraising of spiritual leaders. We betray our trust if we fail to explore the various ways in which the youth who come to us may learn to appreciate spiritual values, whether by the example of our own lives or through the cogency of our philosophical arguments. The simple and direct way is through the maintenance and upbuilding of the Christian religion as a vital part of university life [italics added].

What did Mr. Seymour mean when he said "I *call* on all members of the faculty..."? Did he mean he would be personally obliged if they would only give Christianity a break? Was "I call on all members of the faculty," perhaps, just a figure of speech which meant nothing more than that Mr. Seymour was certain the faculty would be interested in what were his own personal views? Or did he, perhaps, mean: "As the educational leader of this University, feeling as I do that the exposure of Yale students to Christian values is indispensable to the honorable discharge of my responsibilities, I am directing you to assist me in this task; if you cannot in good conscience further this cause, you must understand that you will not long remain in Yale"?

Now this interpretation is clearly untenable, given the persistent antipathy to Christianity and spiritual values on the part of so many of Yale's "thinking body," as described in the first section of this book. Therefore, President Seymour must have made this statement either as a personal, unofficial plea to the faculty, or else as a rhetorical exposition of his own personal convictions. In the latter case he might as well not have said it at all.

A final alternative explanation is that he may have changed his mind during the course of his career as president. This looms as a possibility; though it does not, of course, imply that Mr. Seymour has himself wavered in his appreciation of Christianity. He may simply have decided that his personal attitudes were of no concern to the faculty.

Another question: *Has* Yale, in the opinion of President Seymour, betrayed her mission by her failure exhaustively "to explore the various ways in which the youth who come to us may learn to appreciate spiritual values"? It would seem, on the face of it, that she has. And if this is the case, no one, surely, regrets this more than Charles Seymour, whose unstinting devotion to the University is a matter of record.

6. THE GOALS OF YALE

The administration of Yale makes constant reference to the goals of the University. Witness the report of the president to the alumni (1948–49):

> [It is important that the policies of the law school not be] at variance with the *educational ideals* of the university [p. 33, italics added]. A faculty member must make plain that it is his own opinion that he expresses, and not the *official position* of the university [p. 36, italics added].

An injunction such as the last seems nonsensical since nobody really knows what is the "official position" of the University, or even whether it has one.

I have already mentioned that the value attitudes of the members of the Corporation and the president are similar. They might, loosely, be used to construct the "official position" of Yale. On the other hand, if the members of the Corporation are to observe the mandates of the academic freedomites, no "official position," i.e., a position that is to pervade value attitudes at Yale, is permissible.

As for the University's "educational ideals," not much meaning can be read into the term other than "knowledge of the facts," "a taste for learning," and "proficiency in an area of studies," that is, unless by examining other official statements, we move forward from one confusion to another.

At the conclusion of his 1948–49 report, President Seymour reminded the alumni that Yale "has remained constant to the ideal of training future citizens *in behalf of the public welfare*" (p. 47, italics added).

Now I happen to know (and it is not a closely guarded secret) that President Seymour believes that socialism is distinctly *not* "in behalf of the public welfare." In fact, I am confident that he believes collectivism to be emphatically inimical to the public welfare; and yet, there are faculty members at Yale who, as we have seen, encourage various degrees of socialism, and the textbooks they use are of the same persuasion. So far as Mr. Seymour is concerned, they are teaching, albeit with good intentions, *against* the public welfare, and to the extent that these professors influence students, they are influencing them to *act against* the public welfare. In fact, Yale is paying these professors to do just that. It would seem that if Yale's "ideals" are the same as Mr. Seymour's, then, unhappily, Yale has not in all cases "remained constant" to them.

In his final baccalaureate address, President Seymour told the graduating class, "To [you] . . . there is given the opportunity of public influence, whether for good or for evil."

Mr. Seymour has definite ideas about what is good and what is evil. In part, we may be sure, he was awarded the presidency because of his eloquence in behalf of good and against evil.

Good and evil are, in our society, words without fixed meaning; but it would be absurd to conclude that the civilized world, as a whole, does not know what it means by good and evil, for example, in the field of morals. I am certain that President Seymour, especially as a practicing Christian, would be the first to agree.

He reminds the graduating class, then, that its influence will be far-reaching "whether for good or for evil," and the presumption is of course that, *gratias Yalensi*, it will be for the good.

How does the faculty cooperate in this? For example, a Yale professor of anthropology, George P. Murdock, speaking at a panel discussion at the thirty-seventh annual meeting of the American Social Hygiene Association, on February 1, 1950, expressed graphically and at some length the opinion that ethical and religious sanctions against premarital sexual intercourse were nothing but a "censorious insistence on an unrealistic and outworn code."* As a professor, Mr. Murdock has wide influence, and it cannot be expected that his remarks and attitudes will have no influence on his students. And an influence in this direction obviously runs directly athwart Mr. Seymour's conception of what is "good"; but again, it seems he was powerless to combat it.

A final illustration of interest: in the spring of 1950, President Seymour consented to answer a series of questions for the *New Haven Register*. One of these was: "In the light of financial difficulties do you think the privately endowed university will eventually disappear?" Mr. Seymour answered: *"The privately endowed university will certainly endure so long as it meets its obligation to serve the public welfare."*

Now this was really an incomplete answer, and yet in one respect, an astonishingly shrewd answer. Mr. Seymour is well aware that the privately endowed university will endure only so long as enough of its alumni and friends can afford to sustain it. They could not conceivably afford to sustain it under socialism, which would make support of Yale a luxury impossible to indulge. Since it is well

---

* Professor Murdock made clear in preliminary remarks that his observations were "exclusively scientific," that they were based on a study of sexual attitudes of 250 different societies, and that he realized that there exist cultural and ethical standards of morality. Thus he sought immunity as a scientific investigator. But rather than content himself with personal observations as to the social damages of premarital abstinence, he explicitly advocated a change in the Christian moral code to accommodate his "scientific conclusions," thereby advocating societal rejection of divine laws. By so doing, he aligned himself with the secularists, who diagnose the problems of the world and put forward measures toward their solution without any reference to limitations imposed by religious ethics.

known that Mr. Seymour attaches great value to the continuation of the privately endowed university, it is again clear that to serve the public welfare is to preserve an economy which, among other things, makes possible its continued existence.

But this brand of public welfare is not the brand that Yale's economists and textbooks are urging on future policy-makers. Instead, the student is impressed with the ethical economic imperative of higher and higher graduated income and inheritance taxes,* capital levies through government-manipulated inflation, the abolition of capital gains exemptions—in short, the impoverishment of every imaginable financial supporter of Yale, except the government (which is not impoverishable).

Mr. Seymour has unequivocally ruled against accepting government money. The consequences of this he regards as disastrous. But there will be no other money for Yale if the points of view of many Yale teachers and texts finally blossom into legislation—that is, to a greater degree than they have already.

In other words, Yale is not only working *against* the public welfare, as Mr. Seymour understands the public welfare, but she is also working toward her own destruction, i.e., to the day when some future Yale president, fedora in hand, will knock at the door of some politician with palm outstretched. This day, of course, means the end of Yale as a private institution.

The list of anomalies is endless. The president and many members of the faculty are working at cross-purposes. Much of the tragedy lies in the appalling fact that President Seymour, as a Christian and an individualist, had far less influence upon the students of

---

* But Yale stubbornly persists in decorating much of the literature she distributes to alumni with the following obsolescent message: "In answer to many inquiries from alumni and friends of the University who plan to remember Yale in their will, the following forms are suggested. . . ."

Yale than many professors. I think I know what Mr. Seymour stands for—from listening to him and from reading closely a number of his speeches and reports. The average member of my class, on the other hand, heard him on only two occasions, upon matriculating and upon graduating. But ask the average member of the class of 1950 about the late Mr. Kennedy's views on religion. Several hundred members of the class listened to him three hours a week for 32-odd weeks, and hundreds went on for more. Ask the average student what his teacher in basic economics thinks about the welfare state, or how Mr. Lindblom deals with capitalism in his course on Comparative Economic Systems. They will have ready answers. As to similar inquiries about President Seymour's values, they will shrug their shoulders.

It is plain that the president of a university cannot transmit to the students his own values directly. His duties are so extensive that to conduct classes on a large scale is a practical impossibility. He must therefore utilize intermediaries, men of similar convictions, to do the job. This academic freedom forbids. It is therefore an appalling yet indisputable fact that because of the restraints of "academic freedom," the president of Yale has far less influence on the student body than have scores of influential professors who are allowed—in fact encouraged—to teach just as they will, to traffic, within loose limits, in whatever values they choose.

It is curious that the Corporation spends so much time and effort in selecting a president.

7. SOME OBJECTIONS
TO VALUE INCULCATION

President Seymour devoted a major part of his final baccalaureate address to expounding the reasons behind his inflexible opposition to those who believe ". . . it is the duty of the university to establish a certain standard of convictions or creeds and to exclude from its teaching force those who hold doctrines which do not conform to such a standard." The address represents a valuable synthesis— eloquently written and fervently spoken—of most of the arguments against value inculcation. An analysis of some of the objections he raised may throw light on the controversy.

"*Nothing is more certain* [President Seymour insisted] *than that such a policy would produce the most arid sort of scholasticism.*"

The most unflattering metaphorical definition of "scholasticism" that I can find is the Oxford Dictionary's "narrow or unenlightened insistence on traditional doctrines and forms of exposition," and it is this meaning that I assume Mr. Seymour intended to convey.

To begin with, I believe that, through the use of such emotive language, Mr. Seymour fell back on rhetoric where analysis would have been more appropriate. Even then, it is hard to understand the designation of "arid scholasticism" to describe the propagation of the most esteemed values of a responsible and educated body of men. If we join in insisting that religion and individualism are neither anachronistic nor intellectually untenable; if we go on, rather, to describe them as noble doctrines whose ascendancy is the best guaranty of man's freedom and man's selfless dedication to the good, we are hardly guilty of a "narrow or unenlightened insistence on traditional doctrines."

What Mr. Seymour must have meant is that it is inevitable that should the university subscribe to such a theory of education, it would *some day* drift into "arid scholasticism." The presumption, of course, is that the values behind individualism and Christianity will not endure, and that therefore, Yale, stubbornly clinging to an outworn creed, would one day find itself a desert inhabited by deadened and spiritless intellectual prostitutes.

This is a crucial point. It is, moreover, the most frequently cited defense of *laissez-faire* education. If we were to adhere to a formula of education such as yours, the argument runs, wouldn't progress halt? Wouldn't we still be teaching Copernicus, fundamentalism, and divine right of kings, instead of Galileo, evolution, and republicanism?

To explore the charge calls for a preliminary distinction between *refining* a given set of values, and *displacing* them altogether in favor of others. It is true that a college must, ultimately, be flexible enough to do both.

Now, I see no problem as regards *refining* our values, modifying them, and reinterpreting them, under the educational philosophy I envision. There is great and decisive freedom to be found within the sense-making limits of orthodoxy. Free enterprise can and should be examined, criticized, and fashioned from the heart of an institution nevertheless dedicated, until something better comes along, to preserving its general outline. Similarly, no one can criticize a Christian whose allegiance and devotion to his faith lead him to criticize and to seek to reform the temporal, ritualistic, or even organic inadequacies of his religion.

The critics of any orthodoxy, of value inculcation, are quick to presuppose a rigid, insensitive administration as a necessary feature of such an institution. I fail to see why this assumption should be valid, just as I fail to see why there is reason to believe that the wide powers conferred by the Constitution on the Congress of the United States will inevitably be misused. Ultimately we are all at the mercy of the collective action of men. There is no alternative to faith that men will act reasonably. If pessimism about this prevailed, societal life would be impossible.

It is to be borne constantly in mind that the alumni of a private educational institution are the ultimate overseers of university policy. They can be presumed sufficiently human, sufficiently sensitive to new experience and changing situations, to move along, if circumstance warrants, to "new ideas," even if this means the complete displacement of previously cherished values. In fact, to intimate otherwise, to predict a rigidity of ideas in face of overwhelming contradictory evidence, is to gainsay in the most dramatic sense the validity of democracy. For if we cannot rely on the elite among our citizenry—the beneficiaries of higher education—to accommodate newly perceived truth and to adjust their thinking and acts correspondingly, there is little to be said for conferring on the people at large the reins of our destiny.

But who will advance these new ideas if the faculty is constrained to teach existing ones? Who will unearth them? This raises the question of *who will do research*, while our concern here is with the question of *who will do the teaching*. The tradition that the same men do both bears reexamination, and is discussed below. But we can rest confident that the governing body of an educational institution composed, we presume, of sensitive men of good faith, will honestly confront new experience as it is unearthed, wherever it is unearthed, and will be always prepared to jettison traditional ideas if the situation warrants.

President Seymour's most frequently quoted statement is "We shall seek the truth and endure the consequences." Unimaginable though the advent of such a truth is, I too should be willing to face the consequences of new experience that, for example, rendered individualism infeasible. *But this hasn't yet happened.*

In the meanwhile, at any given time, society is confronted with value alternatives, as with atheism versus faith, collectivism versus individualism. One value or the other, after thoughtful examination, ought to be embraced.

The wife of a prominent professor at Yale once told me that "Yale ought to have a course on Communism, and this course," she added earnestly, "should be taught by a man who is neither pro-Communist nor anti-Communist." Her thinking points up vividly, it strikes me, Richard Weaver's definition of a "liberal" as "someone who doubts his premises even while he is acting upon them." Even President Seymour has written that skepticism has utility *only* when it leads to conviction. Thus, a responsible, reflective man must, soon in life, cast his lot with the Communists or against them. He may change, to be sure; but at any given moment, if he and others like him embrace certain values, as civilized men who recognize that they are "involved in mankind," they must cherish and advance them with fervor. Their values ought to be advanced by individual and collective action in the pulpit and in the marketplace, on the street corner and in the living room, in the caucus chamber and in the legislature. And they ought to be advanced in the classroom.

"A major obligation [of the educator] is to train our youth in the understanding and practice of American democracy whether in the classroom or in our campus life," Mr. Seymour told a newspaper reporter.[9] Mr. Seymour therefore believes the classroom to be an appropriate stage for value inculcation.

In an absolute frame of reference, can the wrong value be embraced? Unquestionably. Wrong values have been embraced in the past by men of profound vision and noble intent. It will happen again. But hazard of error cannot be used as an argument against thoughtful action. Great solace, too, should come from the knowledge that the incidence of error should diminish all over the world as the wisest men, i.e., the educators, we presume, adopt an aggressive attitude in propagating the values toward the selection of which they bring to bear the distilled power of trained minds and the noblest impulses of expansive hearts. H. G. Wells has written that "human history becomes more and more a race between education and catastrophe." But Justice Robert Jackson showed greater insight when he blasted indiscriminate education by pointing out that "It is one of the paradoxes of our time that modern society needs to fear...only the educated man." Aristotle implied the same thing a long time ago when he wrote, "To *know* does little, or even nothing, for virtue." It is what a man is impelled to do with his knowledge that justifies or indicts his education.

To continue with President Seymour's baccalaureate address:

> Even more disastrous [than an arid scholasticism] would be the failure of the university to train the student to form convictions reached by his own effort of reason. It is our function to put him in a position where he must learn to make up his mind. . . . In the formation of convictions there is greater danger in the menace of credulity than there is in agnosticism. . . . An important aspect of the university function is to train its students in the habit of skepticism. . . . "Who never doubted never half believed.". . . The road to settled conviction can never be discovered by attempting to by-pass around doubts.

I have no quarrel with Mr. Seymour with respect to the foregoing, although I should be perhaps less categorical—enough so, for example, to allow me to express preference for a credulous Democrat over a profoundly convinced Communist.

But our discussion must center around Mr. Seymour's intimations that value inculcation would breed unthinking, unreasoning, credulous disciples. I do not see why this should be the case. An indispensable part of education is training in how to think, how to analyze. This thinking, this analyzing, must unquestionably be brought to bear on the values the university espouses. We can surely assume that the faculty will have gone through similar reasonings and analyses in the course of arriving at the values the university will try to foster. They should surely be competent to oversee and to insure exhaustive examination of these values by their students.

It is the attitude of the teacher that is apparently in question. Mr. Seymour is implying that if, let us say, all the teachers of economics side with capitalism against socialism, the student cannot arrive at any profound, reasoned convictions of his own—he simply adopts the teacher's point of view as unquestionable dogma.

The president cannot have thought through the implications of his assertions and their irreconcilability with the university policy which he has sanctioned.

For example: Yale offers only *one* course in basic sociology. For years it was taught by a virulently anti-religious professor. He did not alternate with a colleague sympathetic to religion. As is customary, he taught the course from beginning to end. It was all the sociology hundreds of students ever received at Yale.

Yale offers only one course in Comparative Economic Systems. It is taught by a collectivist. It is the only course in economic theory, aside from the basic course, which is also collectivistic, to which many students are exposed.

But President Seymour did nothing about the monolithic prejudices of these courses. To be true to his platform, he should not have tolerated them because their one-sided pleading would lead to "unreasoned credulity" as to the merits of secularism and collectivism. And yet he did tolerate them. It must be that he tolerated them because he was confident that the student would exercise some discretion, some independence of thought.

So, I insist, could and would a student remain the final arbiter under the system I propose. Under no circumstances should he be shielded from the thought and writings of men with different values; but the professor should do his earnest and intellectual best to expose the shortcomings and fallacies of such value judgments. This cannot be too disturbing a suggestion to Mr. Seymour, who, in answer to the question put to him in the spring of 1950 by a reporter from the *New Haven Register,* "What is the most effective way of fighting Communism on the college level?" answered, "I am sure that Communist ideas ought not to be outlawed from college teaching. Rather they should be analyzed, discussed and *deflated*" (italics added).

That's all I am talking about. President Seymour is not, as we can see, disturbed at the prospect of asking his faculty to "deflate" Communism. This must be because he considers Communism to be evil. If he considers socialism or atheism to be evil, I shall never be able to understand why he should have caviled at instructing his faculty on these issues as well.

I cannot sufficiently stress the responsibility of the faculty to insist upon student examination of other and even unfriendly creeds; but notwithstanding, again I find myself in accord with Mr. Seymour when he says: "In the intellectual and in the moral, our teachers cannot be either subservient or neutral."[10] I hasten to dissociate myself from the school of thought, largely staffed by conservatives, that believes teachers ought to be "at all times neutral." Where values are concerned, effective teaching is difficult and stilted, if not impossible, in the context of neutrality; and further, I believe such a policy to be a lazy denial of educational responsibility.

I believe, therefore, that the attitude of the teacher ought to reveal itself, and that, assuming the overseers of the university in question to have embraced democracy, individualism, and religion, the attitudes of the faculty ought to conform to the university's. Consequently, while reading and studying Marx or Hitler, Laski or the Webbs, Huxley or Dewey, I should expect the teacher, whose competence, intelligence, and profundity I take for granted, to "deflate" the arguments advanced; similarly, I should expect an institution whose alumni sought to promulgate different values to seek out a competent faculty whose concern would be to deflate Locke and Jefferson, Smith and Ricardo, Jesus and Paul.

Ultimately, of course, the student must decide for himself. If he chooses to repudiate the values of his instructor, he is free—and ought to be free—to do so. No coercion of any sort, whether through low examination grades, ridicule, or academic bullying, would be tolerable. The teacher must rest his case after he has done his best to show why one value is better than another. He can do no more. The institution can do no more. Neither should try to do more. Both have discharged their responsibilities to steer the student toward the truth as they see it. But can they do less than that?

8. THE HOAX OF ACADEMIC FREEDOM

I have left for the last a direct examination of the term "academic freedom," that handy slogan that is constantly wielded to bludgeon into impotence numberless citizens who waste away with frustration as they view in their children and in their children's children the results of *laissez-faire* education. We must determine whether freedom is violated by the administration of a private educational institution which insists upon a value orthodoxy.

The hoax to which so many of us have succumbed can only be understood after a fastidious analysis of the functions of the scholar. *We must bear in mind that the scholar has had not one but two functions, and that, further, they are not inherently related.* These pursuits are (1) scholarship, and (2) teaching. They are related solely by convenience, by tradition, and by economic exigency. This would seem clear: a man gifted in research in genetics is not thereby gifted in the art of *transmitting* to the pupil his knowledge of biology. In fact, this is periodically brought to mind in widespread student resentment at the retention by many universities of scholars who, while often distinguished in research, are miserably inept in teaching.

However, since the scholar, like his fellow man, must earn his keep, tradition has it that in the afternoon he will utilize the university's libraries and laboratories, generally to satisfy his own desires, while in the morning he will use the classrooms to satisfy other people's desires. In short, the student pays not only for the scholar's morning work, of which the student is properly the direct beneficiary, but also, in effect, for his afternoon work, which may concern or interest the student not at all.

Now, the implications of this double role are manifold. We have in focus the methodological confusion that impedes purposive discussion of "academic freedom"; for in today's controversy, the critic is taking exception to *unlicensed teaching*, while the professors are actually basing their case on the rights of *unlicensed personal scholarship*. And while the two sides are constantly at loggerheads, they should not be at all, for both are right.

Let us remember that it is *the scholars* who have systematized the modern conception of academic freedom. They have constructed an appealing and compact philosophical package, labeled it "truth," and tossed it for enshrinement to that undiscriminating fellow, the liberal. It is understandable that the modern rationale of "academic freedom" originated with and is a product of the scholar. To the pure scholar, the bread of life is research, theory, creation. It is horrifying to him—as it ought to be to anyone who respects the individual—that anyone other than himself should seek to prescribe the method or the orientation or the findings of his research—except, of course, in those cases where he is hired to perform a specific service.

His position here is certainly unassailable.* A researcher ought to be free to seek out his own conclusions, to make his own

---

* I do not imply, of course, that scholars are always successful in shedding their own prejudices when they embark upon research projects. Nor do I believe that the researcher's autonomy in any way implies a duty on the part of other persons to subsidize him in his work. This I shall elaborate later.

generalizations on the basis of his discoveries. To think otherwise is, at best, to think awkwardly. It is a self-contained paradox to endow a researcher or a research organization with funds and to assert simultaneously what shall come out of the investigations for which the funds are to be used. For obviously, under such a formula, there is no reason for the investigation to be undertaken at all.

But, legend notwithstanding, the proverbial long-haired professor can, at the margin, take stock of the facts of life, and these are that *research* is in large part subsidized by the consumers of *teaching*. Therefore, cannily, he distends the protective cloak of research to include his activities as a *teacher*, thereby insuring to himself license in the laboratory, which is right and proper, and license in the classroom, which is wrong and improper.

The educational overseer—the father who sends his son to school, or the trustee who directs the policy of the school—is violating no freedom I know of if he insists, let us say, that individualism instead of collectivism be inculcated in the school. Rather, he is asserting his own freedom. For if the educational overseer, in the exercise of his freedom, espouses a set of values, his is the inescapable duty and privilege to give impetus to these values in the classroom* just as he does, from time to time, in the polling booth.

But, it will be objected, if no one supports the teacher of socialism, he will be out of a job; hence, in effect, will he not have

---

* In the case of the father, such supervision is imperative if he acknowledges responsibility for the education of his son. It is impractical for the parent to administer education himself; in the circumstances, he delegates his responsibility to someone else, and pays him for services rendered. He cannot delegate the responsibility to educate his son to someone he considers unqualified by reason of bad judgment or incompetence or false values. The parent is thus himself the indirect consumer of teaching, for it is he who is exchanging his money, which represents his goods and services, in exchange for the teacher's services.

been persecuted for his beliefs? Yes. Similarly, if no one votes for an incumbent, he too will be out of a job. He, too, in the realistic analysis, will have been persecuted for his beliefs. In a democracy it is proper that, in this sense, he should be. And yet we have affirmed the sanctity of independent research. There is no contradiction here. The researcher must satisfy consumer demands during those hours of his working day during which he earns his income. Research may occupy him as an avocation, as it has so many scholars. More likely, far-sighted individuals will continue to contribute funds to autonomous research. We can assume, or at least we can hope, that there will continue to be "consumers" of "untrammeled research."

Even if this is problematic, it must be affirmed that every citizen in a free economy, no matter the wares that he plies, must defer to the sovereignty of the consumer. It is of the essence of freedom that citizens not be made to pay for what the majority does not want, and there is no exception to this rule that does not entail a surrender of freedom and a substitution of minority for majority rule.

It follows, then, that where the school is concerned, the educational overseer is paying for the transmission of knowledge and values. He is not *necessarily* interested in paying for autonomous research. If he *is* interested in this activity of scholarship, let him endow a research center (and let him not, as a man of intelligence and probity, stipulate what shall be the findings of research not yet undertaken).

I promised in a previous section to discuss the sources of "new ideas" if the college came to insist, as I believe it should, on a value orthodoxy (narrower, that is, than the orthodoxy to which at least Yale already subscribes). To begin with, I assume that new ideas will come in the future, as in the past, from individual research.

Who is going to pay for this research? My answer to this is, in the simplest terms, whoever wants to. Most researchers today work at their research part time. There are, though, a considerable number that work at it full time. These are subsidized, by and large, by research foundations, private corporations, philanthropists, and, in some cases, by the government. Most, I repeat, are part-time researchers whose work is subsidized by the consumers of teaching.

Let us examine the situation of Mr. John Smith, a socialist professor of economics at Yale, and survey his fate under my proposed plan. First of all, let us bar him from teaching because he is inculcating values that the governing board at Yale considers to be against the public welfare. No freedom I know of has yet been violated. We still cling to the belief in this country that, acting in good conscience, we can hire whom we like.

But before Professor Smith is discharged, let us assume that the department chairman calls him up and says: "Look, Smith, you unquestionably know economics and there is much you can teach these students. I don't believe in the values you foster, and neither do the governors of Yale. In the circumstances, we cannot conscientiously allow you to advance these values in our classrooms. But suppose you go on teaching, and you advance not your own, pro-socialist values, but our, pro–free enterprise conclusions. You are well aware, of course, what these are and what is the intellectual justification of them. This way, we can retain you. What about it?"

Now this is an alternative, horrifying as it sounds, that deserves examination. I am opposed to its being offered for reasons that will ensue. But I am not as shocked as a great many people might be, for I see similar situations, many that are applauded, in operation in the civilized world today. The civil service (particularly in England) is an outstanding case in point. Permanent public servants are supposed to help to implement the policies of the legislature, and their personal convictions are, quite properly, deemed utterly irrelevant. Such is the situation, therefore, that a civil service employee in England who considers socialism the most pernicious of all conceivable economic doctrines might find himself, following the dictates of the government in power, drawing up plans for the nationalization of steel. He has been hired to do just this and *no freedom has been abridged so long as he is at liberty to quit his job*.

A more commonplace example can be brought forward as taking place every day in every community. A man may be skilled in masonry but he may intensely dislike working as a mason. He may prefer, let us say, to take pictures. But if no one will hire him to take pictures, and if there are consumers for masonry, he must turn to bricks, even if he is bored by the very thought of it. He must, what is more, even as the civil service worker must, perform his job well. If not, he will be fired.

Therefore, it can be argued that Professor Smith, a socialist teaching individualism, would be under no extraordinary duress. Even if he were enjoined not to publish under his own name the results of his off-hours research on the virtues of socialism (on the grounds that his hypocrisy would then become patent, and his subsequent teaching ineffective), it could be said that he would not be any the worse off than the civil service worker who would be summarily dismissed if he published an indictment of the government in power.

Nevertheless, I should be opposed to this alternative's being given to Professor Smith. I should be opposed because I believe that even though value inculcation is just a part of education, a major portion of which has to do with the relaying of knowledge, method, and so forth, it is such an important part that it must be approached with the greatest sensitivity and delicacy, and with keen and genuine enthusiasm. I have no doubt that just as there exist debaters who can uphold a resolution against which they have strong feelings and do it with the most convincing finesse and ardor, there must be many teachers who can do the same.

Still and all, the knowledge of it would make me restless and unhappy, and I would advise against it.

Professor Smith is, then, relieved of his teaching duties.

His first recourse, I should think, would be to seek employment at a college that was interested in propagating socialism. But let us say that all these are already staffed. If this is the case, Mr. Smith is the victim of the kind of world he lives in, of an excess of supply over demand, and his recourse is identical with that of anyone else who plies a trade for which there are, at present, no consumers. He must move to something else until an opening turns up. At any rate, Yale is under no obligation to keep him.

Suppose, better still, that there are *no* consumers for socialist teachers? Professor Smith's fate, then, would be similar to the approaching fate of the Communist teacher. There are no bidders. He must join ranks with the teacher of companionate marriage or of fascism. If the people are to retain their sovereignty, they cannot relinquish their right to impose unemployment upon the trader in commodities or ideas for which there is no market.

No freedom has yet been abridged in the case of Professor Smith. Rather, the freedom of the consumer has been upheld.

On the other hand, suppose a foundation, or an individual, decides to subsidize Professor Smith in his research. Any number of motives might underlie such a decision. Perhaps the donor feels that as a result of the professor's criticisms, some hitherto unanalyzed shortcomings of capitalism will be exposed, and that appropriate modifications can then be made. Or maybe a foundation will feel that further research and discovery by Professor Smith will make socialism a demonstrably better system than capitalism to live under. Either way, anyone is at liberty for any reason he likes to subsidize Mr. Smith. I repeat that in most situations only pennywise thinking and inherent dishonesty would lead to a prescription by the subsidizer as to the outcome of research. This would be tantamount to a cigarette company's granting money for research into cancer, with the stipulation that it shall not be discovered that tobacco is in any way conducive to the spread of the disease.

But if Professor Smith found no takers whatsoever, he too would have to turn to masonry and take pictures in his spare time.

Now if the governors of Yale determined to maintain a full- or part-time research center for scholars for whose teaching there were no consumers, I should find this a reasonable decision. I should insist, on the other hand, that separate books be maintained by the Yale research center, so that a contributor to Yale should be given the clear option of subsidizing the teaching part of the University or the independent research section. It is possible that the trustees would refuse the University's facilities to some researchers for a number of reasons, but the merits of each case should be given *ad hoc* attention.

One thing is clear: it is time that honest and discerning scholars cease to manipulate the term academic freedom for their own ends and in such fashion as to deny the rights of individuals. For in the last analysis, academic freedom must mean the freedom of men and women to supervise the educational activities and aims of the schools they oversee and support.

Chapter Five

THE PROBLEM OF THE ALUMNUS

Small wonder that educators, looking at what men choose for themselves and the values they honor in the middle of the century, are asking as never before: "What do we honor and nourish in our schools and colleges?" "What chance do the highest values have there for adequate study or expression?" They know how vital colleges and universities are in giving leading ideas to our national life—all down the line. They know that education is eventually a kind of dynamite. They have clearly seen that "education is the most Fascist aspect of the Fascist Revolution, the most Communist feature of the Communist Revolution, and the most Nazi expression of the National Socialist Revolution." They now realize with new force that "the moral, intellectual, and spiritual reformation for which the world waits depends, then, upon true and deeply held convictions about the nature of man, the ends of life, the purposes of the state, and the order of goods." They wonder if higher education has given decent room to the beliefs that have fostered the great convictions of the Western world.

—*Howard Lowry*, The Mind's Adventure[1]

T he academic community has no illusions about its importance. It may be that this self-recognition is in part responsible for the willingness of so many men and women to suffer the vicissitudes of an incredibly capricious and inequitable pay-scale. There is some reason for the dedication of the educator; primarily, it must stem from his devotion to his work. But in some measure, he is unquestionably fortified by the knowledge that despite the trials and penury of his existence, he is shaping, more directly than the members of any other profession, the destiny of the world.

The educator is the last to underestimate the importance of his work, and he is not reluctant to rhapsodize, from time to time, on his influence. President Griswold has written:

> What happens at Yale and the small company of American, British and European universities that share a historic role with her will determine the whole course of education in those countries during the next half century; and it is not too much to expect that the character of their political and social institutions will reflect the character of their schools and universities.[2]

Mr. Griswold was not exaggerating. It dazzles the imagination to attempt to calculate the national and international influence that Yale alone has exerted even in the past half century. To illustrate this more meaningfully than could be done by reciting a list of prominent statesmen, politicians, authors, industrialists, and barristers who spent four or more years in New Haven, we can point to the single year 1936—at which time the presidents of fifty American colleges and universities were graduates of Yale, and 2,600 alumni were engaged in educational work.[3] There is no more graphic indication of the extent of Yale's *influence*. Add to Yale that "small company of American, British and European universities," in fact add to Yale the entire complex of the Western world's educational institutions, and you have in your grasp the nerve center of civilization.

It is the guardians of this sustaining core of civilization that have, in so many cases, abdicated their responsibility to mankind. And what is more depressing, they have painted their surrender with flamboyant words and systematic sophistry in their efforts to persuade us that far better things are really in store for the world by virtue of their inactivity.

What has happened, in effect, is that the educators of the democracies have neglected to exploit the value-educability of man. The results of *laissez-faire* education were starkly exposed two decades ago by a wise old man, Albert Jay Nock:

> Nature takes her own time, sometimes a long time, about exacting her penalty—but exact it in the end she always does, and to the last penny. It would appear, then, that a society which takes no account of the educable person, makes no place for him, does nothing with him, is taking a considerable risk; so considerable that in the whole course of human experience, as far as our records go, no society ever yet has taken it without coming to great disaster.[4]

I have attempted to establish a number of points specifically relating to Yale and probably applicable to hundreds of schools like her, and to expose, as I understand them, several of the assumptions that underlie *laissez-faire* education. I have said:

1. The responsibility to govern Yale falls ultimately on the shoulders of her alumni.

2. Yale already subscribes to a value orthodoxy.

3. At any given time, a responsible individual must embrace those values he considers to be truth or else those values he deems closest to the truth.

4. Truth will not of itself dispel error; therefore truth must be championed and promulgated on every level and at every opportunity.

5. A value orthodoxy in an educational institution need not lead to inflexibility in the face of "new experience."

6. A value orthodoxy in an educational institution need not in any circumstances induce credulity in the student, nor deny the value of skepticism as a first step to conviction.

7. Freedom is in no way violated by an educational overseer's insistence that the teacher he employs hold a given set of values.

My final point is that alumni and friends cannot support an institution that encourages values they consider inimical to the public welfare if they wish to be honest in their convictions and faithful to the democratic tradition.

Some months ago I received an appeal for funds from the Yale Club Scholarship Committee of New York. The letter featured one sentence, italicized and in bold type, which best illustrates my concern: *"We are confronted with an opportunity actually to invest in future Yale men and in the future leaders of this country."*

That is my point. Preliminary to endowing such future leaders of this country *we have some obligation to speculate as to the direction in which they will lead us.**

---

* A recent article about another private educational institution, in *Holiday* (May 1951), is illustrative: "A wistful respect for the unorthodox is ingrained in the Vassar mentality. . . . The effect of this training is to make the Vassar student, by the time she has reached her junior year, look back upon her freshman self with pity and amazement. When you talk to her about her life in college, you will find that she sees it as a series of before and after snapshots: 'When I came to Vassar, I thought like Mother and Daddy. I was

I shall be plainer and more specific. If the majority of Yale graduates believe in spiritual values and in individualism, they cannot contribute to Yale so long as she continues in whole or in part to foster contrary values. I go even farther. If the majority of Yale's governing body is elected to narrow the existing orthodoxy along the lines I have sketched, I should not expect that the minority of the alumni who believe atheism and socialism to be values superior to religion and capitalism could in good conscience continue to support Yale.* Let me make a final qualification: the minority could and should continue to contribute if they believed the values at stake were not important. But no one not apathetic to the value issues of the day, I repeat, can in good conscience contribute to the ascendancy of ideas he considers destructive of the best in civilization. To do so is to be guilty of supine and unthinking fatalism of the sort that is the surest poison of democracy and the final abnegation of man's autonomy.

Conversely, should the administration of Yale recast her educational attitude and make a conscientious effort to imbue her students with those values that her educational overseers cherish, she ought never to want for support. She ought never to be distracted from her noble purpose by concern over the mechanics of

---

conservative in my politics.' . . . With few exceptions the trend is from the conservative to the liberal, from the orthodox to the heterodox." Typically, the author of this article, while extensively describing and analyzing Vassar education and young alumni attitudes, never inquires whether Mother and Daddy, whose support keeps the college operating, approve of the trend from the conservative to the "liberal," from God and man to nature and the state.

* Minority discontinuance of support is no disparagement of majoritarianism; the minority would have to accede to the wishes of the majority in respect of the values to be taught at Yale, but they would no more be impelled to *contribute* to Yale than a defeated Republican would feel he had to donate funds to the Democratic Party.

operation. Her alumni could not afford not to support to the limit of their resources an institution of demonstrated efficacy, devoted to the preservation of our civilization.

The chairman of the Yale Alumni Fund, Mr. George Herbert Walker Jr., gave the administration of Yale a stern warning at Alumni Day, in February 1951, in the presence of over a thousand graduates. Whether his message impressed an administration grown confident of the malleability of the alumni remains to be seen. Mr. Walker said,

> I believe Yale alumni are looking for—and will respond whole-heartedly to—a re-emphasis of the spiritual and moral values that 250 years ago led to the founding of this University. . . . What is desperately needed? Strong moral and spiritual leadership and a constant reaffirmation of fundamental and eternal values. . . . I say to you that an enlightened University with a high purpose and with the will, the courage, and the conviction *to imbue her students with that same purpose* will evoke the overwhelming support of a militant alumni. . . . To fortify Yale adequately in future years, we must all feel a greater loyalty—*and in my opinion only a dedication by the University to developing the highest values in the characters of men will evoke that loyalty* [italics added].

I do not intend to hazard what I believe to be the validity of my case by proposing a specific formula for Yale and for similar universities to follow. I do believe in more decisive action than, for example, is recommended by such able and learned bewailers of the state of religion in the college scene as Howard Lowry, Merrimon Cuninggim, and Sir Walter Moberly.[5] These men believe action of the sort I advocate to be "spurious remedies toward a spurious unity." I respect these men, but I also note that nothing much has come or in my opinion will come from their forbearance; it may be that I have greater faith in the power of man to shape his own future—a faith perhaps born of youthful and inexperienced brashness, but then again, perhaps not.

I shall not say, then, what specific professors should be discharged, but I will say some ought to be discharged. I shall not indicate what I consider to be the dividing line that separates the collectivist from the individualist, but I will say that such a dividing line ought, thoughtfully and flexibly, to be drawn. I will not suggest the manner in which the alumni ought to be consulted and polled on this issue, but I will say that they ought to be, and soon, and that the whole structure of Yale's relationship to her alumni, as has been previously indicated, ought to be reexamined.

Far wiser and more experienced men can train their minds to such problems. I should be satisfied if they feel impelled to do so, and I should be confident that the job would be well done.

Appendix A

Religion and Sociology

༚

In condensing some of the scholarly observations on religion in this field, I shall, in most cases, lump together under "sociology," both sociology and cultural anthropology. I do so confident that for the purposes of this discussion, the merger is warranted. I add that in this section and in ensuing notes on philosophy and psychology, I make no claim whatever to profound knowledge or insight into the bearing of religion on the social sciences. Nor should these passages imply a blind reliance on authority. I hope, simply, to relay some scholarly observations on the alleged irreconcilability of social science and religion, and on textbook treatment of religion.

As a subject of study, sociology began to flourish contemporaneously with Darwinism. At the end of the century, the field had definitely established itself as a major area of study, and today the sociology department holds forth as one of the largest in any college or university.

In a review of college readings in sociology,[1] Professor Robert L. Sutherland points out the well-known emotional drive that has conditioned and continues to condition the otherwise objective outlook of so many social scientists: "The desire of these early sociologists to become 'scientific' led many of them to shy so far away from anything moralistic or theological as to confuse agnosticism in religion with scientific method in sociology."[2]

Elsewhere, Sutherland states,

> Perversity of youth is not the real reason why sociology some-
> times forgets its debt to religion. More to the point is the fact
> that the fledgling entered the academic world at a time when
> the college atmosphere was distinctly biased: biased in favor of
> science. Sociology's lusty growth...occurred during the period
> when laboratories and scientists were the local deities, if not the
> supreme being, in academic life.[3]

Of the thirty-odd widely used source books in sociology, Professor Sutherland found that "one or two of the texts examined
had an outright 'sidecracking' manner; more gave religion the
silent treatment; and still more used the scientific treatment!"[4]
Professor Margaret Mead, in her treatise on cultural anthropology, does not deal with specific deficiencies in specific books, but
does treat of the general pitfalls of textbook writers in their treatment of religion, emphasizing how these difficulties are com-
pounded by unimaginative and hostile lecture presentations.

As an example of the sarcasm with which so many sociologists deal with religion, if they deal with it at all, Professor Sutherland points out the treatment that Willard gives to funerals.[5]

> The larger group always more or less assumes control of the situ-
> ation created by death. The ritual which it imposes is unyielding
> and complete in every detail: the group does not know how to
> adapt its ritual and usually ends by preaching the dissenter into
> heaven unless he has taken unusual precautions against this anti-
> climax to his life.

Miss Mead points out that even where this is not the intention of the instructor, an excessively clinical inspection of the

religion of primitive societies, and comparisons with modern religion drawn with the same detachment and aloofness that is brought to bear on an examination of other cultural traits, can lead the student to believe that his own religion is "to be equated, and so demoted, to the realm of 'primitive superstition.'"[6] In fact,

> The older evolutionary view of the nineteenth century anthropologists, which regarded primitive religions as stages towards the development of our own higher forms of monotheism and ethics, in a sense did more to support an interest in and respect for contemporary religions than does a partial application of the modern form of anthropological approach which regards primitive societies as contemporary rather than vestigial, and current primitive forms of religion as functionally analogous to current forms of great religions. However, the chance of the student making such an inference is to be regarded as one of the hazards of bad and inexperienced teaching rather than as a necessary consequence of the anthropological approach.

Elsewhere, she presses her analysis still further:

> When religion is so used by an instructor without feeling or interest for contemporary religious forms, or sympathy with religious experience, the effect may be to alienate the student—as a student—from further interest in religion.[7] [It is my contention, as I explained in the first section of this book, that both this cause and this result are discernible at Yale.]

Continuing, to point out that extensive material on religion in textbooks does not necessarily breed understanding or sympathy with religion, Miss Mead states,

If the instructor is uninterested, the mere bulk of description on religious behavior in studies of primitive societies is not in itself sufficient to assure much interest on the part of the student.[8]

In conclusion, Miss Mead charges a number of her professional colleagues with using a superficial and obsolete approach:

> ...the student of anthropology is confronted with a mass of detailed, often bizarre, rich description of religious behavior, which differs strikingly from anything which he has experienced in his own culture. When there is any theoretical discussion it is oriented to preoccupations which are triply out of date, in terms of twentieth-century religious thought, current psychological thought, and current anthropological interests. This is very likely to result in an alienation of the students' interest in religion as a subject for study, an alienation which is of course intensified by the secularization of psychology and sociology. While it is a usual method of teaching primitive kinship to focus the students' attention on our own kinship system, and to compare primitive economic and political forms with our own, there is a very slight attempt to get students to examine and value our contemporary religious forms.[9]

Professor Sutherland believes that the value and relevance of religion are slowly impressing themselves on many important sociologists, as for example,

> ...Apart from its dynamic possibilities for good, then, religion itself may create problems of social policy. Sociologically, we are vitally interested in the effect of religion on the individual's social conduct and welfare.[10]

Religion takes such varied forms that it is to be expected that there will always be controversy as to its origin as a major source of human behavior. There is much greater unanimity as to the present function of religion on the modern social level. In it we find the attainment of cosmic security, motivation for benevolent service, authority for practices and beliefs, means of bringing an end to personal conflict, and the providing of compensations in careers that seem relatively empty.[11]

The mystic identification with powers outside oneself may off-set or balance the disappointments, heartaches, and pain of daily living, in which half measures, compromises, and self-denial are common. It is easy for the critic of religion to point out that this sort of thing is "an escape from reality," a mass neurosis, or a mere "illusion," as Sigmund Freud ... argued. But this will hardly do. It is our contention that cultural reality is not something material nor made up out of biological reactions to food, drink, and sexual objects. It is at heart mental and psychological. It is a question of beliefs, attitudes, ideas, meanings. It exists in the minds of men. One cannot, therefore, with Freud blandly dismiss religious experiences as an unfortunate illusion without at the same time raising the problem as to whether art, philosophy, and most of the fundamentals of social organization and family life are not likewise "illusions."[12]

Professor Sutherland summarizes his survey by stating that while

sociology texts ... are not written with the student's own development in mind ... nevertheless students now find that sociology texts neither ignore nor discredit religion. Rather they make a serious attempt to understand how religion functions in modern life.... Some [sociologists] will continue to deal with religion anthropologically; some will continue to be fascinated by emotional excesses in religious group activities; others will count religion as though numbers of churches and members were significant; others will trace the churches' adjustment to ecological change. But increasingly sociologists are not limited to these approaches. They are finding themselves free to deal with the basic elements of religious experience as they become a part of and condition all experience in the lives of individuals.[13]

I detect in Professor Sutherland's analysis, and in the writings of a goodly number of current sociological writers "sympathetic" to religion, a lingering resistance to recognizing a personal God of the nature that a Christian worships. It is altogether a different matter to analyze and appreciate religion as a cultural phenomenon or a psychological necessity than it is to approach it with the faith and attitude of a believer. The evidences to which Professor Sutherland directs attention, not to speak of his own sympathies, augur well; but it would occur to the average Christian that there is yet much to be desired even from such marginal allies as Read Bain. Writing in *Trends in American Sociology* (in 1929), he states that the "almost non-existent, or negative interest of sociologists in religion and ethics will be replaced by a vital and fruitful revival. This will sound like scientific heresy to many, but I trust the future will justify it." He continues, however, almost as if he could not risk his professional reputation by an implied alliance with Christianity, to contemn the bases of most modern religions:

And it is... evident that supernaturalistic, other worldly conceptions of religion are being and will increasingly be replaced by naturalistic, this-worldly conceptions.... The values that were formerly related to hypothetical gods and heavens and hells and supernatural agencies must be integrated with the validated findings of science. We know enough about social psychology of conversions, visions, intuitions, morals, suggestions, and repressions, to interpret "religious experience" in naturalistic terms. So the relation of sociology to religion will be in the nature of a redefinition and revaluation of values.[14]

But the object of our investigation here, as has been stated, is to ascertain whether or not competence in the fields of sociology and anthropology presupposes skepticism toward a belief in God. We are at least entitled, on the basis of the foregoing, to conclude that neither the silent treatment nor the tongue-in-cheek treatment toward religion is appropriate, or even academically justified, either in textbooks or in classroom presentations. On this score alone, Yale, at least, is guilty for reasons cited in the first section of this book.

The question arises whether or not the objective sociologists can entertain an active belief in a personal God without losing academic caste. The answer again seems to be that he can. There are no inherent contradictions between sociology and religion. To mention just one sociologist who firmly believes in a personal God and needs bow to none of his colleagues in mastery of the field, N. S. Timasheff of Fordham, formerly of Harvard, stands out. Timasheff is a member of the Russian Orthodox Church. There is cause to remark upon Timasheff's religious affiliations, since the Russian church is, in dogma, more exacting than most other Christian religions. And this notwithstanding, he has scaled the heights of his profession without finding belief in God and objectivity in sociology in any way internecine.

Sample Communications
Relating to the Kennedy Controversy

Published by the Yale Daily News

ॐ

March 11, 1949
To the Chairman of the NEWS:

I should like to take issue with the views in the NEWS editorial concerning Professor Kennedy's treatment of religion. Granted that Professor Kennedy's flippant treatment of many people's sincere beliefs may not be in the best of taste, I feel that from an academic point of view it is entirely justified. The editorial states that "It is the duty of the anthropologist to deal dispassionately with religion as a societal factor of major importance." One aspect of this is obviously the question of why people believe in religion. If it is true, as Professor Kennedy maintains, that religion is essentially an irrational and unscientific phenomenon, then the recognition of this fact is a necessary prerequisite of any attempt to explain the psychological causes of religious belief. Professor Kennedy never denies the existence of God; he merely attempts to show the irrationality of belief in God, since if the existence of God can be scientifically demonstrated, it is obviously absurd to look for explanations in terms of ghost fear and father complexes.

   The quotations from Mr. Kennedy's lectures given in the editorial are all either attempts to show the irrationality (not necessarily the falsity as judged by standards of faith and intuition) of certain religious beliefs, or statements of the relationship between primitive and modern religion. The latter are obviously part of the legitimate subject matter of sociology, and I have demonstrated the importance of the former in any adequate treatment of the sociological aspects of religion. The opinions which Professor Kennedy expresses may or may not be correct, they may or may not be expressed in the manner most appropriate to so serious a subject, but as long as they represent his honest convictions and those of other reputable sociologists, it would be absurd to ask him to suppress them. To the extent that his remarks are mere witticisms directed at aspects of religion which no one nowadays takes seriously, they may be enjoyed and then forgotten; to the extent that they represent genuine criticisms of modern religion, they deserve consideration by all believers. If anyone's faith is so shallow as to be destroyed by Mr. Kennedy's superficial satires, it is hardly likely to be a faith worth keeping.

WINFRED F. HILL, 1950

March 11, 1949
To the Chairman of the NEWS:

I'd like to speak out for the large number of Sociology 10 alumni who completely endorse yesterday's editorial. . . .

Leaving aside the matter of the questionable good taste of many of Mr. Kennedy's remarks I should like to discuss only his method of dealing with the subject of religion.

I personally have no objection to any honest attack on religion from a lecture platform, but I do object to the use of propaganda techniques. By playing on the emotions instinctively one wants to be associated with something which is being subjected to ridicule.

Kennedy apparently makes his point without having to rely on naked facts and cogent argument. It is my contention—and I have seen this influence at work—that Kennedy's technique does not serve to free the student's mind from boogeymen, but rather serves to rob many students of the use of rational thinking in coming to extraordinarily important decisions concerning their own spiritual lives.

Defenses of Kennedy to the effect that a strong belief will not bow to his snipings are beside the point. It is the man who is worried about religion who deserves fair tactics. At the age when most people are exposed to his course, they are often reexamining their own religious notions. It is right that they should hear a variety of viewpoints honestly expressed. They are being cheated, however, if they are thrown off balance emotionally by a bombardment of snide remarks from the lecture platform, especially when they are made under the guise of scientific revelation.

In its editorial, the NEWS has done the undergraduate body and Mr. Kennedy a great service. Students are liable to be lulled by a smooth amusing line, and a teacher by its success as measured in laughter and applause. Honest criticism of a professor's teaching methods is salutary and does not in any way justify a hysterical hoisting of the banners of Academic Freedom.

T. J. KENDALL

❧

March 10, 1949
To the Chairman of the NEWS:

At this time when there is a tendency to be intolerant of opinions with which we don't happen to agree, it is vital that we take pains to safeguard the free exchange of ideas. If certain teachers provoke some students to reexamine their beliefs, if some professors manage to penetrate the intellectual smugness of most of us, they are furthering the objective of a college education: the cultivation of a spirit of tolerance, a "receptiveness" towards new ideas.

The ghost-fear or dream theory of the origin of religion presented in Sociology 10 is good sociology in the minds of many. Certainly, whether or not we happen to agree with it, Mr. Kennedy has the right to expound it. And quite naturally he expresses his ideas through his own medium—his personality. Judging from his class response, most of his students find him quite stimulating. The implication of the editorial that Mr. Kennedy subtly insinuates derogatory remarks about religion into his lectures is quite unjust. Following the suggestion of the editorial, he makes his bias explicit and at the same time shows a realization of the limitations of sociology. Thus, in his opening lecture, he said: "Although *sociologists can't disprove* the existence of the soul, they consider it one of the strange phantasies of the human mind." A few lectures later he said: "A scientist (and Mr. Kennedy claims to use the scientific method) isn't an atheist; he's an agnostic. For him the questions of the origin of the universe and of life are unanswerable." Of course, therefore, Mr. Kennedy never makes the statement that God doesn't exist; he states quite explicitly that this question is out of the realm of sociology. . . .

Obviously it is the task of each student to distinguish the objective from the subjective elements of each lecture and to evaluate it for himself. If any student is willing to accept uncritically every opinion and interpretation with which he is confronted, he doesn't deserve to be at Yale.

For the most part, moreover, Kennedy's presentation of what is potentially dull subject matter is sincere, straightforward, amusing, and informative, and always more objective than yesterday's editorial. In my opinion all undergraduates would do well to take his course in basic sociology sometime during their four years at Yale.

WILLIAM J. C. CARLIN, 1950

❦

March 12, 1949
To the Chairman of the NEWS:

I want to congratulate you on today's editorial, "For a Fair Approach"—for the care and restraint which you used in discussing a subject which by its nature will expose you to the abuse of those who will not have read the editorial with the care it deserves, and by those who have never taken a course under Jungle Jim.

You . . . gave him deserved plaudits for conducting an extraordinarily stimulating and entertaining course. But the plain fact remains—and I'm glad someone has finally aired it—that Mr. Kennedy, perhaps unintentionally, uses loaded phrases, insinuation, and ridicule with the net effect that while posing as a scientist, he is dishing out half-truths which a great number of people don't have the background to evaluate.

Mr. Kennedy is perfectly within his rights to attack any institution, and to make his course as funny as he wants. I do, however, question his right to rely on emotional sleight-of-hand in lieu of direct and intelligent discussion.

WILLIAM C. COLTON

❦

To the Chairman of the NEWS:

The editor deserves congratulations for his fine article on Professor Kennedy's teaching procedure. Mr. Kennedy is abusing his position of authority when he weaves violent anti-religious assertions into his discussions of sociological facts. True, those who cannot separate the grain from the chaff may not deserve to be at Yale, yet may there not be some who, accepting Mr. Kennedy's sociological teaching as gospel, also take intensely seriously his statements on religion?

Though his teaching method is an expression of his personality it is not therefore above reproach. Nor does his being "quite stimulating" exempt him from criticism.

I was shocked at Mr. Davie's remark about "standards of journalism." Certainly if any criticism of teaching at Yale is to be voiced, what organization provides a better medium than the NEWS? It is the business of that paper to deal with matters pertinent to the Yale scene and the business of its editor to bring relevant issues into the open.

Finally, I would like to hear an opinion voiced from a member of the Department of Religion. This question is important and should be discussed from various points of view.

DAVID S. STARRING JR., 1950

March 11, 1949
Finally—[Second Editorial in the *Yale Daily News*]

Conscious that a large part of the Yale community may be bored with the whole thing, we are prompted nevertheless to make a few additional comments in regard to the interpretation of Wednesday's editorial "For a Fair Approach." To assert that it is our desire to impose censorship upon Mr. Kennedy is alarmingly ridiculous.*

That Mr. Kennedy performs his job is an undebatable fact. That he could conduct his course as objectively, as provokingly, as scientifically by curbing personal and irrelevant emotional bias on the question of religion is also a fact. We believe that were he to cast aspersions on democracy, on Jews, on freedom of speech, on Negroes, when such aspersions were indirect and impertinent to the course material, he would arouse resentment from unbiased and tolerant men. Why should religion play the underdog?

A large number of communications point out that if a man's religion is so baseless as to be easy bait for Mr. Kennedy's indirect assaults, the religious belief should rightfully be cast aside. For these people we would summon the historical success of the demagogue. The sturdiest beliefs have been cast aside because of the persuasiveness of the orator. It is not our opinion, for example, that the German people are congenitally depraved, violent, rapacious, and anti-Semitic. We believe that for a number of reasons, not the least of which was the compelling character of Nazi oratory, they cast aside moral values and took part in a crusade that led to wholesale human slaughter. Before we go any further, relax: we cite the efficacy of the spoken word, not a comparison between Mr. Kennedy and a Nazi. Most definitely we believe in individual self-reliance, in the responsibility of the undergraduate to separate the wheat from the chaff. We maintain, nevertheless, that since anti-religion is not a necessary element of sociology, obsessive personal bias need not be a necessary element of Sociology 10.

Finally, there is a finer point to be considered. For a large number of students the subject of God is a personal and a sacred thing. Quite naturally their beliefs are constantly challenged by a

---

* My views here are qualified in Chapter Four.

secular environment. Their religion should certainly be intelligently challenged and they should be in a position to cope with such challenges. But by the same laws of good taste, tolerance, and understanding, the laws that prevent us from ripping the veil from a Moslem woman and giving a Bronx cheer, the same laws that restrain you from calling up Mr. Truman to tell him he is a son of a bitch, the same laws that keep you from introducing your roommate as a member of Skull and Bones—so, it would seem, should these laws apply in lecturing to a class, in ridiculing institutions when such ridicule is not necessary to the objectivity of the course.

Philosophy
and Religion

❧

M uch of the antagonism between philosophy and religion
is similar to that described above in connection with sociology and religion. By and large, animosity seems to spring from
the notions that nature and supernature are irreconcilable, and
that man's dependence on the supernatural is restrictive of the
potentialities of man. The antagonism often takes its rise from
sheer ignorance of the metaphysics and meaning of Christianity.

Discussing "Problems of Philosophy," Professor Peter A. Bertocci concludes,

> Accordingly, writers of this outlook [the naturalist] have con-
> centrated on the practical and intellectual disvalues of religion.
> Whatever values might seem to reside in religion have been
> given a surer and "modern" foundation. These men have, how-
> ever, neglected the serious portrayal of religious philosophies
> which have attempted to reinterpret the data of science and reli-
> gion. They have acted on the inarticulate assumption that the
> good which has attended religious belief was an accident rather
> than an essential consequence of true religion. They hold that
> religious beliefs at their best are hardly necessary to effective
> human living and at their worst are morally and intellectually
> vicious. Religious experience has not been denied but it has been

reinterpreted in the light of naturalistic categories.... The present intellectual scene, it may be suggested, is a sad commentary on the theoretical and spiritual problem of our time.[1] [Mr. Bertocci goes on to point out that many theologians and religious persons have been driven, unhappily, to find a "deeper antithesis" between naturalism and religion.]

In dealing with textbooks on the history of philosophy, Professor Robert L. Calhoun begins by insisting that no treatment of philosophy is in any sense comprehensive or even adequate without a full treatment of religion:

> Unlike books on the natural sciences, on economics, or civil government, or on logic or the rudiments of a foreign language, books on the history of philosophy deal with material in which the problems of religious thought are a major and inescapable factor, material to which the religious or anti-religious convictions of the philosophers treated are nearly everywhere relevant. It is not possible for the historian of philosophy, whatever his own predilections, to by-pass the religious aspect of the development of Western thought without giving a seriously defective, not to say distorted and misleading account of what has happened since Thales and his successors restated the problem of understanding man and his world.[2]

Mr. Calhoun finds neutrality and disregard in a few books (e.g., Schwegler and Weber),[3] "active and dogmatic disparagement" in others, e.g.:

> It was only after the French Revolution that he [Spinoza] came into his own.... But by then Christianity had ceased to be a

dominant intellectual force and had become what it is today, a folk-belief.[4]

Mr. Calhoun concludes his review of textbook treatment of religion by saying that

> If the apparent results of this survey are dependable, there is ground for acute dissatisfaction with the treatment of religion in too many of the usable text-books, but also ground for expecting real improvement. The inadequacies found in most of the books examined seem to arise from defective understanding more than from hostility to religion. Superior scholarship and philosophic competence in these books are associated, by and large, with discerning rather than disparaging or uncritical treatment of religion.[5]

It seems almost unnecessary to stress the fact that, even more evidently than in the field of sociology, conversance with philosophy by no means presupposes naturalism or atheism. No man could possibly justify the generalization that either mastery of the history of philosophy or pioneer work in the problems of philosophy requires agnosticism or disparagement of religion. After all, a list of the famous religious philosophers since the beginnings of Christianity would fill most of the pages of a *Who's Who* of the field.

It is at the same time true that the breadth of philosophical inquiry is such as to necessitate a thorough exploration by the student of any number of philosophical conceptions that run counter to religious precepts. But this has little bearing on our thesis; our exclusive concern here is with whether or not philosophical objectivity must go hand in hand with skepticism, and the answer is, clearly, that it need not do so. The naturalists, the logical positivists, the empiricists, the solipsists are all important, and their contributions are important; but these can be explored, explained, and properly analyzed and oriented with a view to meeting their conclusions face to face and refuting them.

Appendix D

Religion and Psychology

༄

The field of psychology, textbook wise, seems to be the most uniformly antagonistic to, or oblivious of, religion. It is even a nose ahead of its cousin, sociology.

Professor Gordon W. Allport's section on psychology in *College Reading*[1] analyzes sixty-four standard works in the field. Fourteen of these, including "some of the most widely used textbooks in psychology," contain no mention whatever of religion:

> A student assigned one of the following [14] textbooks would probably never encounter the word religion in any one of them; certainly he would obtain from them no idea that religion plays any significant part among the motives or interests of mankind.[2]

What is more,

> The most widely used of all, F. L. Ruch's *Psychology and Life*[3] [used in the basic psychology course at Yale in 1949] mentions religion in only one of its pages: "It is interesting to note that when the part of his brain thought by the phrenologists to be the center of religion is stimulated, a man twitches his leg." The jibe is directed not at religion but at phrenology, yet it is perhaps symbolic of a common state of affairs that tens of thousands of

students who make contact with psychology only through a single text find the sole reference to religion buried in a context of absurdity.[4]

Not all the books examined confine themselves to the "silent treatment" where religion is concerned. Some, notably J. F. Brown's *Psychology and the Social Order*,[5] are overtly hostile, and raise the traditional objection that science and religion are not compatible. "While claiming a strict spirit of impartiality," notes Mr. Allport, Mr. Brown writes:

> Natural science and religion cannot be accepted side by side. . . . Metaphysical arguments for the existence of God have all been shown to be invalid by competent philosophers.

"In one and a half pages," Mr. Allport continues,

> the author disposes of all arguments for the existence of God or a soul, and says, "Consequently, we must conclude that there is not the slightest proof either for the existence of God or for the immortality of the soul. . . . Therefore science may just as well take the atheistic position which denies the existence of God and the position which denies the existence of the mind without the body."[6]

Emphasizing the damage that textbooks of this nature can inflict on students, Mr. Allport comments:

> College students are seldom critical enough to resist the lure of an iconoclastic writer provided he calls himself scientific. The tightness of reasoning behind the words is not examined. When an author, presumably an authority, declares religion and science

to be completely incompatible (and the former to be a mere illusion), the student who has been toying with this same oversimplified dichotomy and conclusion is pleased to have his suspicions confirmed. Henceforth he can simply *accept* science and *reject* religion. What could be simpler as a solution of his perplexity?[7]

As a final comment on the treatment of religion in basic college textbooks, and this despite the fact that of the books reviewed by Mr. Allport he had himself written two,[8] he concludes,

> To be more concrete, the historical Christian faith has today and has had throughout the ages a colossal impact upon human personality. Yet no textbook in our list depicts this faith or examines the mental functions that are involved in its widely adapted pattern of affirmations. Some authors, perhaps, take it for granted as the background of our culture, and one, Klein,[9] mentions the merits Christianity has in common with democracy and mental hygiene. But no text in general use presents the pattern as a common and important form of mental organization and aspiration.[10]

The question arises: if there is apparently no altogether suitable textbook, how can a department of psychology cope with the situation? Still further, does not the fact that there is no suitable textbook available indicate that the overwhelming majority of experts in the field do not find religion a relevant subject, or that if they do, it is only to point out its fallacies in the light of psychological advances?

To begin with, while Mr. Allport believes that there are no completely satisfactory texts (as of the date he wrote), he indicates that some are better than others. Deficiencies in the books themselves might be compensated for by the lecturer—if, of course, he is of the persuasion of Mr. Allport. But even surveying only the books Mr. Allport describes, there is a remarkable polarity in outlook between, let us say, J. F. Brown, and D. B. Klein. While Mr. Allport does not end his article with the note of cheery optimism that anticipates improvement in basic texts, it must surely be that adequate textbooks will sooner or later see the light of day.

As to the incompatibility between psychology and religion that the present situation might suggest, again a generalization is groundless. Systematic psychology is a new field and seems to suffer from the same belligerence toward religion that has characterized its sister social sciences in their irrational and thoughtless struggle to "emancipate" themselves. This notwithstanding, there exist even today several scholars of acknowledged eminence who find, we repeat, no stultifying restrictions imposed upon their work by reason of their faith in God. And this list includes Roman Catholics, who accept dogmatic requirements of unusual stringency. A partial list of these and others is Vincent V. Herr, Thomas Verner Moore, Rudolph Allers, and, of course, Gordon W. Allport.

Cuninggim on
Religion at Yale

❧

U nder the chapter heading "Significant Programs,"[1] Professor Cuninggim discusses specific religious programs in
nine colleges and universities. In describing Yale's, he cites the
religious tradition of the University, and quotes Anson Phelps
Stokes, who in 1901 wrote of "The Present Condition of Religious
Life at Yale,"

> The university church, at present worshipping in the Battell
> Chapel, and the Christian Association, with its centre in Dwight
> Hall, are the two most important factors in the student religious
> life. The importance of the former shows that the authorities of
> the university recognize the Christian religion as a powerful fac-
> tor in education; that of the latter is evidence that interest in
> matters religious is strong among the students themselves.[2]

Cuninggim then says, "Though the years have wrought many
changes, Stokes's statement is still substantially true." I have maintained that the statements here are only superficially "substantially
true." In the last analysis, I am interested (and so is Professor Cuninggim) in whether or not the net influence at Yale is religious or
irreligious. Curiously enough, despite Mr. Cuninggim's general
approval above, Yale does not meet the requirements which he

later specifies (Chapter Seventeen) as necessary for an "adequate religious program."

I do not intend to convey that the author of *The College Seeks Religion* gave Yale a clean slate; he did nothing of the sort, but he cited it as a college more hospitable to religion than a great many others. As a student of comparative college religious programs, he is eminently entitled to do this; and since I confine myself to Yale, the only educational institution with which I am well acquainted, he must surely understand if I am less contented than he about the state of affairs. As I have said, our interest should focus not on whether Yale is better or worse than other colleges, nor on whether it is better or worse than at the turn of the century, but rather on how good *is* it?

Undelivered Address

Prepared by the Author for the
Yale Alumni Day, February 1950*

༄

I t is a great honor for me to address you on this occasion. I consider it an especial privilege in view of the fact that no topic for
my talk was stipulated by Woodbridge Hall, and hence I was quick
to assume that so long as I am presentable, I am acceptable. Therefore I plan to use good grammar, not to split an infinitive and not
to end a sentence in a preposition: and I plan to unburden myself
of one of the problems that is uppermost in my mind, as it must
be in yours, and as it must be in the minds of all those men and
women who contemplate the dilemma of mid-twentieth-century
liberal American education.

I say I plan to unburden my mind because I hope for guidance
and because I defer to the seasoned and inquisitive and concerned
alumnus to help to solve this problem and to point out the way
for Yale University.

Yale was founded to educate young ministers for the Congre-
gational Church. We read with interest and even with amusement
of the rigors of college life during the eighteenth century, when the
bright and heartening rays of the enlightenment began to illumine
men's minds, when that great optimism that accompanied the Age

---

* The circumstances surrounding this speech are described in
  Chapter Three.

of Reason made its way felt in every corner of the civilized world. These were the days when students were required to converse in Latin, when public whipping was the obvious disciplinary recourse, when the curriculum was narrowly prescribed, when the sense of direction of the faculty and the fellows was forcibly imposed upon the young mind, when the college had a very explicit mission, narrow though this mission was.

And the nineteenth century served as the relaxing transition toward today, when the University seems to have no mission.

Only a few years ago the administration of Yale expanded its required courses for Yale College, reasoning that an educated man must know something about social science, must have grappled with exercises in formal thought, must be aware of the texture of a foreign language, must engage in some concern for a natural science. Some deemed this policy reactionary, and it is indeed in a large sense out of tune with the Yale of 1950, because Yale imposes little directed discipline, because Yale's mission is not articulate except in so far as an agglomeration of words about enlightened thought and action, freedom and democracy, serve to define the mission of Yale.

No, this is the university of "free and untrammeled inquiry." This is the university where extremes of thought are presented. This is the university which harbors professors who decry God and nature, capitalism and socialism, puritanism and moral laxity; this is the university which serves as the headquarters of a magazine devoted exclusively to metaphysics and another concerned entirely with an analysis of French existentialism. This is the university that reifies and projects all thoughts, arming them for the battle in the "arena of public and conflicting opinion"—and may the best thought, the best idea, the best concept win, and let the graduate decide for himself which cause to espouse. Yale has presented every side with equal vigor.

And this is the great puzzle for me. It is, I am certain, consciously or unconsciously the great puzzle for my classmates. And I hope that the implications of this extraordinary policy have puzzled you, because the problem is a real one, and somebody must resolve it.

This is what I want to know: Does not this policy of educational *laissez-faire* imply that the standards and convictions of the president and fellows of the Yale Corporation are no better *for Yale* than those of any faculty member who devotes his energy and his time to proselytizing conflicting views? Does this mean that it is of no importance that President Seymour is a practicing Christian and Professor Smith is a professional anti-Christian, because President Seymour's opinion on this subject is no more valid than Professor Smith's? Does this mean that although the members of the Corporation of Yale believe that modified free enterprise is the best course for Americans, their opinion on this is of no more value than that of Professor Jones, who urges modified socialism upon his students? Are we not led to the inescapable conclusion that the only function of the administration is in fact to administer, to raise money, to elect presidents, to confirm appointments, but to be ever so careful to refrain from letting personal convictions affect their educational policies? Does this mean, in effect, that the president and the Fellows of Yale, while of course reserving to themselves the right to cast personal value judgments on the issues of today, may not impose their guidance on the students of a university over which they nominally preside? Doesn't this indicate that the term "educational *leader*" is in fact a gross misnomer, a hazy and farcical semantic device applied to a body of men whose only apparent prerogative is to set up a curriculum and to maintain within the University a certain amount of working harmony?

But the case is overstated, you will say. After all, didn't President Seymour last spring state that he would not knowingly appoint a Communist to the faculty? Most certainly he did. (It is interesting, too, that his assertion was considered audacious.) But against what did the president rule? Against an extreme extreme. He might with equal daring have ruled against student polygamy. What steps is the administration allowed to take to show up socialism, the blood brother of Marxism? What steps are taken to rule out polygamy as a *moral*, rather than a merely sociological evil? Certainly these questions are rhetorical, because so long as Yale professes this uncurbed, all-encompassing, fanatical allegiance to *laissez-faire* education she will lead her students nowhere. She leads them only to confusion; she prolongs and prolongs and prolongs through her young graduates that struggle in the arena of free thought, never contributing to the ascendancy of one of the protagonists, regardless of what he stands for—because to do so would bring from the liberals the cry of educational totalitarianism, and Yale is very, very allergic to criticism from the liberal, who is the absolute dictator in the United States today.

The dilemma is frightening. Suppose the administration of Yale were to formulate in unambiguous terms its educational credo. Suppose this credo were to assert that Yale considers active Christianity the first basis of enlightened thought and action. Suppose it reasserted its belief in democracy. Suppose it asserted that it considered Communism, socialism, collectivism, government paternalism inimical to the dignity of the individual and to the strength and prosperity of the nation, save where the government and only the government could act in the interests of humanitarianism and national security. Suppose Yale were to go on to say that whereas every student must recognize and explore conflicting views and of course ultimately formulate for himself his own credo, nevertheless the University would not *sustain* prominent members of the faculty who sought to violate the explicit purpose of this University by *preaching* doctrines against which the officials of the University had cast judgment.

There would come a great hue and a cry. A hundred organizations would lash out against Yale. They would accuse her of traducing education, of violating freedom. These charges would be loud, pointed, violent, and superficial—superficial because Yale is a private institution and acknowledges responsibility to her alumni, her community, and herself. She would be best acknowledging this responsibility by following the course which would lead, in her opinion, to a better America and to a better world. Would Yale be toying with means to achieve an end? Certainly not. Her faculty must hold certain opinions. Why not opinions that, in general, tally with those of the trustees of the institution, and that hold, with the trustees, a common goal?

And so we saw in eighteenth-century Yale a thesis in education. Two hundred and fifty years later we see the antithesis, and perhaps the time has come to resolve the two and proceed to the synthesis: the modern, free, enlightened University *with a purpose*, and with the will, the courage, and the conviction to imbue her students with that same purpose. This is a purpose which you and I and presumably the officers of Yale consider magnificent and noble. It is certainly their right to desire and to insist that in so far as it is possible this purpose be passed on to succeeding generations—at least to that portion of succeeding generations that is processed by Yale.

Appendix G

Colleges and Universities Using the Basic Economics Textbooks

๛

The following is an incomplete list of colleges and universities other than Yale that have adopted the basic economics texts reviewed in Chapter Two.

Samuelson, *Economics, An Introductory Analysis*

Allegheny College
American University
Amherst College
Atlantic Union College
Aurora College
Balboa University
Baldwin-Wallace College
Bates College
Bell Iles College School of
    Commerce
Berea College
Birmingham-Southern College
Boston University
Bowling Green State University
Bradley University
University of Bridgeport
Brooklyn College
Bryn Mawr College
University of Buffalo
Butler University

University of California
University of California, Los
    Angeles
University of California, Santa
    Barbara
California College of Commerce
Cambridge University (England)
Carnegie Institute of Technology
Carroll College
Case Institute of Technology
Catholic University of America
Cedar Falls, Iowa, State Teachers
    College
Champlain College
University of Chicago
Chicago Institute of Design
Chico State College
City College of New York
Cleveland College
Colgate University

College of St. Thomas
University of Colorado
Colorado State Agricultural College
Colorado State College of
    Education
Columbia University
Cornell College (Iowa)
Davidson College
Dartmouth College
University of Delaware
Denison University
DePaul University
Drake University
Drexel Institute
University of Dubuque
Duke University
University of Florida
General Motors Institute
Golden Gate College
Grinnell College
Harvard University
Haverford College
Heidelberg College
Hillyer College
Hobart College
Hofstra College
Howard University
Hunter College
Idaho State College
University of Illinois
Illinois Institute of Technology
Indiana University
Iowa State College
Ithaca College
Johns Hopkins University
John Muir College
Junior College of Connecticut
Kalamazoo College
University of Kansas City

Kenyon College
Knox College
Lafayette College
Larson College
Lincoln University
Los Angeles City College
Louisiana State University
University of Maine
University of Maryland
Massachusetts Institute of
    Technology
McGill University
Miami University
University of Michigan
Milwaukee School of Engineering
Milwaukee State Teachers College
University of Minnesota
Mississippi State College
University of Missouri
Mount Holyoke College
New Jersey College for Women
University of New Mexico
New York University
Northeastern University
Northern Illinois State Teachers
    College
North Park College
Oberlin College
Ohio State University
University of Omaha
Paterson, N.J., State Teachers
    College
University of Pennsylvania
University of the Philippines
Philippine College of Commerce
Philippine Military Academy
Philippine Union College
Pomona College
Princeton University

Purdue University
Queens College
Quincy College
Reed College
Rhode Island School of Design
Roosevelt College
Rutgers University
St. Francis Xavier University, N.S.
St. Olaf College
Sampson College
San Bernardino Valley College
University of San Francisco
San Luis Obispo City Schools
Sioux Falls College
Simmons College
Smith College
South Dakota State College
Southern Methodist University
Stanford University
Stevens Institute of Technology
Swarthmore College
University of Tennessee
University of Texas
Texas A. & M. College
Texas College of Arts & Industries
Texas State College for Women
University of Toledo
University of Toronto

Trenton, N.J., State Teachers
  College
Trinity University
Tri-State College
Tufts College
Union College
United States Coast Guard
  Academy
United States Naval Academy
Upper Iowa University
Vanderbilt University
Vassar College
Vermont Junior College
Wake Forest College
Washington State College
Washington University
University of Washington
Washington & Jefferson College
Waynesburg College
Wayne University
Wesleyan University
Western Reserve University
Western Washington College of
  Education
Williams College
Wright College
University of Wyoming
Yale University

Tarshis, *The Elements of Economics*

American University, Washington,
  D.C.
Baldwin-Wallace College, Ohio
Beloit College, Wis.
Birmingham-Southern College, Ala.
Bluffton College, Ohio
Boston College, Mass.

Boston School of Pharmacy, Mass.
Brownsville Junior College, Tex.
Catholic University of America,
  Washington, D.C.
Colgate University, N.Y.
College of William and Mary, Va.
Columbia University, N.Y.

Converse College, S.C.
Cornell College, Iowa
Cornell University, N.Y.
Dakota Wesleyan University,
   S. Dak.
Dean Junior College, Mass.
Denison University, Ohio
De Pauw University, Ind.
Drake University, Iowa
Draughon's Business College, Ark.
Drexel Institute of Technology, Pa.
Duke University, N.C.
General Motors Institute, Mich.
Goucher College, Md.
Grinnell College, Iowa
Hardin-Simmons University, Tex.
Harvard University, Mass.
Hobart College, N.Y.
Howard University, Washington,
   D.C.
Hunter College, N.Y.
Illinois Institute of Technology
Iowa State College
Kemper Military Academy, Mo.
Laredo Jr. College, Tex.
MacDonald College, Canada
Manchester College, Ind.
Mississippi State College
Missouri School of Mines
Mount Royal Jr. College, Canada
New York University
Nichols Junior College, Mass.
Northland College, Wis.
Occidental College, Calif.
Ohio State University
Ohio Wesleyan University
Oregon State College
Otterbein College, Ohio
Pomona College, Calif.

Rutland Junior College, Vt.
Sacramento College, Calif.
St. John's University, Minn.
Santa Barbara College, Calif.
Simmons College, Mass.
Sir George Williams College,
   Canada
Southwest Texas Junior College
Stanford University, Calif.
S.T.C., Lock Haven, Pa.
S.T.C., Milwaukee, Wis.
Texas Technological College
Tufts College, Mass.
U.S. Department of Agriculture,
   Graduate School, D.C.
University of Alberta, Canada
University of Arkansas
University of Buffalo, N.Y.
University of California at Los
   Angeles
University of Connecticut
   Extension: Fort Trumbull
University College, Ill.
University of Illinois
University of Kentucky
University of Puerto Rico
University of Texas
University of Toledo, Ohio
University of Toronto, Canada
University of Wisconsin
Upper Iowa University
Utah State Agricultural College
Virginia State College
Washburn Municipal University of
   Topeka, Kans.
Washington College, Md.
Washington University, Mo.
Wayne University, Mich.
Wesleyan University, Conn.

Westminster College, Mo.

William Jewell College, Mo.

Williams College, Mass.

Yale University, Conn.

Bowman and Bach, *Economic Analysis and Public Policy*

Adelphi College

Arkansas Polytechnic Institute

University of Arkansas

Babson Institute

Baker University

Bowling Green State University

Bradley University

University of Buffalo

Butler University

University of California, Berkeley

University of California, Los
   Angeles

Carleton College

Carnegie Institute of Technology

University of Chicago

City College of New York

Columbia University, New York

University of Denver

Drew University

Drexel Institute of Technology

Emory University

Florida Southern College

Florida State University

Golden Gate College

Haverford College

Highlands University

College of Holy Cross

University of Houston

Illinois College

University of Illinois, Champaign

Illinois Wesleyan University

Iona College

Iowa State College

Kenyon College

Knox College

McGill University

Marquette University

University of Maryland

Michigan State College

Missouri School of Mines

Montgomery Junior College

Muhlenberg College

New York University

North Dakota Agricultural College

North Park College

Oberlin College

Occidental College

Oklahoma City University

Rockhurst College

College of St. Thomas

S.T.C., Edinboro, Pennsylvania

S.T.C., Superior, Wisconsin

Suffolk University

Swarthmore College

Syracuse University

University of Tennessee, Knoxville

University of Tennessee, Nashville

Utica College

University of Utah

Vermont Junior College

University of Vermont

University of Virginia,
   Charlottesville

Washington State College

Wayne University

Wilmington College

Willamette University

Xavier University

Morgan, *Income and Employment*

Univ. of Calif., Berkeley
Univ. of Calif., Los Angeles
Univ. of Calif., Santa Barbara
C.C.N.Y.
Colorado Col.
Columbia Univ.
Univ. of Dayton
Elmhurst Col.
Iowa St. Col., Ames
Univ. of Kansas, Lawrence
Lincoln Memorial Univ.
Marietta Col.
Merrimack Col.
Univ. of Miami, Fla.

N.Y.U.
Univ. of Oklahoma, Norman
Princeton Univ.
San Diego St. Col.
Seton Hall Univ., S. Orange
Univ. of Southern Calif.
Temple Univ.
Utah St. Agric. Col.
Wayne Univ.
Wash. Univ., Mo.
Wash. & Lee Univ.
Univ. of Wash., Seattle
Western Maryland Col.
Westminster Col., Mo.

Notes

❧

CHAPTER ONE: RELIGION AT YALE

1. Merrimon Cuninggim, *The College Seeks Religion* (New Haven: Yale University Press, 1947), 237.

2. Ibid., 149, 237.

3. Ibid., 256.

4. *College Reading and Religion* (New Haven: Yale University Press, 1948), 292.

5. Howells, *Mankind So Far*; Murdock, *Our Primitive Contemporaries*; Mead, *From the South Seas*; Benedict, *Patterns of Culture*; Keller, *Starting Point in Social Science*, and *Societal Evolution*; Tuck, *Not with the Fist*; Gillin, *Ways of Men*; Yang, *Chinese Village*.

6. *Yale Daily News*, issue of October 10, 1950.

7. New York: Odyssey Press, 1935.

8. *College Reading and Religion*, 60–62.

9. Ibid., 16–17.

10. E.g., Schlick, *Philosophy of Nature*; Otto, *Science and the Moral Life*; Edel, *Theory and Practice of Philosophy*.

11. R. M. Dorcus and G. W. Shaffer, *Textbook of Abnormal Psychology* (Baltimore: Williams & Wilkins Co., 1934, 3d ed. 1945); L. F. Shaffer, *The Psychology of Adjustment* (Boston, New York: Houghton Mifflin Co., 1936); F. L. Ruch, *Psychology and Life* (Chicago: Scott, Foresman & Co., 1937); and O. Klineberg, *Social Psychology* (New York: Henry Holt & Co., 1940).

12. 1946–50.

13. *College Reading and Religion*, 82.

14. Ruch, *Psychology and Life*, 5.

15. *College Reading and Religion*, 90.

16. Ibid., 108.

17. John S. Nason, president, Swarthmore College, *Educational Record* (October 1946).

18. Ibid.

19. Albert C. Outler, *College, Faculties, and Religion* (Hazen Pamphlet, January 1949), as cited by Howard Lowry, *The Mind's Adventure* (Philadelphia: The Westminster Press, 1950), 61.

20. Norman Foerster, *The American State University*, 263–64, as cited by Cuninggim, *The College Seeks Religion*, 260.

21. Paul J. Braisted, *Religion in Higher Education*, 11, as cited by Cuninggim, *The College Seeks Religion*, 256.

22. Cuninggim, *The College Seeks Religion*, 24.

23. "Yale Interprets the News," August 15, 1948.

24. Cuninggim, *The College Seeks Religion*, 259.

25. Ibid., 260.

26. E. Fay Campbell in address, as cited by Lowry, *The Mind's Adventure*, 54.

27. *General Education in a Free Society*, Report of the Harvard Committee (Harvard University Press, 1945), 76.

28. Lowry, *The Mind's Adventure*, 54.

29. *General Education in a Free Society*, 39.

30. Ibid., 65.

31. Lowry, *The Mind's Adventure*, 55.

32. Ibid., 133–34.

33. Cuninggim, *The College Seeks Religion*, 65.

34. Ibid., 235.

35. *Yale Alumni Magazine* (March 1950), 8.

CHAPTER TWO: INDIVIDUALISM AT YALE

1. I am indebted to the *Educational Reviewer* for an excellent review of Samuelson's text (issue of October 15, 1950), and for an equally valuable analysis of *A Grammar of American Politics—The National Government* by Binkley and Moos (issue of April 15, 1951). I am also grateful to the National Economic Council for its telling analysis of the Tarshis book (*Review of Books*, August 1947).

CHAPTER THREE: YALE AND HER ALUMNI

1. See Hubert Park Beck, *Men Who Control Our Universities* (New York: King's Crown Press, 1947).

2. *Yale University Organizations*, pamphlet issued by the Alumni Board, June 1950.

3. *President's Report to the Alumni*, 1949–50, 38.

CHAPTER FOUR:
THE SUPERSTITIONS OF "ACADEMIC FREEDOM"

1. Published under the title *Freedom and the University* (Ithaca: Cornell University Press, 1950).

2. Ibid., 5.

3. Ibid., 121–22.

4. Ibid., 117–19.

5. *The Jerome Davis Case*, "Final Report of an Investigation Conducted by the American Federation of Teachers into the Proposed Dismissal of Professor Jerome Davis from the Stark Chair of Practical Philanthropy at the Yale Divinity School," Chicago, Illinois, 1937.

6. November 1935.

7. Lowry, *The Mind's Adventure*.

8. Oregon School Cases 268 US 510, 534.

9. *New Haven Register*, March 1950.

10. Baccalaureate Address, June 1950.

CHAPTER FIVE: THE PROBLEM OF THE ALUMNUS

1. Inside quotation is from I. L. Kandel, in the *New Education and Religion*, 1, Associated Press, 1945.

2. Quote from *New York Times Sunday Magazine*, issue of February 26, 1950.

3. "Presidents of American Colleges and Universities Who Are Yale University Graduates," *School and Society*, XLIII (June 13, 1936), 809–10.

4. *The Theory of Education in the United States* (Chicago: Henry Regnery Company, 1949, 2d ed.).

5. Lowry, *The Mind's Adventure*; Cuninggim, *The College Seeks Religion*; Sir Walter Moberly, *The Crisis in the University* (London: SCM Press, 1949).

APPENDIX A: RELIGION AND SOCIOLOGY

1. *College Reading and Religion* (New Haven: Yale University Press, 1948).

2. Ibid., 275.

3. Ibid., 263.

4. Ibid., 264.

5. Willard Waller, *The Family* (New York: Cordon Co., 1938), 12.

6. *College Reading and Religion*, 291.

7. Ibid., 292.

8. Ibid., 292.

9. Ibid., 297.

10. John Lewis Gillin, Clarence G. Dittmer, Ray J. Colbert, and Norman M. Kostler, *Social Problems* (3d. ed.; New York, London: D. Appleton Century Co., 1943), 338.

11. Ernest R. Groves, *The Family and Its Social Problems* (Chicago, New York: J. Lippincott & Co., 1940), 60.

12. Charles H. Cooley, *Human Nature and the Social Order* (New York: Charles Scribner's Sons, 1902), 503.

13. *College Reading and Religion*, 283.

14. George A. Lundberg, Read Bain, and Nels Anderson, *Trends in American Sociology* (New York: Harper & Bros., 1929), 112–13.

APPENDIX C: PHILOSOPHY AND RELIGION

1. *College Reading and Religion*, 75.

2. Ibid., 5.

3. Albert Schwegler, *Geschichte der Philosophie im Umriss* (Stuttgart, 1870); Alfred Weber, *A History of Philosophy* (New York: Charles Scribner's Sons, 1860).

4. George Boas, *The Adventures of Human Thought* (New York, London: Harper & Bros., 1929).

5. *College Reading and Religion*, 24.

APPENDIX D: RELIGION AND PSYCHOLOGY

1. *College Reading and Religion*, 80–114.

2. Ibid., 82.

3. F. L. Ruch, *Psychology and Life* (Chicago: Scott, Foresman & Co., 1937).

4. *College Reading and Religion*, 5.

5. J. F. Brown, *Psychology and the Social Order* (New York: McGraw-Hill Book Co., 1936).

6. Ibid., as quoted in *College Reading and Religion*, 85–86.

7. Ibid., 87.

8. In explanation of this, Mr. Allport wrote me, in December 1950, that he considered his book *Personality* "hospitable to the religious sentiment and to the Christian ethos." He added, though, that he had "not done justice to the enormous importance of the religious value in some lives." An effort to offset this deficiency was made in his latest work, *The Individual and His Religion*, which Professor Allport published in 1950.

9. D. B. Klein, *Mental Hygiene: The Psychology of Personal Adjustment* (New York: Henry Holt & Co., 1944).

10. *College Reading and Religion*, 108.

APPENDIX E: CUNINGGIM ON RELIGION AT YALE

1. *The College Seeks Religion.*

2. A. P. Stokes, "The Present Condition of Religious Life at Yale," Chapter Seven in J. B. Reynolds et al., eds., *Two Centuries of Christian Activity at Yale* (New York: G. P. Putnam's Sons, 1901), 117–18.

Index

Note: Page references followed by "*n*" indicate footnotes.